Democratic Transgressions of Law:
Governing Technology through Public Participation

International Studies in Sociology and Social Anthropology

VOLUME 112

Democratic Transgressions of Law: Governing Technology through Public Participation

Edited by
Alfons Bora and Heiko Hausendorf

TUTA SUB AEGIDE PALLAS · 1683 ·

BRILL

LEIDEN • BOSTON
2010

Cover image: Richard Schindler

This book is printed on acid-free paper.

Library of Congress Cataloging-in-Publication Data

Democratic transgressions of law : governing technology through public participation / edited by Alfons Bora and Heiko Hausendorf.
p. cm. -- (International Studies in Sociology and Social Anthropology ; 112)
Includes index.
ISBN 978-90-04-18043-7 (hardback : alk. paper)
1. Technology and law. 2. Technology and state--Citizen participation. I. Bora, Alfons. II. Hausendorf, H. (Heiko)

K487.T4D46 2010
344'.095--dc22

2009052174

ISSN 0074-8684
ISBN 978 90 04 18043 7

PRINTED IN THE NETHERLANDS

CONTENTS

INTRODUCTION

GOVERNING TECHNOLOGY THROUGH PUBLIC PARTICIPATION

Alfons Bora and Heiko Hausendorf

Science and technology have long been regarded driving forces of modernisation and central factors of prosperity and welfare. However, in the second half of the 20th century it has emphasized that they also produce risks and dangers. Especially the most far-reaching innovations, namely high technologies, are therefore often socially contested. During the last decades, major social conflicts were triggered by technological innovations such as nuclear power and biotechnology, or by the effects of scientific and technological progress such as the ozone layer or major desertification processes. Against this background, the necessity of social regulation of science and technology emerges from the double need of socially promoting desirable innovations on the one hand and of controlling risks and socially unwanted developments on the other. This double need fosters a post-interventionist understanding of science and technology policy. Regulation in the broad sense of both promoting and controlling science and technology takes place at every stage of the innovation process, from basic research, selection processes in innovation networks and economic marketing decisions, to the classical forms of state intervention by political and financial support on the one hand, and legal control on the other.

Regulation is frequently discussed in the theoretical context of *governance*. Although the concept of governance is itself not undisputed, it can nevertheless serve as a heuristic tool in order to identify the peculiarities of science and technology policy. In contrast to classical regulatory approaches, the perspective of governance emphasises a more complex understanding of recursive, multi-level and multi-actor relations in regulatory networks. It indicates that new forms of non-hierarchical, de-centralized, co-operative, 'enabling' regulation replace older models of hierarchical intervention. Accordingly, the concept of governance indicates the need for political, legal, and social regulation beyond markets and hierarchies. Governance thus describes the coordination of new forms of social cooperation, i.e. more horizontal activities between state institutions, non-governmental organisations, private enterprises, and individual actors. In this perspective, governance covers aspects of the state, the market, and civil society, including the general public. Consequently, it comprises various forms of citizen participation as a tool for decision-making in the process of governing science and technology.

Having mentioned these more institutional aspects, it is important to see that the participatory turn in governing technology has substantive motives too: Participation, i.e. the trend to involve citizens or the general public, is conceptually based on a critique of expertise and on a discourse about 'democratising expertise'. 'Big Science' has been realised as a major challenge for governance (Fuller 2000). The critique that experts are not neutral in political processes and that their advice, in principle, is embedded in a grid of techno-normative discourses (Bora forthcoming), has led to an extended debate about the role of laypersons and experts in political and legal decision-making (Liberatore & Funtowicz 2003). Against this background it is argued that participatory procedures could help to overcome the bottleneck of 'technocratic' policies. They are expected to evoke the motivation to engage in decision-making, to broaden the base of knowledge and of the values involved, to initiate learning processes, to produce new possibilities of conflict solution, to realise common interests, and last but not least, to increase the acceptance and legitimacy of a decision. Therefore, participatory procedures are supposed to improve governance in contrast to older, 'technocratic' models.

Moreover, the conception of the role of science and technology in society has changed in the scholarly debate. Against an older, linear model of technological innovation proceeding from scientific invention to useful application, technological innovations are now viewed at much more in the way of 'mode 2' (Nowotny et al. 2001), namely as outcomes of social networks that incorporate a wide range of social actors, including users. Under such presuppositions, it seems obvious that citizens should be involved in decision-making processes.

Due to these reasons (among others), the participation of concerned actors and of the public in general has become a genuine part of contemporary governance models. On the other hand, participation itself has never been uncontested. It has been argued that participatory procedures generate empirical and normative problems. It is questionable, according to the critics, whether participatory exercises will elicit sufficient commitments from all participants unless they lead to a real win-win-solution. From the democratic perspective it might even be doubted whether these procedures are actually legitimate with respect to their political representativeness. In addition, the involved citizens' lack of power has also been criticised. Last bust not least, the manner in which participatory procedures can be integrated into the system of representative democracy is unclear in some cases (Abels & Bora 2004).

All in all, there is an on-going controversy on participatory governance. The contributions collected in the present volume will critically scrutinise central aspects of this controversy. As was briefly indicated above, the main interest in political science and in sociology lies on new participatory *fora* and procedures, i.e. on *alternative procedures*, such as citizen juries, consensus conferences, scenario workshops, public consultation exercises etc. These models represent alternative forms insofar as they normally are not part of the institutions of parliamentary politics. On the contrary, they are often meant as political alternatives to the political institutions that have developed in the 19th and 20th century.

We do not deny the relevance of these alternative forms. In the present volume, we nevertheless focus on *regular, routine forms of participatory governance*. These forms can be found at the heart of political power, namely in all kinds of administrative, i.e. executive procedure. The usual forms of decision-making procedures in public administration contain numerous interactions between government and citizens. Such interactions occur in everyday contacts between the two sides, and especially in those forms, which provide for a certain amount of citizen participation. What then comes into focus are not only and not primarily the legal conditions and the administrative directions, but above all the empirical ways by means of which these conditions and directions are manifested and communicated within the participation process itself. The claim of citizen participation, in other words, promises a slot for participants acting as citizens to take part in the decision making process: As a social place, where citizens have every-day experiences with state organisations, administrative procedures provide an explicit frame with pre-structured – and in a strict sense: 'legalised' – participation concepts for each of the participants. If we want to assess the theoretical and empirical chances of public participation as a relevant dimension of governing technology, we first of all have to study participatory exercises at the heart of existing political institutions. This is actually the place where participation plays an important role and where it can be investigated *in situ*.

Therefore, the theoretical assumption is that governing technology through public participation is neither exotic nor alternative. It is rather a genuine part of the everyday life of state and government institutions in all contemporary democratic societies. In studying such phenomena we concentrate on the legal and political situation in Europe. This is not due to a disregard of the circumstances in other parts of the world, let alone on global level. In fact, the study of European countries is motivated by the intention to reduce theoretical and empirical over-complexity and to identify at least some of the factors that make participatory governance a difficult undertaking. Nevertheless, we hope that concentration on the European situation will create a basis for further, even more comprehensive, comparison.

What can be learned from these normal forms of participatory governance is a deeper understanding of the relation between political subjects and political power, between periphery and political centre. The particular quality of these participatory forms consists in the fact that, in constitutional democracy, they are inevitably governed by the rule of law. That means that in any case of participatory procedure a legal framework lies behind the involved actors' concrete actions. The current volume critically examines these means of governing technology through participation, mainly in the realm of the legally framed public administration. It also touches upon alternative forms of participation, but always from the perspective of the routine procedures of political power.

In methodological and conceptual respects, the current volume continues an argument that has been opened by the editors in an earlier contribution (Hausendorf/Bora 2006). Having tried to show the methodological fertility of a socio-linguistic approach to examining micro-structures of governance in that previous book, the theoretical emphasis was therefore mainly put on questions of citizenship. We, therefore, developed the conceptual idea of 'communicated citizenship'. Given this background, the current volume focuses on more general questions of governance. Combining sociological and linguistic analyses it tries to give answers to some of the conceptual suggestions and questions that were raised in the previous book. Most of the authors of the chapters have been cooperating with each other in a number of research projects during the last ten years. Hence, the authors have been in intensive, interdisciplinary communication with each other when preparing this volume. The current book, therefore, is the result of almost a decade of fruitful discussion. It also demonstrates the potential of a cross-disciplinary approach that stretches from *sociology*, via *political science* and *jurisprudence* to *hermeneutics, linguistics* and *conversation analysis.*

The volume presents its general argument in three parts The first part mainly follows theoretical aims. In chapter 1, *Patrick O'Mahony* opens up the theoretical horizons of the volume by discussing the relationship between public participation and sociological theory. He critically examines all relevant theoretical approaches – namely pragmatic, discursive and differentiation-theoretical – in order to investigate the potential for a synthesis of differentiation and pragmatic traditions. The starting point of the analysis is *Habermas's* later writing – in particular, "Between Facts and Norms" (1996) – in which Habermas elaborates on the idea that the moral foundations of communicative rationality have been institutionalised in the basic legal institutions of modern democratic societies. Whereas Habermas's intention – in contrast to his earlier "Theory of Communicative Action" (1984) – is aimed at legal theory and thereby withdraws from sociological analysis to a certain extent, *Boltanski and Thevenot* ("De la Justification", 1991) draw attention back to the empirical foundations of legal rationality. O'Mahony introduces this theoretical strand in order to build the foundations for a constructivist approach to the discursive and evaluative basis of politics. Both theories are, however, not comprehensive for explaining societal structures from a general point of view. A sophisticated sociological approach, as O'Mahony argues, has to combine both normative and empirical perspectives. At this point, he introduces *Niklas Luhmann's* sociological systems theory (Luhmann 2002, Bora 1999) in order to gain a comprehensive perspective on the normative organisation of modern society. He then develops a mediating position between normative pragmatic and systems theory. This model contains three levels – the macro-level of form, the meso-level of activity, and the micro-level of cognition. Public discourse located on the normative dimension is closely intertwined with cognitive innovation and normative justification on the micro-level on the one hand, and with social structures on the macro level on the other. Public participation can be viewed at as cognitive innovation and as a set of procedures for testing and socially implementing such innovations. Introducing this approach, the chapter offers a novel view on participation beyond the classical perspectives of normative pragmatic and systems theories. At the same time, it adverts to the importance of micro-structures and communications analysis while embedding both aspects in the macro-perspective of culture and political institutions. The chapter thereby creates a comprehensive theoretical perspective for understanding the following steps of our argumentation.

In Chapter 2, *Giuseppe Pellegrini* takes up the challenge of theorizing participation in biotechnology regimes from the point of view of political sociology and political theory. Against the background of current biotechnology policies – which are from an empirical standpoint the field of reference for this volume – he strongly argues in favour of alternatives or 'supplements' to the routine forms of public governance. This argument is based on the observation of democratic deficits in the routine forms. It suggests that alternatives such as the consensus conference, for instance, might help to overcome deficits that have been introduced above under the header of 'democratising expertise'. The chapter gives an extensive account of the relevant studies in this field (Gaskell, Bauer, Durant, Callon, for example) and then focuses on question of legitimacy. In the field of European policy-making, a critical analysis of representative mechanisms is developed. In order to assess political instruments in the governance of technology, a model for the politics of knowledge is applied, in which more closed mechanisms (knowing and evaluating public opinion) are contrasted by more open ones (public engagement, public participation). The latter should allow for the kind of cognitive innovation and normative justification mentioned in chapter 1. The need for these open types is deduced from the above mentioned analysis of political deficits. Finally, the concept of consensus conference is suggested as a participatory method that could perhaps overcome the difficulties in governing modern biotechnology. In basing his argument on the ground of political practise, Pellegrini clearly shows where the demands for enhanced citizen participation are directed at in the wider context of democratic institutions. On the other side – by suggesting the advantages of consensus conferences over the routine models – he also shows the necessity to carefully study the deficits and shortcomings in the routine procedures. Only on the basis of such an analysis – namely the opening of the black box of participation in routine procedures – can the possible function and performance of any alternative be judged. Finally, the chapter also indicates the necessity to carefully look at strengths *and* weaknesses of the proposed alternative procedures.

In chapter 3, *Les Levidow* takes a comparative perspective by asking how it is possible to democratise the regulation of agro-biotechnology.

He examines four alternative models – the Danish consensus conference (Joss 1989), the German 'TA' exercise on genetically modified herbicide resistant plants (Bora 1999a), the French citizens' conference on GMOs (Marris/Joly 1999) and the British 'GM Nation' case. The author rather critically assesses the alternative procedures by claiming that in all cases the alternative forms have rather led to a biotechnologised democracy, instead of democratized technology. These procedures, as Levidow says, have perhaps enhanced the accountability of governments with respect to regulatory criteria. They have, however, not improved innovation prospects from a democratic point of view. The reasons for this regulatory failure are manifold. Firstly, the integration of the participatory exercises in neoliberal policy frameworks counteracts the institutionalisation of democratic procedures. Secondly, ambiguous and contradictory aims of the participation – such as democratisation of the procedure, education of the public, institutional reform, or conflict resolution – hinder the development of clear structures. Last but not least, there is still a remarkable dominance of experts, even in the selection of layperson-participation. The problem definitions they bring in influence the procedures to a certain extent. The author concludes that 'state-sponsored' participatory procedures do not complement representative democracy but rather neoliberal models. Democratic accountability, as Levidow says, will more likely be realised in autonomous forms of participation beyond state-sponsorship. The chapter altogether presents an important argument for the book, because it clearly accentuates the current state of the art in most parts of the debate on participation in sociology and political science. It puts emphasis on the relationship between empirical structures and normative consequences. In accordance with the first two chapters of part I, it thereby prepares the ground for the following – in general rather critical – argumentation of the volume.

Altogether, the first part of our book draws the picture of a controversial theoretical argument. Strong assumptions are brought forward in order to support the enhancement of participation in all fields of science policy and legal decision-making. Nevertheless, a certain theoretical scepticism is formulated and – led by a comparative view on participatory exercises – critical questions about the effects of participatory governance are raised. The first chapters therefore give reason to open the black box of participatory procedure and to have a closer look at the dynamics of communication in the micro-structures of participatory governance.

In the second part of the volume, this micro-perspective becomes the focus of theoretical interest. The theoretical perspective is embedded in studies in the field of agro-biotechnology. In chapter 4, *Peter Münte* takes up the theoretical opening and shows by a detailed analysis of an administrative decision-making process, how and why the deficits mentioned in chapter 3 occurred. Based on a detailed analysis of documents stemming from a licensing procedure on GMO plants – such as the official announcement by the competent authority, the written objections that concerned citizens raised and the final decision of the authority – Münte shows how the discursive positions in the course of the legal procedure are transformed into 'legitimate' arguments. Any communicative aspect that does not fit into the logic of the 'techno-scientific normativity' (Bora, forthcoming) of the procedure will be excluded. The analysis also makes clear that these deficits are structurally motivated and to that extent are inevitable on the basis of a legally framed procedure. These findings, obviously, have consequences for the theoretical approach. They give reason to assume that exactly the conditions of constitutional democracy and the rule of law – front-ranking evolutionary achievements in modern society, of course – are responsible for the deficits observed in participatory procedures. Münte discusses this point with respect to a number of international documents that represent the participatory turn in science, technology and innovation Policy. Very similar to Levidow's argument, Münte shows the intrinsic ambiguity of these documents, which deeply subverts participatory governance. Authorities do not act according to the normative model and the discursive expectations formulated by citizens do not comply with the normatively relevant frames. Moreover, even the legally intended model, as Münte argues, bears a deep rooted misconception of the procedure itself. It neglects the fact that, at least to a certain extent, the communicative rationality expressed in the citizens' expectations goes far beyond the legal rationality of the procedure. In fact, it covers O'Mahony's level of participatory innovation. From the inner-legal point of view, these expectations appear as transgressions of the legal frame. From a political point of view, they could be taken on board as contributions to social innovation processes, if they were only embedded in political contexts. In the given situation, however, they can only produce irritations to the procedure. Therefore, they lag far behind the legislative intentions. Münte, therefore, suggests paying more attention to the sociological dimension of

Herrschaft and to ask from that point of view, what the particular contribution of participatory governance could be.

As far as these findings can be confirmed, the consequences for the theory of participation as discussed in chapter 1 and for arguments in political science like the ones presented in chapter 2 are up for debate. From different points of view the following chapters circulate around this question.

As we have seen from the previous chapter, the legal framing of participatory governance has a significant influence on the communicative micro-structures that shape the performance of participation. Against this background, *Matthias Baier* critically examines the relation between law and participation from the perspective of Law and Society Studies in chapter 5. The data give reason to assume that legal provisions might be dysfunctional with respect to political participatory ambitions. Baier even goes further in saying that participatory elements in the law may have paradoxical tendencies, namely to exclude citizens even when the legal situation is designed to include them. This argument is supported by data from Swedish environmental law with respect to plant GMOs. An overview across the scholarly debate in the Nordic countries shows a general tendency of the law to use participatory mechanisms to actually exclude citizens. Therefore Baier asks for a theoretical approach that allows for a fruitful conceptualisation of these findings. Following Gunther Teubner (1993), he distinguishes formal, substantive and reflexive law with respect to the dimension of rationality. The Swedish GMO regulation has, accordingly, to be characterised as substantive law that is embedded in framework legislation. All provisions are focussed on the licensing decision. Therefore, citizens' rights are limited by this general orientation. Reflexive elements have been introduced in this legislation implementing the cooperation of new authorities. Accordingly, Baier speaks about a 'legal hybrid', a description that is actually appropriate for most of the national regulations in Europe and that is clearly representative of the overall situation. Baier's particular point is that in the course of a concrete participatory exercise, the legal framework creates different *social positions* with different types of communicatively constructed interpretations (*Deutungsmuster*). They refer to questions of GMOs, but also to the procedure and its legal and political contexts, e.g. to the understanding of democracy and citizenship. The crucial point with respect to the law is that it selects some of these positions and rejects others, thereby including and excluding the respective rationalities. In the concluding part of the chapter, Baier relates these findings to legal theory by applying Kaarlo Tuori's 'critical legal positivism' (Tuori 2002). Formal, substantial and reflexive law, in this perspective, are ordered historically with the latter being the most recent form. Yet, the participatory positions are still not perfectly compatible with the deep structures of the law, as the results show. Baier, therefore, places his hopes on the further development of legal rationality.

In chapter 6, *Henrik Rahm* shows from a socio-linguistic perspective that the concept of citizenship underlying the idea of participatory governance in itself might be a contested concept. The empirical reference of the chapter is also the Swedish case, which allows for a direct connection with the socio-legal argument in chapter 5 (Baier). Rahm applies the methodological and theoretical approach of Critical Discourse Analysis (Fairclough 2003). He studies the actors' views on a particular aspect of the Swedish licensing procedure for GMOs, the referral process. Methodologically, the analysis is grounded in Fairclough's distinction between discourse (representation of the world), genre (acting in the world) and style (identification of self and others). The analysis shows that on the institutional level the principle of transparency and the system of referrals pre-structure a kind of 'represented citizenship'. By this expression Rahm describes the fact that the citizens' arguments are only brought into the procedure via organizations. Against this background, different discursive practices are identified in which particular social 'voices' are articulated. These voices very significantly differ from each other in the ways in which they communicatively frame the procedure and discursively construct types of citizenship. Interestingly, also in the interviews with critical activists, the above-mentioned type of representative citizenship is dominant, although it might take the form of 'public' citizenship. Rahm critically notes that in the current data no example of what he calls 'individual' citizenship could be found, due to the limited interest of the mass media in the GMO issue. However, as Rahm convincingly argues, the data also show the great potential of the Swedish legislative tradition that offers more options to engaged citizens than most other European legislatures. The trail to success is blazed by the opportunities of Swedish citizens to obtain information. These opportunities are unique compared to what we find in all other countries.

The next step of the argumentation draws attention to the social and cultural context of participatory procedures. In Chapter 7, *Elena*

Collavin gives a striking example of the importance of cultural factors as they were theoretically outlined among other aspects in chapter 1 (O'Mahony). Although in Italy the GMO legislation in general and the provisions for citizen participation in particular significantly lagged behind developments in many other European countries for a couple of years, a country-wide opinion against GMOs emerged from mainly local initiatives. The national legislation – interestingly due to its time lag with respect to European developments – was directed in a clearly anti-GMO direction. The chapter unfolds the normative background of participatory procedures and depicts some of the 'mainstream' procedures in participation. It then explains the legal situation in Italy, which for a significant time span was characterised by a very slow and incomplete implementation of the EU legislation on GMOs. In spite of these encouraging institutional conditions, the author shows that there has been a really effective and far reaching political mobilisation in Italy against plant GMOs. The characteristics of this development are in sharp contrast with all models of participatory governance. Italy is an interesting case for our investigation, because the political impetus seemingly did not arise from formal participatory exercises, but rather from a deep-rooted cultural structure that became manifest in different activities on local and community level. In the end, the contribution of the public came from outside the legal frame, as Collavin argues, namely via local and regional deliberative exercises. The case, therefore, shows the rather low steering effect of the law in a social, cultural and political situation, where a broadly shared interpretive scheme (*Deutungsmuster*) prevails. The political 'sovereign' (in the sense of Münte, chapter 4) came into play as soon as local and regional authorities – in fact *contra legem* – became aware of their scope of actions. Collavin, therefore, suggests broadening the concept of public participation by including local institutions, which take up issues beyond their core domain. The argument complements the findings of the previous chapters insofar as it stresses the importance of cultural identities on the community level. These identities are important factors also for the implementation of national and EU legislation. Italy, from this point of view, becomes an example of bottom-up participation developing outside all legally framed and politically routinized procedure. The case, therefore, shows how some of the participatory impasse described in many parts of this book can be avoided, if only the political-cultural ground is fertile for a 'wild' public, as Collavin puts it.

In chapter 8, *Zsuzsanna Iványi, András Kertész, and Kornélia Marinecz* show that every cultural impetus needs institutional support. They demonstrate what happens in a situation in which the constitutional framework of modern democracy is not yet completely institutionalised *and* in which the cultural dimension shows a different face from what was reported in the Italian case. By applying the theory and methods of socio-linguistic conversation analysis, the chapter studies the communicative construction of governance in the context of a legally framed decision-making procedure. In so doing it creates a methodological link to chapters 4 and 6 (Münte and Baier), while simultaneously complementing the argument presented in chapter 7 (Collavin). In the beginning, the chapter lays out the theoretical ground for understanding governance as a communicative achievement. With the instruments of conversation analysis, it then analyses the communicative structure of the relevant legal provisions in Hungarian GMO law. The legal act provides for a number of *social positions,* which are altogether very strictly limited by the purpose of deliberate release of GMOs. Concepts like 'the public' or 'participation' are defined from that point of view and are more or less restricted to the right of information. In the following steps, on the basis of oral data, the analysis is extended to the *positioning processes* arising in the course of the procedure. Detailed accounts of the involved positions, their images of self and others and their concepts regarding subject matters allow for a deeper understanding of the dynamics that are developing between these positions. A fine-grained sequential analyses of a TV show communication about genetic engineering is presented that gives an instructive insight into the communicative construction of a certain type of 'public'. The reader can witness with which communicative means the discursive construct of the 'public' is downplayed. The communicative slots opened by the legal provisions, the authors argue, are being filled only in a very restricted sense and in neglect of the genuine expectations of some social positions. Thus, the chapter gives a very illuminative picture of the processes described in chapters 4 (Münte) and 5 (Baier). In particular, the effects of legal provisions can be judged more precisely against the background of the empirical observations in this chapter. We can examine how 'quasi-citizenship' is being constructed within a legal frame that to a certain extent complies with the requirements of the rule of law in a modern democratic society.

Together with the Italian case (chapter 7), this chapter provides an important argument in the context of this volume. Both cases not only show the importance of the interplay between cultural factors and democratic *practises* – the Italian in their realisation *contra legem*, the Hungarian in their incomplete development – but they also demonstrate the crucial relevance of democratic *institutions*. Chapter 8 makes clear that the problems and shortcomings of participatory governance cannot be avoided in bypassing the routine forms of the rule of law and of democratic basic institutions – a conjecture that might be inspired by some arguments in the foregoing chapters. On the contrary, every attempt to de-regulate the governance of technology in this sense will create even stronger problems, because institutional voids cannot be filled without democratic culture. Vice versa, as the chapter clearly shows, it is difficult to build a democratic culture without a complementary legal framework that clearly specifies normative goals.

The contributions to part three of the book reflect upon the possible future of participatory governance from theoretical and practical perspectives. In chapter 9, *Gabriele Abels* takes up the tension between institutional frames and participatory culture, which came out as being critical in chapter 8. Abels critically scrutinises the case of 'democratic' or 'participatory' technology assessment (pTA) that is probably the most wide-spread and thoroughly discussed example of governing technology by public participation. The chapter depicts the normative, epistemological and empirical background of participatory technology assessment and develops a comprehensive analytical frame for integrating pTA in the institutional context of representative politics. Today, as Abels argues, pTA is broadly located in an 'institutional void', a fact that also affects the potential impacts of this kind of participatory exercise. The author, therefore, tries to demonstrate, how pTA in particular and participatory procedures in general could be related to the institutional system of representative politics. In a comparative overview over a broad range of participatory settings, the chapter assembles substantive evidence for the presence of an institutional void. The subsequent view on democratic theory shows that pTA is not necessarily linked to a certain type of democratic theory. Rather, the normative grounds for pTA are heterogeneous and manifold. Therefore, as Abels argues, different forms of pTA can go along with different normative reasons. Moreover, the self-limitation to a certain strand of democratic theory limits our ability to see possible linkages between pTA and representative politics. Given the fact that pTA in its core is a form of policy advice, the question arises how pTA can be related to its social environment. On three dimensions – the level of activity, the appropriate participants, and the scope of potential addressees – the chapter presents a wide ranging overview over different procedural settings and their respective impacts. They all show particular capacities as regards representative institutions. Although taking a critical view of the excesses of euphoric expectations of participatory alternatives, Abels briefly argues for a case-by-case examination – similar to the chapters in part two – and finally anchors participation in the grounds of representative politics. In a wide theoretical sweep the author comes back to the starting point of our book. In political science, she opens theoretical horizons for a normative integration of the *routine forms* of institutional politics and of those forms of participatory governance, which are still widely understood as 'alternatives' to democratic institutions.

In chapter 10, *Alfons Bora and Heiko Hausendorf* look 'beyond participation'. Against the background of the above empirical and theoretical critique and based on experience in comparative studies the authors ask whether it might be advisable to carefully implement incremental changes in the routine mode of citizen participation in administrative decision-making? Theoretically, the chapter presents the idea of participation as communication. The theoretical background of this assumption is a combination of sociological systems theory and socio-linguistic conversation analysis. Both perspectives are grounded in communication theory. Social phenomena are therefore understood as communicative phenomena. The theoretical and methodological focus lies in the analysis of social structures. These structures, according to the basic theoretical assumptions, have to be understood as communicated expectations. Such expectations, as the chapter argues, have the particular property of constituting social positions (Hausendorf 2000). Some of the foregoing chapters have already demonstrated the empirical fruitfulness of this conceptual perspective. Bora and Hausendorf give additional accounts on the viability of the concept. In so doing, the authors study the practice of participatory discourse. With the theoretical instruments developed at the beginning, the social structures of participatory discourse are interpreted as social positions. Examples demonstrate that and show how such social positions are generated in participatory discourse. The interesting point with respect to the theoretical questions raised in the first chapters of this book lies in the fact that the institutional – namely legal – framework of participatory discourse fosters a certain dynamics of social positioning. This fact had already been indicated in chapters 4 and 8 by Münte and Ivanyi et al.

Such dynamics, as was argued, have both inclusive *and* exclusive effects. Participation as such, the central argument of the chapter, neither guarantees a greater degree of democratic culture nor does it compensate for the democratic deficit in modern society. Therefore, some suggestions are developed with respect to further institutional and political-cultural developments 'beyond participation'. Besides the demand for properly informing citizens and the transparency of the participatory procedure, the essence of the recommendations refer to the institutional setting in which participatory exercises are performed. According to Bora and Hausendorf, it is essential for all further endeavours in participatory governance to clearly analyse the *function* of participation in a given institutional context. To this extent, the chapter closely relates to chapter 9 and the discussion about the 'institutional void', where exactly this point was used to outline possible institutional settings for participation. Furthermore – and according to this argument – the role of 'alternative' forms has to be scrutinised very carefully. The theoretical and empirical results support the suspicion that participation – applied without careful analysis – may have serious dysfunctional and contra-intuitive effects (cf. also Bora, forthcoming). Altogether, in spite of this critical keynote, the chapter ends with a rather optimistic foresight: put on a social-scientific and comparative basis, the normative intention of governing technology through participation should not be abandoned. It will rather be supported by a theoretically well-grounded empirical analysis.

As we have tried to sketch out, the present volume assembles contributions of a broad interdisciplinary range within a comparative research programme that opens the black box of participatory governance. The central question is whether and to what extend the regulation of technology in modern, democratic society indeed benefits from public participation. The answer to this question is complex, disenchanting to some extent – at least for those who accord extended participation strong normative preference – and certainly not completely in the mainstream of the political and scholarly perception. In the course of the argumentation, however, the contributions produce numerous detailed results, which can be integrated in some general conclusions worth further discussion:

All contributions to this book confirm the impression that in modern democratic states the situation is characterised by a political-institutional context, which regularly locates citizen participation within the frame of a formal legal procedure. At the same time, the public debate about scientific and technological innovation such as in agro-biotechnology, for instance, is vivid and controversial. This holds true not only for the 'old' western European democracies and the OECD-world in general, but also for 'new' democracies in transition, such as Hungary, for instance. Public debates in all societies aim at political decision-making and at more general issues of collective interest. Therefore, in all chapters evidence is given for the suggestion that in situations where the chains of the legal communication are looser, where the culture is more inclined to public debate, there will be more signs of inclusive dynamics than in the current 'standard' situation, where administrative decision-making is captured in the 'iron cage' of law (Bora, forthcoming). Public debates are closer to legislation and to the parliamentary process than administrative decision-making. It might therefore be advisable to think about chances of transferring participatory elements from the executive (administration) to the legislature.

The cases gave reason to stress certain theoretical issues. With respect to political culture and to the institutional options for citizen participation the Hungarian case (chapter 8) is extremely instructive, because it shows increasing potential for conflict, in circumstances where public information is not widely available and public debate not yet very far developed. Therefore, the Hungarian case also gives support to the above-mentioned conclusion. It clearly shows the problematic effects of the current standard situation given the nature of the "silent" public. On the other hand, the detailed analysis of the Swedish case (chapters 5 and 6), both from a socio-legal and a socio-linguistic perspective, shows the enabling *and* limiting function of law. It also adverts to the changing character of the public debate under the condition of greater transparency. In this respect, institutional and cultural influences merge. The Italian case in turn illustrates the importance of culture and political action in a given institutional context. It, very strongly, points at the importance of a re-politicisation of the legally framed public debate – a suggestion that supports the above-mentioned requirement of a shift from administration to legislation. Given this presupposition, it is perhaps not so surprising, even in a sense self-evident, that participatory forms can – and perhaps should – be closely linked with institutional settings of representative democracy – that, in other words, they should not be understood merely as alternative (chapters 9 and 10). Last but not least, the analysis of micro-structures (chapters 4, 6 and 8) is an important means to understand the communicative logics of participatory settings. It gives reason to go 'beyond participation' in a certain sense: Not that participation as such should be discarded, but rather that it should be critically scrutinised with respect to its structures and potential functions (chapter 10).

Altogether, the findings presented in this volume indicate that the function of participation should be clarified with respect to the particular procedure and with respect to the constitutional and legal framework in any given case. Furthermore, all contributions clearly show that the function of participation should be made explicit in legal statutes. Moreover, any implementation of 'alternative' participatory forms should be accompanied by a precise scientific analysis of the function and structure of participation in the particular model.

The chapters of this book give detailed insight into the social dynamics that are triggered within the activity of governing technology by participation. On the level of concrete communication, these dynamics have turned out to be dysfunctional to the regulatory intentions in many cases. The chapters show empirically and theoretically, where and why social positions get into conflict with each other. Moreover, they demonstrate a certain danger that underlies a wide-spread 'participatory euphoria'. A merely normative approach – insinuating that any 'more' in participation will result in a 'more' of better regulation – may provoke the exact opposite of more *exclusive* dynamics and conflict. One aim of this book is to help avoid such an impasse and to support a constructive debate on further improvements in participatory governance, through the medium of theoretically reflexive, interdisciplinary and comparative research.

References

Abels, Gabriele and Bora, Alfons (2004): Demokratische Technikbewertung. Bielefeld: transcript Verlag.

Boltanski, Luc and Thevenaut, Laurent (1991): De la justification. Paris: Gallimard.

Bora, Alfons (forthcoming): Technoscientific normativity and the 'iron cage' of law. Manuscript. Bielefeld 2007. (Accepted for publication in Science, Technology & Human Values 2009) (http://www.uni-bielefeld.de/iwt/personen/bora/pdf/Alfons-Bora.technoscientific%20normativities.pdf).

Bora, Alfons (1999): Differenzierung und Inklusion. Partizipative Öffentlichkeit im Rechtssystem moderner Gesellschaften. Baden-Baden: Nomos.

Bora, Alfons (1999a): Discourse Formations and Constellations of Conflict: Problems of Public Participation in the German Debate on Genetically Altered Plants. In: Patrick O'Mahony (ed.), Nature, Risk and Responsibility. Discourses of Biotechnology. London: Macmillan, 130–146.

Fairclough, Norman (2003): Analyzing Discourse. London & New York: Routledge

Fuller, Steve (2000): The Governance of Science: Ideology and the Future of the Open Society. Open University Press, Buckingham, UK.
Habermas, Jürgen (1996): Between Facts and Norms. Contributions to a Discourse Theory of Law and Democracy. Cambridge: Polity.
Habermas, Jürgen (1984): The Theory of Communicative Action. Boston: Beacon
Hausendorf, Heiko (2000): Zugehörigkeit durch Sprache: eine linguistische Studie am Beispiel der deutschen Wiedervereinigung. Tübingen: Niemeyer.
Hausendorf, Heiko and Bora, Alfons (eds.) (2006): Analysing Citizenship Talk. Social positioning in political and legal decision-making processes. Amsterdam: John Benjamins. Discourse Approaches to Politics, Society and Culture 19.
Joss, Simon (1998): The Danish consensus conferences as model of participatory technology assessment. In: Science & Public Policy 25, 1, 2–22.
Liberatore, Angela and Funtowicz, Silvio (2003): 'Democratising expertise', 'expertising' democracy: what does this mean, and why bother? In: Science and Public Policy 1 June 2003, 146–150.
Luhmann, Niklas (2002): Die Politik der Gesellschaft. Frankfurt/M.: Suhrkamp
Marris, Claire and Joly, Pierre-Benoit (1999): Between consensus and citizens: public participation in technology assessment in France. In: Science Studies 12, 2, 3–32.
Nowotny, Helga, Scott, Peter and Gibbons, Michael (2001): Re-thinking science: knowledge and the public in an age of uncertainty. Cambridge MA: Polity Press.
Teubner, Gunther (1993): Law as an autopoietic system. Oxford: Blackwell.
Tuori, Kaarlo (2002): Critical Legal Positivism. Aldershot: Ashgate.

PART I

THEORETICAL CONCEPTS AND QUESTIONS

CHAPTER ONE

DISCOURSE, PARTICIPATION AND SOCIOLOGICAL THEORY

Patrick O'Mahony

The following is an exploration of the relevance of sociological theory to an acute modern societal problem, the problem of participation in democratic societies. Extended forms of political participation are called for on a wide variety of fronts as a possible contribution to the solution of highly complex and often partisan issues of collective decision-making and coordination. Today, there is a re-estimation of the importance of participation in institutional contexts. As an example, transnational governance regimes and organizations such as the European Union and the OECD support enhanced participation, albeit chiefly in the form of expanded consultative arrangements with a relatively limited remit (European Union 2001; OECD 2001). In addition, a more ad hoc structure of participatory innovation has emerged in democratic countries such as public hearings and forms of citizen deliberation, often as a response to pressure from civil society. Most western European countries manifest elements of such experimental participatory innovation, yet they are nowhere coherently institutionalized within the general cultural and structural framework of deliberative and decision-making arrangements (Abels and Bora 2004; Bora 1999). These developments signify a renewed interest in participation that extends beyond pluralist and corporatist models of interest group bargaining. They reflect a growing concern with the management of the spiraling complexity of modern societies and the twin phenomena of political alienation on one side and political conflict on the other.

The present volume addresses participation in the context of a pressing and divisive societal issue in contemporary European countries, that of GM plants. This issue is not simply a commonly experienced problem in different European societies, but is one that also raises the question of the balance between transnational co-ordination and national autonomy. As a divisive social issue, GM plants currently takes the form of an indivisible conflict in which compromise is hard to envisage and for that very reason calls forth the idea of expanded participation as a possible remedy. In the European Union, participation on the GM plants issues in inextricably bound up with trans-national policy making arrangements. All EU countries have to implement a structure of participation laid out in two Directives, 1990 and 2000, one succeeding the other, the latter significantly enhancing the consultative dimensions of participation. The Directives specify limited participation as a component of risk assessment procedures within the political-administrative system, procedures that also include a licensing system and a post-release monitoring regime, respectively decided upon and supervised by means of expert committees. The participation allowed for within this regime is comprised of written objections to a decision to grant a license within a specified period. It is therefore a limited form of citizen consultation, though the fact that the expert committees also have lay members could itself be regarded as a form of participation. Beyond this political-administrative regime and for the present largely superseding it, the issue has ignited a major public debate in European countries that has resulted in a climate of public opinion largely hostile to GM foods. This debate in its turn has generated further, more elaborate forms of participation, most notably the kinds of organized public consultation that has taken place with different formats in Ireland, France, Netherlands and Britain. What is striking about this debate and consultation exercise is the interdependence between public opinion and consultation procedures. The authorities in all countries have to find a path forward that satisfies their distinctive national publics, a process that in turn circumscribes the room for manoeuvre of all other countries as the European legislative context requires unanimity before GM crops can be commercialized in any one country. Given the interdependence, the issue provides a test case on the nature and functioning of a European public sphere (Durant et al. 1998).

In this essay, I will not address the specific characteristics of this example. Instead, informed by its exemplary background value for problems of participation, I will examine the relationship between public participation and sociological theory. On the whole, the new forms of participation have not been extensively theoretically addressed in sociological or political theory. I take up and seek to combine – at least in argument – a number of frontlines in sociological theory, viz, the status of the normative given the rise of discursive sociology and the associated relationship between what I describe below as normative-pragmatic theories and the strong theory of differentiation represented by Luhmann. I will suggest that there is potential for a critical synthesis of differentiation and pragmatic traditions in order to propose some ideas on how participation in contemporary democracies can be sociologically addressed from the standpoint of discourse and political structure formation.

A. Normative Pragmatic Theory, Democracy and Participation

A pragmatic theory of agency with a normative import at root draws on the republican idea of a collective good that can be known and at least potentially realized.[1] As against strong republican theories that aim at substantively elaborated versions of the good, sociologically informed pragmatic theory at most operates with weak specification of the good but with strong articulation of the mechanisms whereby it finds plural definition and achieves selective stabilization. Such a theoretical standpoint may be contrasted with systems theories that regard any common good standard as unrealizable in contemporary society and thence confine themselves to a procedural account of legitimacy (Willke 1992) or with post-structural theories that describe mechanisms for the stabilization of contingency according to a situation-relative standard of rationality (Rose 1999). Pragmatic theory with normative import is obliged to concern itself with the at least minimal specification of common goods to ground the epistemic and practical relation between *conscious* collective coordination and the production of expected outcomes. Without such a relation, necessarily articulated in modern societies as a cognitively related set of goods rather than a good (Walzer 1983), democratic institutions would be unable to understand and shape their societal environment and modern societies could consequently not be guided in any meaningful sense by collective will formation (Joas 1993). It is, of course, a major question of contemporary societal diagnostics where such standards can in fact be practically realized. Nonetheless, I venture to offer it as a prerequisite of an adequate normative pragmatic theory.

[1] Habermas (1996a) distinguishes his own deliberative model of democracy from republican and liberal models. He claims that republican theories, especially in their communitarian incarnation, over- substantialize and hence narrow public discourse by presuming an overarching common good. However, it can plausibly be argued that Habermas proceduralizes the republican version of the good in his consensual deliberative theory and remains committed at least to the idea that deliberatively realized popular sovereignty becomes socially effective through the medium of law.

A normative pragmatic theory in a sociological register requires two essential components, a theory of mechanisms and a theory of outcomes. The first reconstructs the ongoing and innovative processes of conscious collective choice making by social actors. Such collective choice making as conscious activity is explicitly oriented to ends but it does not follow that the outcomes of such actions conform exactly with the programmes or even the intersection of the programmes of contending actors. It means instead that there is *some* relation between the specification of ends in episodes of political action and the structural outcomes of such action.[2] The link between ends and outcomes opens the way to consideration of the mechanisms that transmute between the two. The second component of the theory, a theory of outcomes, must show the relation between mechanisms and outcomes and also demonstrate that the outcomes are significant in terms of control by democratic institutions of their societal environment.[3] For present purposes, I am applying these insights to the institutional political order; however, it could be applied to any structured form of political governance in which mechanisms of agency seek to shape an environment to allow certain kinds of power to flourish. Such a structured complex in the political system should not be thought of as complete in itself and environment indifferent. Rather, it must constantly respond to the contingency of an external environment that it does not directly control and seek to shape the operation of that environment with available political-administrative mechanisms, norms, rules, incentives and discourses.

In order to respond to external challenges that test its capacity to influence its societal environment, the political system depends on developing an adequate socio-cognitive model of its relation to that environment. This model gives form to the medium of communication

[2] The relationship between the genesis of worldviews and ultimate consequences can be considered through the history of the idea of environmentalism that can be understood as a progression from a relatively unelaborated idea to its potential ultimate realization as a political ideology. (O'Mahony 1996). It is not the case that the end state of environmentalism could have been precisely specified in its early formulations. This would be a metaphysical construct. It simply means that crucial components remain ideologically consistent over time.

[3] The treatment of outcomes is generally poor in social movement theory that otherwise contains much of the material needed for a theory of mechanisms. See an attempt by the present author and Gerard Delanty to conceptualize the relationship between mechanisms and outcomes in the case of the Irish national movement. (O'Mahony and Delanty 2001)

that connects system and environment. We may therefore understand political communication as taking place within a particular socio-cognitive order whose essential feature is to produce world defining and yet operational schemata that effectively couple inputs and outputs. Normative pragmatic theory is committed to the view that actor defined ends are critical inputs and normatively regulated order an indispensable output. There is, of course, a divide between the descriptive semantics of normative philosophy, especially theories of deliberative democracy, and normative pragmatic sociological theories in that the latter must empirically ground and not assume or ideally hypothesize the very conditions of possibility of pragmatic control. One understanding of the division of labour requires that philosophy and political theory propose normative orientations and sociology examine the conditions for their realization. However, that is only one route. Another is to regard sociology as listening for the heartbeat of imaginative change manifested in social practice, clarifying its possible telos and regarding normative theorists not as innovators so much as interested participants in the argumentation process. Up to the present, sociology has an uneven record in constructivist studies of the latter kind, generating a profusion of situated studies of local order as for example in the sociology of science but rarely tackling fundamental questions of normative integration and differentiation in an empirical-theoretical register.[4]

I will briefly consider these questions through the prism of two mature and influential normative pragmatic theories; that of Habermas and of Boltanski and Thevenot respectively. I shall be particularly concerned with how they fare on the two basic dimensions of a normative pragmatic theory in sociological view, the common-good mediated relationship between inputs and outcomes, on the one side, and the way in which this relationship is realized through particular societal mechanisms, on the other.

By contrast to Boltanski and Thevenot, Habermas's normative pragmatic theory is a strong theory articulated both in his – related – sociological work on communicative rationalizaton and political

[4] To be sure, if one wishes to conduct studies of the latter kind, one has to work in the absence of tried and trusted frameworks that have already generated good results and bodies of usable knowledge. In this respect. Boltanski and Thevenot may be regarded as a notable exception. Another major contribution is the work of Ferree et al. (2001, 2002)

philosophical work on deliberative discourse (Habermas 1984, 1987, 1993, 1996).[5] The combined theory specifies the relation between normativity and communication understood as a process of rationalization under the exigency of consensus formation. Habermas combines theories of segmentary, stratificatory and functional differentiation. These processes can be communicatively understood and hence rationalized by subjects within the limits of the distribution of social power. Modern segmentary differentiation, in a way that is at least formally strikingly similar to the late Luhmann, arises in the architecture of the political system organized into core, semi-periphery and periphery.[6] Stratificatory differentiation, increasingly disconnected from a theory of class, is based upon the access conditions to the public sphere of institutionally advantaged– core and semi-peripheries – and institutionally disadvantaged – peripheral – collectivities. The stratificatory theory is now a weak one but remains in the sense of differential capacities, even in the periphery, to articulate and hence politically respond to societal needs. The functional differentiation theory, strongly developed in the sociological work of the eighties, is less central in the later work, perhaps testament to the immense difficulty of combining plausibly structure and actor approaches. The later, more political work, translates one aspect of the earlier differentiation thesis, the separation and mediation of system and lifeworld, advancing significantly the theory of juridification sketched towards the end of that work, into a political theory of periphery and core (Habermas 1996). In this process, functional differentiation is re-coupled to the public sphere as the embodiment of civil society and made to respond to a normatively inspired theory of periphery-driven learning.

Periphery driven learning is carried in the form of discourses of various kinds of which morally significant ethical discourses are given primacy in social evolutionary terms. Habermas's work is pragmatic in the sense of an intersubjective account of the formal conditions of

[5] I distinguish between the two theories as strong or weak or the normative plane. Habermas claims to *reconstruct* the normative content of modernity as a progressive rationalization of the universal pragmatic bonds of intersubjective communication. Boltanki and Thevenot's work, by contrast, has no such normative connotations and therefore may be regarded as *constructivist* in analyzing the orders of worth that flow into argumentative discourse.

[6] In Habermas's case, the idea is idea of the circuit of political power between the political core, the semi-periphery of delegated autonomy and the societal periphery of the public is taken from Bernhard Peters (1993).

communication and its transposition onto the societal-evolutionary plane of communicative rationalization by means of a theory of democracy. Its strength lies in the retrospective reconstruction of the immanent normative potential of modernity to institutionalize moral univeralization via deliberation. Habermas is able to demonstrate that the moral premises of communicative rationality have become decisively institutionalized in the procedural forms of contemporary democracies.

Sociologically, however, while raising many fruitful questions this remains a limited reconstructive perspective in relation to the contingent direction of societal development. In this regard, the actual societal implications of periods and kinds of communicative rationalization built into institutionalized procedures of deliberation must be assessed in the wider context of non-normative structures and processes. For example, it remains a pivotal question, as specified above, whether rationalization instantiated in the legal-political order is mastering or merely finessing functional differentiation processes. From the other side, so to speak, the question can be asked as to what new communicative processes, themes and actors might be attaching themselves to the re-structuring of the political order. The latter raises issues of the direction of the 'guiding semantics' of societal development and the conflictual – pragmatic – fronts that will animate its possible forms. For this task, one cannot commence from the formal, social a apriori of the normative rationality of communication; one has to address the cognitive structures and actor-borne cognitive models that follow either a reproductive or transformative logic shaped in the crucible of public discourse and that vary across space and time.[7]

On the basis of these sociological remarks, it is possible to observe on some limitations of Habermas's account of institutionalization as communicative rationalization for sociological analysis and further theory development. The idea of the common good or goods as rationality criteria and substantive ends, indispenable to a normative pragmatic theory, survives in the later Habermas in the form of the outcomes of procedures of communicative rationalization that he understands now as carried in the political circuit of power (Habermas 1996). It is

[7] For a good account of the fluid social spaces that generate new capacities for agency, see Emirbayer and Sheller (1998). Hans Joas also addresses this question in *The Creativity of Action* and *The Genesis of Values* (1996 and 2000 respectively).

therefore a proceduralized thesis of the common good, the common good emerging from procedures to specify the good. However, this does not address the semantic and cognitive question of the common good as the immanent and explicit specification of societal ends that emerge from its conscious self-objectification. Put simply, it does not address the question of how society can *think* about the actual trajectory of its own development. Strydom, drawing attention to Habermas's limitations in this cognitive frame, speaks of his failure to attend to discourse synthesis. For Strydom, this present itself as a question of understanding the cognitive structures consciously generated from societal processes of argumentation. From a constructivist standpoint such cognitive structures, at first exploratory, emerge from conflict between innovating cognitive models; later they may become institutionally anchored in stabilized cognitive structures such as a regime of justice or ecological responsibility. It follows from this that Habermas world understanding is too normative and gives insufficient attention to either the cognitive structures that encompass the substantive specification of the common good or goods or the mechanisms whereby such a collective cultural order is discursively generated (Strydom 2006). The crucial point is that the world specification and learning processes build into cognitive structures are open to reconstruction on the temporal plane of social action and that once consolidated as structures have radical implications for societal organization. Normative order is therefore first cognitively elaborated rather than the other way around. Moreover, normative rationality remains continuously cognitively interpreted and elaborated. Following the above logic, then, it may be submitted that Habermas's approach works on an evolutionary reconstructive plane, but it is not elaborated on a projective, constructive plane.

Boltanski and Thevenot (1991) explicitly call for the re-moralization of sociology. However, they start from a standpoint of entrenched differences built into various historically formed evaluation regimes rather than Habermas's strategy of grounding the possibility and necessity of moral universalization as a learning potential built into the telos of rational communication itself. While Habermas's strategy is *consensual* in the sense of substantially grounding democratic principles through inclusive deliberative procedures, Boltanski and Thevenot are instead orientated to *compromises* between the foundational orders of worth – modes of evaluation – established in modern society, namely, industrial, civic, market, domestic, fame and inspiration.[8] These orders of worth form the basis for comparative analysis of their incidence and strength in different political systems and in this sense could be described as constructivist (Lamont and Thevenot 2000; Moody and Thevenot 2000; Thevenot, Moody and Lafaye 2000). Lamont and Thevenot (2000) provide a comparative, general account of repertoires of evaluation in France and the United States. The nearest conceptual analogue to their use of 'repertoires of evaluation' is 'political culture'. However, repertoires of evaluation are conceived theoretically and methodologically on a different basis. Theoretically they refer to philosophically delineated interpretive traditions as opposed to politically relevant public belief systems and methodologically they are derived from the analysis of texts rather than survey data. Repertoires of evaluation also have a constitutive dimension in the sense that their utilization potentially generates new relational patterns that suggest the idea of fluid – at least in the combination of different repertoires in specific polities – rather than unchanging components of 'political culture'.

The above remarks suggest there is some value in using the core ideas of Boltanski and Thevenot, and associated writers such as Lamont, as a projective, constructivist account of the discursive and evaluative basis of political systems. However, recognition of any such value must be tempered by the equal recognition of some limitations. In the first case, the concept of repertoires of evaluation is tied very closely to the discourse positions of protagonists in political conflicts; to each participation, one repertoire (Moody and Thevenot 2000). By contrast, what is frequently interesting about such positions in periods of conflict is how they combine different semantic dimensions or keeping consistent terminology how they would combine repertoires.[9] Such acts of combination are particularly the case in periods of symbolic conflict when agents are struggling to generate innovation, combining

---

[8] Giegel (1992) identifies three dimensions of the 'consensus concept' in the background consensus of the lifeworld in the sense of Schutz, results oriented consensus or compromises and consensus arrived at by means of argumentation not achieved by results but by the grounding – or procedural rationality – whereby a result is achieved. The latter two rather well relate to the distinction between Boltanski and Thevenot and Habermas.

[9] The specification of orders of worth are good approximations of what could be understood in the conceptual register of frame theory as 'symbolic packages', ie, packages of discursively coherent frames that confront one another in public discourse.

established cultural beliefs and values with new ones. In the Boltanski/Thevenot approach, the orders of worth and the actors who carry them are not conceived pragmatically as intersubjectively operating and interactively open; hence, from the outset, it does not bestow adequate attention upon mechanisms of variation. It is only by adding an interactive dimension in this sense to the basic theory that it truly becomes of value as a constructivist undertaking.

In the second case, their approach does not systematically address general political normative structures and their cognitive foundations. The work points in this direction in the reconstruction of dimensions of the French and US systems (Lamont and Thevenot 2000) but does not address regimes of political normativity in a systematic fashion. This task would require more than, for example, reference to chracteristic republican and liberal features of the two polities but a willingness to address the respective ideological and intersubjective foundations of normative commitments. In an essay on John Rawls, Habermas distinguishes between the universal, obligatory commitment of norms and the preferential ordering of cultural goods represented by values (1995: 115). The strength and yet the weakness of this school of sociology lies in its promising treatment of justificatory values. However, it does so without addressing the general normative context in which such values are located. As currently developed, their work may be regarded more as the sociology of normative pragmatic regimes rather than a normative pragmatic sociology in the more emphatic sense. To acquire the latter standing something like Habermas's account of discursive, norm-forming procedures and their outcomes is a necessary complement to the constructivist value of orders of worth that can be empirically operationalized.

These normative pragmatic approaches in certain respects complement one another, while even together they leave much unresolved from a sociological perspective. Habermas's approach is strong on outcomes, communicatively established and replenished democratic normative structures, but short on mechanisms, dynamics, and the evaluative trajectories embodied in discourse ('discourse synthesis'). Boltanski and Thevenot do by contrast identify empirically reconstructable pragmatic regimes but in their relatively rigid form they come at the cost of considering interaction dynamics, at least in a fine-grained sense, normative innovation and even more fundamentally than Habermas, discourse synthesis as a cognitive learning process. The last three dimensions are pivotal to the sociological theorizing of participation and while they can be better *theorized* from the Habermasian perspective it suffers from the sociological-constructivist limitations described above, limitations that become clearer when the attempt is made to move onto the methodological plane. The normative-pragmatic theories of Habermas and Boltanski and Thevenot advance an important perspective for sociological accounts of participation with the regulative idea that collective agents acting within normatively organized structures can in defined historical, territorial and institutional contexts impose order on contingencies generated by social and natural processes. Habermas goes further. The historically achieved capacity to embody *the right* in democratic governance arrangements is capable in benign conditions of also maintaining and advancing *the good* of society.

Neither the normative pragmatic theories of Habermas or Boltanski and Thevenot are by themselves sufficiently comprehensive theories with which to conduct societal diagnosis on the sociological plane. The question of how free are normative pragmatic structures and forces to shape their societal environments in deliberative arenas or by public discourse is not simply a question of concluding there is some measure of pragmatic autonomy shaping social structures; it is also a question of continuously exploring the limits of this autonomy. Today, the question of autonomy in sociology is less presented either in the classical philosophical sense after Kant of the conditions for the autonomy of the individual will or in the sense of classical sociology on a notion of collective autonomy that is dependent on the differential play of social power between groups. These questions have not gone away, but they have been joined, and in sociology partly superseded, by the question of the extent to which formal organizations and steering media curtail or remove altogether the autonomy of human actions (Peters 1993). This is a complex dialectic whose outcome does not univocally point in one direction only for systems confer not simply constraints but freedom too. This has been explored in critical theory in Habermas's two-track theory of system and lifeworld and in Offe's idea of the desirability of uncoupling social spheres to relieve the spiral of complexity (Habermas 1984, 1987; Offe, 1987).

Hence, in the first place, there is a requirement to consider the point of view that *relatively* autonomous systems confer not simply efficiency gains but indirect normative advantages, ironically by disburdening over-stretched pragmatic capacities. In the second place, reaching beyond Boltanski and Thevenot's idea of pragmatic regimes, no less than Luhmann's and Habermas's respective accounts of social movements as peripheral mobilizations, lie the organizational and discursive issues of how such movements or other collective social forms come to be, what social needs do they embody that reach the form of a collective understanding of the world that animates discursive explication? And this applies not simply to social movements but to all collective social positions that can be argumentatively mobilized. The idea of socially interpreted needs can be combined with that of natural or social constraints to generate the requirement that modern societies must be capable of unceasing social innovation. Social innovation comprises both the ongoing explication of needs under conditions of constraint and the possibility that they can be realized by means of transformed practical social rationality.

Social innovation can be viewed from either the standpoint of the empirical manifestation of new need interpretations and associated rationality structures or from the normative register of rationality standards that judge what counts as socially feasible, just, responsible, tolerable and desirable. A sociological normative pragmatic approach must combine the two, the one constructive and the other both reconstructive and future-oriented. These two dimensions therefore combine an empirical and normative approach to episodes of social innovation. This approach involves the application of a constructivist reconstructivism in which the generation of potentialities is first constructively identified and the reconstructive implications of these potentialities are then social theoretically elaborated. In turn, these reconstructive implications then direct inquiry into the chances of realization of the identified potentialities in given situations. The normative pragmatic approaches sketched above suggest the existence of collective will formation – regimes of moral justification in Habermas's sense, of evaluative justfication in Boltanski and Thevenot's – built into political institutions. In the case of the matter at issue in this paper, the normatively informed reconstructive idea is that society is capable of organizing a different level of public participation and the reconstructive task of a normative pragmatic theory is, firstly, to show the ways in such an idea is either positively or negatively embedded in the consciously comprehended schemata of actors and, secondly, to examine the contexts of these schemata in order to assess the prospects for realizing participatory innovation in the complex conditions of modern societies.

B. Normativity and Autonomy: Systems Theory and Participation

The first sociological issue that opens up from the previous section is whether contemporary society can be normatively organized at all? The related question is how intrinsic is public participation to this process? Both the above positions, Habermas quasi-transcendentally and explicitly, Boltanski and Thevenot empirical-theoretically and implicitly defend the idea that normative order is an intrinsic component in the reproduction of modern societies. Such a contention, however, does not answer the question of its efficacy in constituting society as an agreed – by consensus and compromise – normative reality in its contemporary modern form. What both strains of work bring to the fore is that the cognitive schemata that underpin any such normative reality determine the underlying possibility of normative order. What opens up in relation to the question of participation from this understanding is how such schemata, or their sum in the form of idealizations, relate on the one hand to the problem of complexity in modern societies and on the other to the question of extended participation as a solvent of unmanageable complexity.

In order to address these questions, I will first of all address the opposing view that society cannot any longer be normatively integrated according to society-wide democratic idealizations, following Bora's (1999) version of systems theory, a view that nonetheless foresees the possibility of expanded participation under certain conditions. For Bora following Luhmann, the historical logic of differentiation means that social systems have become autonomous and therefore achieve operative closure from their environment constituted by other social systems and contingent processes. Social systems themselves and not the actors who populate them advance social evolution. However, Bora's approach does not abandon normative innovation, echoing the remarks above on systems as normatively creative. He describes a process of 'pluralistic norm-building' that can occur as a consequence of a social system reflexively observing its effects on its environment. Participatory arenas can help with this process of pluralistic norm building by bringing the communication codes of systems into closer relation with one another (see Willke 1992 for a broadly similar formulation). These participatory arenas, as is commonly but mistakenly supposed, do not serve the function of consensus building so as to reshape the internal procedures of social systems. Instead, participatory procedures offer a means for systems to externalize *norm-building* processes. The outcomes of these processes may then influence *norm application* procedures *within* the given system. The latter can only occur, however, in line with its semantic codes and operational rules. Participatory procedures, then, provide a lens whereby systems can observe their resonance on other systems and build the results of this observation into their internal operational procedures.

Bora seeks to decisively differentiate his approach as a system-environment one from the alternative actor-structure approaches that enjoy wide influence in contemporary sociology in the work of figures such as Giddens, Etzioni Bourdieu and Archer These writers seek to join together macro- and micro-sociology by exploring how actors and structures reciprocally influence one another. At lease in the view of Hans Joas (1996: 230–238), the first two of these writers, plus a host of others including Etzioni, Randall Collins and Touraine can be grouped together under the loose rubric of 'constitution theory' with the aim of the 'democratization of differentiation'. The essential point in Bora's detailed but negative consideration of this approach is that its 'dualism' presumes that actors can influence structures, a position he finds untenable because actors cannot be elements of social systems. The view that actors cannot be elements of systems derives from the system theoretical distinction between social and psychic systems. Social systems depend on social processes of communication. By contrast, individuals are psychic systems and as such can only belong to the environment of social systems, even if apparently animating communication. Sociology cannot be concerned with the intra-psychic processes of these individuals. Individuals influence social systems only by 'irritating' the communication codes of these systems forcing them into further semantic distinctions. The construction of new patterns of system semantics – the specific systemic logic of distinctions - then objectively confronts individuals and directs their possible actions. This categorical distinction between actors and systems demands of social theorists to base their theoretical frameworks on the side of social systems, rather than as in structuration theory to assume mediation between actors and systems.

Participation emerges from this account as a process that improves the reciprocal resonance of social systems. Social communication in participative arenas can be understood as the encounter of the semantics of different social systems in the light of the potential for further autopoiesis, the generation of new semantic distinctions and the setting in train of the further evolution of those systems. It is the semantic codes of systems that adapt or learn when actors from different institutional milieus encounter one another in participatory arenas rather than the individuals, who can only learn indirectly by triggering and then observing the autopoiesis of these systems.

Bora considers but rejects Schimank's attempt to reconcile actor and systems approaches (Schimank 1996). Schimank distinguishes three kinds of actor perspective with respect to social systems: the most general level comprising of the perceptual horizons of actors that shape preference formation in social sub-systems and that have the function of reducing the complexity of such systems for the actor; the middle-level of rule systems that have the function of guiding action; and the most specific level of the interactive coordination of actor's intentions. Schimank's three levels roughly correspond with the, by now conventional, formula of distinguishing social life into macro, meso and micro levels. According to Bora, Schimank confines the self-organization that he regards as essential to understanding integration in dualistic actor-structure theories to the micro level of actor interaction described above, but interaction on this level generates adaptation on the other two levels.

Schimank's approach amounts to a bridge between action theory and systems theory that remains close to the systems theoretical tradition. Essentially, he raises the possibility that the explicit, rational understanding of social systems by social agents can partly shape their structural organization and semantic codes. Actors perceptions in this view are not merely local and one-dimensional but absorb and reconstruct abstract cognitive orders. Actually, Schimank's position is only one of a range of attempts at reconciliation of actors and structures that includes Joas's idea of constitution theory – leaning to the primacy of action – and Habermas who grants systems substantial autonomy but gives primacy to the socio-cultural order of the lifeworld (Joas 1996; Habermas 1984, 1987). Notwithstanding its leaning to systems theory, Bora considers Schimank's approach untenable as it mixes system and actor perspectives with the outcome of rendering it unclear how actors – understood here strictly as individuals – could belong to social systems in the first place. In essence, Bora's point is how could actors direct the evolution of social systems without dissolving the autonomy of these systems?

The difference between these two authors lies on the fault-line of contemporary social theory. What Bora describes as dualistic actor-structure theories do lead into the kinds of problems he describes since in one way or another everything has to be led back to the actor. This in turn leads to a constrained apprehension of society as an ensemble of structures that has always to be understood in terms of the projects of actors. This objection acquires particular force if the actors in question are considered to be, as Bora infers to Schimank's position, strictly individual actors as opposed to collective actors. Bora defends the integrity of the actor-less sociology of Luhmann that restricts actors to the status of psychical systems that can be regarded as distinct from the social. Actors are therefore at best conduits for the kind of communicative variation that is assumed to take place only by means of social systems.

Luhmannian sociology seeks to exclude reasons and intentions from the horizons of actors on the grounds that contra Habermas and others with an alternative linguistic-pragmatic reading of the contemporary world, actors cannot enter into joint intersubjective collective intentionality in communication; instead they can only observe and attribute possible intentions to other actors on the basis of their manifest communication. This orientation gives a decidedly semantic cast to Luhmann's social theory, where learning in the sense of enhanced appreciation of the resonance of system communication excludes the pragmatic dimensions of communicative action. The methodological correlate for this, following Bora, is the social scientific observation of the process of structural coupling of communication in participatory arenas. Such structural coupling occurs between the codes of different social systems and may result in further autopoiesis within given systems; it may also allow for participatory innovation that respects the codes of different social systems.

It is reasonable to regard this as a variation on the general process whereby the semantic structures of public opinion engage with social systems, as Luhmann explores in the *Die Politik der Gesellschaft (2002)* Here, Luhmann, with a structure-periphery architecture somewhat similar to Habermas (1996) sees an important role for social movements operating on the periphery, and thereby with greater environmental sensibility, to induce variation in the political system. For Luhmann, these social systems focalize public opinion in such a way that the periphery is capable of generating a semantics that resonates back on the core of the political system. This is also similar to Habermas's admittedly more normative formulation of the role of the periphery as responsibility demanding via the medium of the public sphere. However, neither author truly addresses the discursive significance of movements, though both see movements as mediating between periphery and core even if they ultimately belong to the periphery. From the Luhmannian perspective, it might even be said that if movements qua movements can influence political agendas, perhaps even political structures, can it not also be said that some kind of collective intentionality can shape political processes? If this were so, and it is more easy to establish at the level of collective rather than individual agency, could it not also be said that movements bring new canons of reason into the institutions of the political core with repercussions for wider social systems? This perspective offers some encouragement to Schimank's explorations described above on the expanded if far from decisive influence of human actions on function systems. In Luhmann's terms, the penetration of new semantics from the periphery transmutes into a problem of the resonance of political communication on system semantics, first within the political system and later between the political and other systems. The problem should not be posed as one of comprehensive normative foundations for social coordination but more in the sense of a restricted normative basis for public reason. How wide ranging such a normative basis should be is hard to prescribe this side of a comprehensive *substantive* theory of rights, justice and responsibility and a specification of how these could be *procedurally* secured.

Here, I arrive at the theoretical core of the essay. The above reflections on systems theory, normativity and participation lead to the following conclusions. Conceived individualistically, it is hard to see how actors can influence the operation and evolution of social systems that recursively structure interaction. However, they can have an aggregative, at least partly unintentional, effect on systems by means of their collective preference formation. I leave to one side this kind of rational action consideration and the degree to which it may be regarded as intentional in favour of another kind of impact of actors on social systems already sketched above; the degree to which in episodes of collective action – loosely conceived – agents come to develop macro-level reasons for substantive and procedural innovation in democratic ideals and arrangements which, if successfully institutionalized, have implications for social organization generally. Apart from the moral core of basic rights and obligations, the mechanisms of modern society do not allow stability on either the substantive plane of political values or the procedural instantiation of these values. Hence, innovative collective ideals that sometimes reach the status of widely shared ideologies constantly re-shape substantive democratic goals and procedures.

The normative pragmatic tradition, whether the attempt to rationally ground norms in the case of Habermas or to empirically specify cognitive regimes as in Boltanski and Thevenot or a variety of other traditions, assumes that actors have the capacity to shape social organization by means of arguments that ultimately stem from the distinctive social positions in which they are embedded. Such a theory must also assume that these differences can both be fully represented and yet transcended by means of rational discourse. Hence, argumentation across social positions in the right institutional circumstances and conditions of discursive openness enables collective learning that takes the form of new cognitive models. These cognitive models in turn can potentially reshape politically relevant cognitive structures such as, for example, ideas concerning the normative desirability and practical achievability of expanded participation.[10] This tradition does not exclude what Habermas calls 'subjectless communication' as issue cultures develop and reach beyond the specific social positions that initially have a certain proprietary hold on them, but at base it depends on the rationalization of society-relevant needs by pragmatically situated agents and their subsequent institutionally supported intersubjective coordination. The systems theoretical tradition, on the other hand, holds that such embedded positions are an illusion and that individual or collective social actors can at best irritate social systems into further autopoiesis but actors cannot directly specify codes or programmes for

[10] It should be noted that this example is largely hypothetical as neither Habermas nor Boltanski and Thevenot make strong arguments for expanded public participation. The former is somewhat ambiguous in this regard as it appears a corollary of the universalization principle of discourse ethics that differentiated publics should be sufficiently involved in political processes that they can give uncoerced assent to proposed solutions to matters that effect them. In *Between Facts and Norms* (1996), Habermas claims the deliberative involvement of the public with a view to meeting this standard can be indirectly met by the communicative structuring of legal-political institutions. However, it could hardly be claimed that multiple publics in contemporary public spheres normally have the means to comprehensive assert their positions given differences of competence, knowledge and access. It is this gap that allows one to assert that Habermas's theory still depends on the real and not simply counter-factual expansion of public participation. This gap, in the case of Habermas, can of course be partly, though not entirely, explained as the difference between philosophical and sociological projects.

these systems. In Luhmann, the very movements themselves are conceived as loose coalitions of discourse drawn up in the free spaces at the environments of multiple social systems and minimally crystallizing an otherwise diffuse public opinion. Further, participation as the coordination of action that would circumscribe the autonomy of systems is theoretically excluded. Prima facie, the ontological and theoretical choices that open up from this divide are almost disabling. Any attempts at mediating positions risk possible incoherence by mixing strongly articulated theoretical premises and elaborations. Nonetheless in the next section I propose to attempt to develop such a mediating position and then to relate it to the question of theorizing public participation.

C. Democracy, Participation and the Societal Environment

Part of the effort of this essay has been to conceptualize how the claims of democracy interpreted as a normative pragmatic social theory can be related to its societal environment comprised of, on the one side, formally organized spheres and, on the other, extra-institutional practices of ideal innovation. In delineating these dimensions more clearly I will speak of the 'three-level model'. This model is composed of (a) self-referential social systems as understood by Luhmann capable of internally processing an external environment on temporal, social and material planes and stabilizing corresponding organized and interactional worlds (b) institutionalized, normatively regulated arenas generating rule systems that deal with 'human-centred' questions of the good and the right in the context generated by (a) above and (c) to follow and (c) combined semantic and pragmatic regimes of associated identity and ideal interpretation systems either managed from the centre or mobilized on the periphery and for which the work of Boltanski and Thevenot offers a degree of approximation, for example in the tentative idea of a green order of worth. These components could be understood to be processually instantiated in a version of the centre-periphery model, variously adumbrated by Habermas (following Peters 1993) and Luhmann, albeit with different normative intentions. The three worlds identified above circulate between *macro-level models of form*, respectively functional coding, normative institutionalization and ideas; *meso-level models of activity*, respectively distinctions drawn by interacting systems, communicative rationalization in institutionally regulated arenas and diffuse learning processes in heterogeneous interaction contexts; and *micro level cognitive models* respectively of expectations, justifications and cultural projections. The relationship between these dimensions are outlined in figure 1 below:

Dimension/ Level	Functional	Normative	Ideal
Macro (cognitive structures)	Codes	Norms	Ideas
Meso (inter-action processes)	Systemic and Inter-systemic Communication	Normative Rationalization Via public Reason/discourse	Common Horizon Formation
Micro (cognitive models)	Expectations	Justifications	Projections

It would be a daunting task, and certainly impossible in an essay of this kind, to properly defend such a theoretical architecture rather than, as I have done, simply deriving it from a reading of the interconnections of social theories. All three of the above levels of theoretical articulation are at work and needed in making sense of the political world. From an applied perspective, both Habermas and Luhmann operate on a strongly future oriented plane. As we have seen above, Habermas offers a universalistic normatively driven theory of communicative rationalization and Luhmann anticipates the global universality of autopoietic social systems, calling forth a secondary normative thesis of universal inclusion in such a global order. Finally, theories concerned with ideal interpretation systems ('constructive ideality') explore how innovative ideas may – or may not – emerge in episodes of collective learning in specific societal conditions as candidates for either functional system formation or normative institutionalization. This ideal innovation can also be thought of in another register as historically sedimented innovation that retains institutionally sanctioned pragmatic force. An example of the latter kind would be identity complexes that retain a 'symbolic surplus', which can be creatively applied in either arguing for or opposing innovative ideas. Even when opposing innovative ideas, these complexes can still be symbolically innovative in the sense of a creative re-use of existing resources to defend existing institutional orders and power balances.

Theories operating at this level of abstraction can only offer general orientations for concrete cases. Normative theories offer a reconstructive dimension drawing attention to the institutionalized forces at work in given situations and a future-oriented dimension exploring the construction of normative problems and solutions. Theories such as Luhmann's, which disavow having normative intentions, nonetheless have normative implications, for example, in the critique of the over-extension of inappropriate norms that impede the evolution of autonomous systems.[11] Theories of constructive ideality emphasise the degree to which the normative order depends on shifting socio-cognitive interpretation systems. Interpretation systems have particular import for the pragmatic dimension of normative pragmatic theory as they are more open to cognitive re-shaping by agents, individual or collective, than either codes or norms. Institutionalized political agents, for example, will develop a normative account of the proper relationship between procedural democratic norms and system codes, perhaps combining restricted rights to public oversight with freedom of innovation in scientific controversies. The conditions of modern society are such interpretations constantly generating unstable particularistic values that mediate between more stable norms and codes. Hence, pragmatic innovations generate substantive orientations towards new forms of differentiation or normative rationalization. If norms and rules are to be justified and applied both the pragmatic condition of *intentional innovation* and the normative condition of *discursive rationalization* must both be met in complementary activities of structure building. It is not enough that norms are somehow there and enjoy mute acceptance; agents must understand them and defend them over time. This does not preclude a multitude of other forms of innovation for every mode of coordination at every societal level outlined in figure 1 above; modern society would be unthinkable without this creativity and autonomy. The normative pragmatic contention is both ambitious and modest. The direction and tempo of modern society bears the form of ethico-moral rationalization and must continue to do so but this rationalization must not over-reach itself, as it does not and must not control other kinds of innovation.

---

[11] See Richard Munch on Luhmann in Munch (1990: 444) who makes a similar point.

The above schema may be used to explain why the practice of public participation in political deliberation and decision meets considerable sociological resistance. From the systems theoretical standpoint participation is possible and desirable provided it does not involve the public directly in shaping the internal codes of social systems. In other words, public participation should not seek to normatively steer social organization. Instead, it acquires a function within political systems that enable decisions to be reached that conform with the imperative – in this sense normative – codes of a given system, primarily the legal and political systems from the vantage point of decision, administrative or legal. Public participation of varying forms hence comes in under the aegis of particular systems and enlightenment is not regarded as extending from public to system but the other way around. The public becomes educated by what it cannot achieve by means of participation; it learns by disappointment. In this sense, it learns to conform to substantive norms and not to procedurally over-reach itself. Procedures conform to system requirements and systems acquire legitimacy by the public learning the nature of such requirements through procedures. Systems are also enabled to draw further distinctions, ie, to continue autopoiesis by learning from the interplay of discourse constellations in participatory settings. Hence, public participation conceived as linked to system logics via procedures has a place in systems theory but it does not have the kind of normative role envisaged for it in stronger theories of participation that argue for the real participation of civil society in societal opinion-formation and decision-making.

In the normative-pragmatic account of Habermas, public participation is also not as classically envisaged. In fact, Habermas restricts the role of civil society and in the formulation of 'subjectless communication' channels the pragmatic force of dynamic components, associations and movements, into terms amenable to deliberatively controlled formal decision procedures. On the one side, Habermas's approach drawing from an ultimately republican wellspring of the liberties of the ancients, participation and communication, crafts a conception of communicatively shaped deliberation that involves a comprehensive, i.e., society spanning, concept of participation. On the other, his polycentric conception of society categorically rejects a thorough going reverse colonization of already deliberatively structured administrative enclaves by civil society through the form of a structure transforming public participation. The influence of civil society, reflecting the concerns of a rationalized lifeworld, is discursively – indirectly – rather than directly realized. Habermas does not erect a barrier between public reason and public discourse, as does John Rawls, and in that sense is able to claim that normative rationalization proceeds inwards to the legal-political core rather than outwards from it. The concept of 'subjectless communication' involves the transmutation of the partial discourses of civil society into an orientational discourse that can be processed in the deliberative reason of law and politics, a process that in turns generates an output rationality in the form of normative steering of their societal environment, allowing the conclusion that society can be regarded as mediately normatively integrated.

This formulation has generated considerable disappointment amongst proponents of stronger participation. One objection, important here, is that the division between core deliberation and periphery agenda-setting instantiates a clear division between the two realms that implies that existing structures can allow the periphery to adequately influence structures of political power. However, theorists such as Fraser with her idea of 'participatory parity' claim that this is by no means the case and that the architecture of contemporary democracy cannot simply be left as it is. But such calls for participation are only articulated normative philosophically; they are neither empirically supported by analysis of participation experiments nor elaborated by means of sociological theory. The absence of the latter is particularly pressing in this essay. On the one side, normative political philosophy and political theory clarifies both reconstructively and projectively the implications of different sets of normative commitments. On the other, the situated study of participation in action illustrates actual normative potentialities or disappointed expectations. Neither address the sociological question of how innovative normatively oriented participation arrangements could contribute to regaining in contemporary circumstances the vitality of democracy as a means of ensuring that society is tolerably normatively integrated on grounds that are both feasible and defensible.

The latter task is clearly a large one and beyond the bounds of this essay to fully address. Surveying the theoretical considerations outlined in the essay so far, systems theory offers a restricted account of participation that is embedded in sociological theory but is neither normative in the sense of a revitalized theory of democracy as a theory of at least minimal normative steering of society nor pragmatic in the sense of allowing an agential role in shaping normative orientations.[12] Deliberative theory in its Habermasian formulation construes *public* participation as procedurally minimal and taking effect mainly in the form of society spanning mechanisms of discursive argumentation. Radical critiques of Habermas expand the normative canvas to include wider question of parity with respect to inclusion, power, voice and so on but do not consider the matter in relation to sociological theory or in consideration of empirically manifest dynamics. Empirical accounts of participation travel light on theory of any kind, guided more by pragmatic intuitions of desirable normative innovation. Boltanski and Thevenot offer a sophisticated version of how social positions with democratic import are pragmatically embedded in ethical worlds but it is not clear how such worlds combine in normative regimes that can be morally justified in line with the requirements of a theory of democratic participation. The potential green world, for example, is adumbrated without attention to the fundamental green axiom of expanded public participation.

As against this, on the one side, largely pessimistic reading of the theoretical state of the art on participation as democratic innovation, I have also advanced the idea that more is to be gained by combining the sum of the parts than regarding them in isolation. In particular, combined sociological theory can advance itself as a needed concomitant to political theory in relation to the task of conceptualizing and also researching issues in democratic innovation, including participation. I have suggested above a basic three-level framework for addressing this task. In the remainder of this essay I wish to consider the positive contribution of combining – at least in the sense of identifying overlapping possibilities – sociological theory traditions towards the task of clarifying the possibilities and potentialities of participation as democratic innovation.

D. Sociological Theory and Innovation in Participation

The first challenge facing a sociological theory of any aspect of democracy, including participation, is to illustrate its relevance. In figure 1

[12] I leave to one side here whether systems theory can actually be reconciled with some variants on a liberal reading of democracy. See Gerhards, Neidhardt and Rucht (1998) for such some suggestive remarks along these lines.

above, I delineate three levels by means of which the sociological contribution may be conceptualized. The central column of the figure corresponds to the democratic function of normative integration. At the centre – the middle column of the entire figure – is the locus in which public participation should be centrally theorized as a component of the interaction processes of public reason and public discourse that carry the burden of normative rationalization. Public reason is distinguished from public discourse by virtue of its constitutional and deliberative remit; it is therefore pivotal to the reproduction of the macro level of norms. Public discourse, on the other hand, relates to the active justification of procedures and outputs of political processes before a public and consists of the formation of political belief regimes that are shared between political actors and the public. Shortly, I will consider how these levels come together to shape a context for understanding expanded public participation but first I need to consider these processes from the vantage point of the levels of reality reflected in the other columns of the figure.

Two pivotal dimensions of these relations need to be considered, epistemic and consequential. From the standpoint of the democratic order each of these may be regarded as transactional in an input-output sense, that is, they involve relations going both ways. From the standpoint of the democratic order, epistemic relations involve feeding the outputs of social systems into *substantive* normative conceptualizations, for example, Rawls idea of a political conception of justice (Rawls 1993). Reciprocally, social systems must be aware of normative constraints on their operations deriving from such substantive normative conceptualizations, both in the more explicit sense of normative rules governing non-normative operations – the classical example is market regulation – and, more indirectly, the normative commitments of actors set within them – participation and information rights to give just two examples. From a *consequential* standpoint, democratic institutions are set within a field of opportunities and constraints established by social systems that substantially determines their horizons of possibility; they depend on economically generated resources, scientifically generated knowledge, legally generated judgements and so on. Correspondingly, such social systems operate quite differently as a result of their embedding in a democratic society than they otherwise might. Democratic norm building imposes on social systems not simply efficiency norms such as fair competition but also distributive norms such as the minimum wage, procedural norms such as participation rights and publicity norms such as information rights.

The third column, reflecting the activity of cognitive innovation, adds exogenous epistemic critique and practical evaluation to societally available reflexive capacity. Both social systems and democratic institutional complexes utilize as part of their epistemic repertoire endogenous reflexive monitoring of different kinds, the one processual-semantic and the other normative-pragmatic. However, beyond such routine acts of adjustment, radical normative change involves the consolidation of alternative epistemic horizons to those either operative as codes or institutionalized as norms. In Touraine's conceptualization, modern societies seek to act on their own historicity and to modify – or transform – it. In contemporary societies, the possibility of revolutionary transformation to a completely new social model is no longer a feasible horizon – at least so long as these societies wish to remain modern. This does not exclude, however, re-evaluations that propose normative innovation and code modification from spaces beyond existing systemic or institutional structures. As long as these are consolidated into associations carrying recognizable ideologies over time, they can be considered the product of collective movements. Recent influential examples of this kind are right-wing libertarianism and green ecologism. As idea systems penetrate from the periphery they gradually lose their exclusive identification with a particular collective movement and begin to resonate with norms – and normative conditions of epistemic agreement as to the right – and with codes – and with conditions of semantic coherence of systemic communication systems. In terms of Boltanski and Thevenot such innovation could involve as with right wing libertarianism the re-evaluation of orders of worth – promotion of market and domestic orders over the civic one, for example – or the introduction of new orders of worth – for example, the green order of worth. Such innovations offer a substantive or cognitive context for the generation of new structures of expectations and justifications that add to or modify the role of existing structures in orienting social action.

There is a close affinity between cognitive innovation, captured in this third column, and the lower and middle dimensions of the second column. Cognitive innovation generated by discursive practices becomes effective first in democratic justification regimes and then penetrates into democratic interaction systems and procedures. By this process, the democratic complex is enabled to absorb substantive innovations and by degrees in successful cases turn them into constitutional and operational norms. Democracy is thereby substantively responsive as well as constitutionally and procedurally accountable. From a sociological point of view, such responsiveness is a key concern in that it enables public agendas to become politically relevant. This is key to focalizing the question of public participation in a sociological register. It is triply framed. Firstly, direct public participation takes place by means of a range of procedural mechanisms that incorporate manifestations of incipient public will formation into democratic procedures. It therefore translates between the third and second columns, between socio-cognitive innovation and normative institutionalization. Secondly, as a set of procedural mechanisms set within the democratic system, public participation ideally translates between the normative core and public justification regimes. Thirdly, public participation takes places within an input-output relation to social systems in that the operational horizons of such systems condition norm-building efforts within contexts of public participation.

The increasing salience of public participation as a solution to governance problems may be explained in terms of the above figure in terms of two related processes. In the first instance, social systems operating with greater pace and intensity have become increasingly disconnected from public oversight. Their self-organizing logics generate innovations that are potentially dramatic in their social consequences, for example, in the economy, in genetics, in modes of individuation, and motivate a call for more responsive mechanisms of regulation than a representative democracy whose ideological cleavage structure appears normatively and epistemically outmoded, The normative core of representative democracies is too minimal to provide confident answers on its own to modern problems and conflicts and its aggregative and indirect membership model generates legitimation problems for its procedures.[13] Transferring decision-making to the legal system will not solve the problem if the issue is grave enough to

[13] For example, in the case of science and technology issues, parliamentary committees are made up of members who by and large belong to parties who strongly favour progress in scientific innovation. In many cases, the public does so too but is more likely in whole or in part to oppose particular innovations that are regarded as having deleterious consequences on various grounds. Political parties locked into comprehensive programmes – employment and economic growth, building a knowledge economy, satisfying mass constituencies – are less likely to differentiate between the risk and benefits of different innovations than sections of the public. The question of public participation is how do the latter acquire democratic voice in a representative system and how can such a voice be reconciled with other voices.

require new statutory foundations that in turn change the context of law. In the latter circumstances, the legal system operates for a time as a specialized kind of argumentative forum but cannot function as the decisive arbiter of societal outcomes until the statutory framing is sufficiently comprehensive and enjoys public legitimacy. In the circumstances, public participation mechanisms – consultations, public hearings, mediation processes – become a means to establish substantive grounds that in the end could be legitimate.

Approached from the other side, the standpoint of cognitive innovation, regimes of public justification are subject to constant emendation in processes of discursive exploration and argumentation. Discursive activity is generated by the ongoing interpretation and question of established norms and codes, both separately and in relation to one another, by crisis-inducing events that resonate with the contradictions, incoherence and inappropriate application of codes and norms and as the outcome of new regimes of prognosis and diagnosis initiated by movements of all kinds. Only the latter is truly exogenous and as such the carrier of projections of transformative social change, especially when such projections evolve from peripheral articulation to the formation of shared horizons amongst a substantial section of the public. Once consolidated into rationalized systems of ideas that have survived public argumentation, initially peripheral mobilizations have the potential to migrate into regimes of public justification that enter into the process of normative justification and rationalization.

Public participation can be viewed from this standpoint as both a cognitive innovation in itself, admittedly one with substantial historical provenance, and as a set of procedures for the amplification and testing of such innovations. As a cognitive innovation, social movements have most assiduously supported public participation as a means of creating permanent opportunity structures for the promotion of ideas and for increasing the political influence of the periphery, rather than operating in an ad hoc, situation-dependent and evanescent manner. As a conduit for widening public involvement and identification with democratic institutions by the transparent and wide-ranging testing of political norms and decisions, existing public participation procedures have so far had relatively poor results. On the whole, they do not enhance governmental legitimacy, reduce conflict dispositions, provide consensual solutions to problems or serve for the reciprocal translation and mediation of codes, norms and innovative ideas and contestations. A systems theoretical argument to explain this state of affairs has been advanced by Bora (1999a; 1999b). In this view, public participation must be strictly aligned with the self-unfolding logics of social systems and any attempts to transcend this logic will be doomed to disappointed expectations as systems, especially the pivotal legal system, re-asserts its own foundational codes and also refuses to tamper with the foundational codes of other systems. On the other side, a stylization of the affirmative movement view of participation would emphasise participation as an least potential medium of a wider spectrum of voices (inclusion), as a forum for addressing a wider range of issues and knowledge perspectives (thematization) and as a procedure for solving disputes in a more even-handed manner (negotiation). Each of these assessments, systems theoretical and movement, only indirectly addresses the relationship between participation and norm formation within the – as argued here – necessarily normative pragmatic register of democratic theory. Seen from such a normative pragmatic democratic standpoint, the rationale for expanded public participation could lie in the form of a democratic response to contemporary problems in the face of social systems that assert their autonomy and persistent conflict between a variously defensive and offensive civil society and the consequences of the increasingly autonomous logics of these systems.

This more positive assessment of the potential of public participation than 'realistic' system theories or movement advocates 'disappointed' with their historic performance may be related to the unfolding of the argument of this essay. Notwithstanding the problems of expanded public participation with respect to representation and legitimation – who should be excluded and included and how legitimate are the outcomes – and with respect to compatibility – with established norms and system codes – it is a needed democratic innovation. In the first instance, it is a means of bringing the discrepant horizons of social practices into some kind of normative relation to one another. Here, public participation is more than Habermas's idea of quasi-autonomous discursive rationalization in the public sphere that 'automatically' lose their pragmatic relevance as they become incorporated into instituted logics. It is an assertion of the need for procedurally organized spaces for the continuation of pragmatically grounded argument within an institutionally resonant context. It is not merely by means of the autonomous logic of discourse alone that substantive norms and themes become absorbed into the grounding and procedures of democratic institutions; it is also by an expanded range of consideration and decision of these institutions induced by wider canons of inclusion.[14] To some considerable extent contemporary political conditions already manifest signs that that such continued pragmatic involvement is taking place in a relatively ad hoc way, for example, in the protracted political arguments over the drafting of multi-level statute law in disputed areas such as the various implications of gene technology or environmental standards. In this light, given the diversification of the public, the endless possibilities of new cleavage structures and the consequent difficulties of finding agreement on traditional or innovative substantive values of democracy – liberty, equality, freedom from endagerment, identity rights – and if democratic institutions are to continue to count, then expanded public participation appears less as an option than a necessity. Apart from the necessity, however, quite how this is to be done is another question. All this essay can show is that notwithstanding poor institutional performance and societal recognition to date, the expansion of public participation remains a big issue of our common democratic future.

References

Abels, G. and Bora, A. (2004) *Democratische Technikbewertung*, Bielefeld: Transcript.

Alexander, Jeffrey, C. (1982) 'Differentiation Theory: Problems and Prospects', in J. Alexander and P. Colomy (eds) *Differentiation Theory and Social Change*, New York: Columbia University Press.

Boltanski, L. and Thevenaut, L. (1991) *De la Justification*, Paris: Gallimard.

Bora. A. (1999a) *Diffenzierung und Inklusion: Partizipative Offenlchkeit im Rechtsystem modernerGesellschaften*, Baden-Baden: Nomos.

Bora, A. (1999b) 'Discourse Formations and Constellations of Conflict: Problems of Public Participation in the German Debate on Genetically Altered Plants' In O'Mahony, P. (Ed), *Nature, Risk and Responsibility. Discourses of Biotechnology*, London: Macmillan.

Brandom, R. (1994) *Making it Explicit: Reasoning, Representing and Discursive Commitment*, Cambridge, MA: Harvard University Press.

Burns, T, and Dietz, T. (1992) 'Institutionelle Dynamik: Ein evolutionarer Ansatz', *Journal fur Soziale Forschung, 32, 3/4, 283–306.*

Durant, John, Bauer, Martin and Gaskell, George (Eds.) (1998). *Biotechnology in the Public Sphere: A European Sourcebook*, London: Science Museum.

[14] To fully explicate the implications of this point, the formulation of Habermas's consensus theory and Rawls separation of public reason and public discourse would at a minimum need to be critically examined as both – Rawls more than Habermas – make it hard to see how a renovation of democracy to address its substantive limitations could take place. I assert this point rather more in terms of the embedded problems of contemporary democracy that in terms of hypothetical ideas of normative rightness.

Eder, K. (1996) *The Social Construction of Nature*, London: Sage.
Emirbayer, M. & Sheller, M. (1998) 'Publics in History', *Theory and Society,(27 (6),* 727–779.
Ferree, M. Gamson, W. A., Gerhards, J. and Rucht, D. (2001) *Shaping Abortion Discourse: Democracy and the Public Sphere in Germany and the United States*, Cambridge University Press.
Ferree, M., Gamson, W. A., Gerhards, J. and Rucht, D. (2002) 'Four Models of the Public Sphere in Modern Democracies' in *Theory and Society* 31 (289–324.
Fraser, N. (1992) 'Rethinking the Public Sphere: A Contribution to the Critique of Actually Existing Democracy', in Calhoun, C. (ed) *Habermas and the Public Sphere*, Cambridge: MIT.
Freeden, M. (1996) *Ideologies and Political Theory: a conceptual approach*, Oxford: Clarendon Press.
Gerhards, Jürgen, Friedhelm Neidhardt and Dieter Rucht (1998) Zwischen Palaver Und Diskurs. Strukturen Öffentlicher Meinungsbildung Am Beispiel Der Deutschen Diskussion Zur Abtreibung, Opladen: Westdeutscher Verlag.
Organization for Economic Cooperation and Development (2001) *Citizens as Partners: Information, Consultation and Public Participation in Policy-Making*, Paris: OECD.
European Union (2001) *European Governance: A White Paper*, Brussels: European Union.
Giegel, H-J. (1992) 'Einleitung' in Giegel, H-J. (ed) *Kommunikation und Konsens in modernen Gesellschaften*, Frankfurt: Suhrkamp.
Habermas, J. (1984) *The Theory of Communicative Action*, vol (1: *Reason and the Rationalization of Society*, London: Heinemann.
Habermas, J. (1987) *The Theory of Communicative Action, vol (2: Lifeworld and System: A Critique of Functionalist Reason*, Cambridge: Polity.
Habermas, J. (1993). *Justification and Application: Remarks on Discourse Ethics* Cambridge, MA: Cambridge University Press.
Habermas, J. (1995) 'Reconciliation through the public use of reason: remarks on John Rawls Political Liberalism' in the *Journal of Philosophy*, XCII, 3, 109–131.
Habermas, J. (1996) *Between Facts and Norm: Contributions to a Discourse Theory of Law and Democracy*, Cambridge: Polity.
Habermas, J. (1996a) 'Three Normative Models of Democracy' in Benhabib, S. (ed) *Democracy and Difference: Contesting the Boundaries of the Political*, New Jersey: Princeton University Press.
Joas, H (1996) *The Creativity of Action*, Cambridge: Polity.
Joas, H. (2000) *The Genesis of Values*, Cambridge: Polity.
Lamont, M. and Thevenot, L. (2000) 'Conclusion' in *Rethinking Comparative Cultural Sociology* in Lamont, M. and Thevenot, L. *Rethinking Comparative Cultural Sociology: Repertoires of Evaluation in France and the United States*, Cambridge University Press.
Luhmann, N. (2002) *Die Politik der Wissenschaft*, Frankfurt: Shurkamp.
Moody, M and Thevenot, L. (2000) 'Forms of Valuing Nature: Arguments and Modes of Justification in French and American Environmental Disputes' in Lamont, M. and Thevenot, L. *Rethinking Comparative Cultural Sociology: Repertoires of Evaluation in France and the United States*. Cambridge University Press.
Munch, R. (1990) 'Differentiation, Rationalization, Interpenetration: the emergence of modern society' in Alexander, J. and Colomy, P. (eds) *Differentiation Theory and Social Change*, New York: Columbia University Press.
O'Mahony, P. (1996) Introduction to *Final Report to the European Commission of Research Project Sustainability and Institutional Innovation* (no: EV5V-CT94-0389), CEC: Brussels.
O'Mahony, P. and Delanty, G. (2001) Rethinking Irish History: *Nationalism, Identity and Ideology*, London: Macmillan.

Peters, B. (1993) *Die Integration moderner Gesellschaften*, Frankfurt: Suhrkamp.
Rawls, J. (1993) *Political Liberalism*, New York: Columbia University Press.
Rose, N. (1999) Powers of Freedom: Reframing Political Thought, Cambridge University Press.
Strydom, P. (2002) *Risk Environment and Society: Current Issues and Future Prospect*, Milton Keynes: Open University Press.
Strydom, P (2006). 'Contemporary European Cognitive Theory' in Delanty, G. (ed.) *Contemporary European Social Theory*, London: Routledge.
Thevenot, L, Moody, M. and Lafaye, C. (2000) 'Comparing Models of Strategy, Interests and the Public Good in French and American Environmental Disputes' in Lamont, M. and Thevenot, L. *Rethinking Comparative Cultural Sociology: Repertoires of Evaluation in France and the United States*. Cambridge University Press.
Walzer, M (1983). *Spheres of Justice: A Defence of Pluralism and Equality*, Oxford: Blackwell.
Willke, H (1992) Ironie des Staates: Grundlinien einer Staatstheorie polyzentrischer Gesellschaft, Frankfurt: Suhrkamp.

CHAPTER TWO

BIOTECHNOLOGIES AND COMMUNICATION: PARTICIPATION FOR DEMOCRATIC PROCESSES

Giuseppe Pellegrini

Biotechnologies have been presented with great emphasis in the public arena, since their first applications, as "one of the most promising frontiers of contemporary science" (Il Sole 24 ore 26/09/99). Their use has allowed the development of products in various fields and proposed as relevant "facts". In medicine, insulin has been produced, in vitro embryos have been created, and prenatal and pre-implant in utero diagnoses have been perfected. In agriculture, with the production of herbicides and pesticides together new plant varieties, there has been an increase in crop productivity. With regard to animals, the characteristics of several species have been improved by overcoming the barriers between them with recombinant DNA technology, and the cloning of several animal types.

Achievement of these goals and the promotion of the advantages promised by biotechnologies have been flanked by a parallel growth in uncertainties concerning their effects on humans and the environment. In particular, the biotechnologies applied to human and vegetable cells have provoked various controversies, especially in the case of GMOs, which, with regard to agriculture and the agro-food industry, have caused great alarm among the public. These concerns are due, in a general sense, to the potentials of biotechnologies: they allow life (human, animal and vegetable) to be changed in a way which thirty years ago was unimaginable, thereby posing situations with uncertain outcomes (Callon 1999; Wynne 1999).

There are other specific reasons for these suspicions. The ability of scientists to modify nature and life using biotechnologies, beginning with the discovery of DNA, has created great expectations in governments and the economic and financial spheres[1]. Since the 1980s a visible growth in investments in the biotechnology sector has occurred,

[1] Recognising the potential of biotechnological applications, the European Union has developed an action plan on life sciences and biotechnology in view of fulfillment

for example, the launching of large-scale research programmes like the genome project. This work has mostly been carried out by private industry, highlighting the self-serving side of science ever more attentive to economic results and therefore to the monopoly in certain innovations, illustrated by taking out patents.

This interest in the use of biotechnologies in the agriculture and agro-food sector has produced an industrial concentration made up of a small number of multinational companies with monopolies on the main patents allowing the use of GMOs in agricultural production. These economic aspects have roused public suspicions, especially when the innovations concern goods for consumption, i.e. food products, for which, especially in the western world, no pressing need is seen. As in the case of other techno-scientific innovations, the world of science is unable to provide political decision-makers with exhaustive safety guarantees on the use of biotechnologies (Pellizzoni 2005), given that the consequences of their application are not easily quantifiable, and there is a lack of studies on the environmental impact.[2] Public opinion is not solely interested in the analysis and evaluation of potential risks according to scientific parameters. It is also interested in ethical and moral factors tied with trust in the regulatory system (Salter & Frewer 2001). Various opinion polls on GMOs, for example, have demonstrated that they are perceived as threats because they are "unnatural" products with which the idea of an unjustified risk is associated. Consequently, it is impossible to refer solely to accurate risk assessments in order to reassure the public; social values must also be considered. If, for example, an emphasis is placed on the benefits for human health, the environment, and fauna, perceptions of risk might be counterbalanced, but only if the requests made for these benefits are realistic (Frewer et al. 1997).

These studies demonstrate the difficulties encountered by the scientific world in meeting the demands of public opinion, given that science often responds to ethical and moral issues in terms of *risk assessment*. For this reason, proponents of the scientific community have on several

---

of the Lisbon 2010 objectives for Europe to become the most developed knowledge-economy area in the world. European Commission, *Life Sciences and Biotechnology: A Strategy for Europe*, Brussels COM 2002, 27 final.

[2] Recent studies have generated uncertainties in several cases of the use of modified agricultural plants. One example is the Farm Scale Evaluation carried out in England on four types of genetically modified plants which obtained different results in regard to impacts on biodiversity: Cordis Focus n. 259, October 2005.

occasions judged the general public to be irrational and ignorant (Salter & Frewer 2001: 9), causing a communicative short circuit between actors in the public debate. In addition, it should be noted that concerns about the effects of biotechnologies have also animated the scientific community, which, at the beginning of biotechnological applications in the biomedical field called for a moratorium on experimental studies at the Asilomar conference; an indication of science's awareness of the limits and range of these innovations.[3] This regime of uncertainty, linked to the ethical and moral apprehensions expressed by the public (also because of the wide coverage given to the subject by the media), has caused a crisis in the role of experts in regards to their credibility. It has also produced a rift in the traditional alliance between the political and scientific spheres, generating considerable controversy and difficulty in the management of biotechnological research and production. The experts in favour of some or other biotechnological innovation are unable to furnish exhaustive and convincing arguments that political decision-makers can put to use in the electorate. This is also because the scientific community has on several occasions been divided in its opinions on the utility of biotechnology, thereby adding further doubts to the public debate. This situation again highlights the fact that the aptitude of science to contribute to social order through mechanisms of forecast and control has lessened over the past twenty years, partially by revealing, on several occasions, its weakness in proof and argument, demonstrated by various emergencies and well-known cases, such as BSE and lipobay, etc. Furthermore, scientists have lost their role as privileged advisors to decision-makers: as politicians have engaged in debate and decisions on biotechnology, they have been more responsive to values matching the needs of the public than to science-based discussion. Politicians and scientists' authority and control over the discussion concerning biotechnology has diminished while public opinion, the media and the organizations of civil society have gained a decisive ability to the use of these innovations – especially in Europe.

These developments highlight the pervasiveness of biotechnologies, given their new and extraordinary capacity to affect the environment and mankind. This potential is simultaneously a limitation and a resource for scientists, people and nations. For scientists, an epoch

[3] International Conference on Recombinant DNA Molecule Research, Asilomar Conference Center, California, 1975. Jasanoff (1995).

has begun in which it is possible to improve health, modify nature even more profoundly, and to direct the life course. However, at the same time, promotional arguments put forward do not satisfy the public. People are confronted by the problem of information and choices regarding new but highly uncertain practices and lifestyles. Governments have the difficult task of simultaneously funding research and creating legislative conditions that favour a promising and highly innovative scientific sector, while taking into consideration concerns the regarding correct use of biotechnologies expressed by several social actors, in particular public opinion. Biotechnologies epitomize the techno-scientific conditioning of contemporary life through the influence exerted on the choices of single individuals. They have roused opposing views, from simple enthusiasm to generalized fear, the most striking example of which is the difference between public opinions on medical and agricultural applications (Durant et al. 1998; Gaskell & Bauer 2001). With regard the public and political debate, biotechnologies are "a platform to discuss and activate conflicts on a wide range of arguments which involve many stakeholders" (Gaskell & Bauer 2001: 3). The obvious difficulties of managing these conflicts and reconciling very different interests are two of the most problematic aspects for democratic systems referable to the issue of legitimacy: who must make the decisions that regulate the use of biotechnologies, and how? Is it possible that only politicians and experts may decide on important questions that modify the existence of individuals and the balance of the environment? How can they find public justification for particular decisions? These are only some of the questions concerning the delicate relationship between techno-scientific innovation and democracy, of which biotechnology is only one of the most significant cases. It is therefore appropriate to look at the ways in which managerial and decision-making processes have been addressed in this area over the past few years.

A. Legitimacy in the Governance of Biotechnologies

The emergence of biotechnologies in the broader context of the so-called risk society[4] requires consideration, comprehension and management

[4] The reference is to Beck's notion of risk in relation to the gap in Western societies between citizens' needs and their representation (Beck 1986).

of a series of social questions in order to justify decisions on potentially risky phenomena – not only with accurate measurement of the possible effects and probabilistic calculations, but also with detailed examination of the political processes able to represent and reflect upon the various sensitivities and attitudes of the actors involved. The case of biotechnology, however, is located in the sphere of uncertainty, in which the probabilities of an event cannot be calculated precisely, due to inadequate information (Pellizzoni 2005: 92). These considerations have induced the European Union to produce several documents containing reflections and guidelines to deal with a general crisis in the legitimacy of the competent authorities, which stresses, amongst other things, the importance of monitoring the impact of biotechnologies in order to devise suitable policy measures. This commitment is mainly due to the increasing legislative output at the community level which influences member states on important issues such as biotechnology. This influence takes places despite the fact that member states have autonomous applicative space to interpret European laws through the implementation of *ad hoc* procedures, as in the case of GMO experimentation, for which various types of citizen and civil organization participation have been designed.[5]

The European countries are liberal democracies founded on the principle of representation, i.e. on the right/duty of the elected to make decisions in accordance with the popular will expressed during elections. Thus, through participation in voting, citizens authorize political decision-makers to govern processes and innovations that are ever more characterized by techno-scientific content. In the case of biotechnology, countries' ability to obtain the trust of their electorate in order to produce adequate legislation has entered crisis, so much so that in recent years many countries have resorted to referendums as well as to parliamentary and popular legislative initiatives.

This has come about coincidentally alongside the controversy surrounding GMOs and the use of biotechnologies in medicine. Trust in decision-makers and in the forecasting abilities of science has diminished: they no longer enjoy the prestige that they had in the past (OST July 1998). Although it was clear in the 1990s that providing incentives for biotechnological innovations without the trust of the public was

[5] In the case of Directive 2001/18/EC on GMO research, member-states have adopted very different procedures with which to consult and involve civil society organizations.

not possible, little was done to analyse the causes by evaluating representational limits in traditional decision-making practices, which fall under the name of "comity"; the contribution of experts, the institution of scientific committees, and the use of scientific knowledge deemed certain and objective in decision-making.

The above practice is derived from a centuries-old tradition which has considered politics to be the exclusive locus of power, and science as an ethically neutral activity which should concern itself only with research, inventions and discoveries – even though science experts have recently played a central and uncontested role in the process of risk assessment and have influenced politicians. This division of tasks has historically excluded a crucial actor of increasing importance in recent years: civil society. Notwithstanding the efforts made at EU level to prevent this separation, the initiatives undertaken have neither been reflected upon adequately with regard to their ability, nor to offer democratic guarantees to citizens.

Amongst these guarantees are those on the enjoyment of rights to counterbalance particularly invasive expressions of techno-scientific power, such as biotechnologies. The right to be informed, the transparency of decision-making processes, and participation in the formation of decisions are some of the avenues through which citizens can include themselves in the context of techno-scientific modernization. These guarantees are also of concern the various interest groups that take part in the discussion and decision-making process regarding biotechnologies, as stressed by studies on participation by civil society and technological innovation. One notes, in fact, that discussion on the life sciences and biotechnologies has excluded numerous actors representing important segments of civil society, generating suspicion towards EC policies (Commission of the European Union 2001: 16; Mayer et al. 1996: 2).

Access to specialised information has increased notably in recent years, yet almost all the scientific data on which experts base their opinions is inaccessible to the general public, due to unavailability or simply because it is difficult to understand. Citizens are implicitly asked for consent supported by trust in the official representatives of scientific knowledge. The explicit request is to acknowledge the credibility of scientists more than to subscribe to the validity of scientific explanations, for which there is disciplinary validation according to the practices of the various scientific communities concerned. It is therefore not the authority of science in question but its self-referentiality.

Transparency is necessary to disseminate the processes of technological transfer and their implications (social, economic, ethical) in order to unravel the complexity of certain applications – for example, by labelling procedures in the food and medical sectors (Dolmetta 2001).

However, this process of transparency does not develop in this way alone; it does also by creating spaces for discussion prior to finalizing decisions. Transparency in this case means ensuring that certain problems are not dealt with exclusively within the restricted circle of scientists, politicians and economic actors. This prompts consideration of modes of communicating with the public, and specifically, consideration of the views of non-experts – inducing the European Community to launch the Eurobarometer programmes for public opinion analysis.

Consideration of the public and of civil society in general is all the more important when initiatives are structured to give voice to the needs, proposals and criticisms of individual citizens and their organizations. In other words, in fostering participation: action recently developed in several directions through procedures and instruments to facilitate the delicate relations among science, political decision-makers, and the general public.[6] The assumption behind this strategic orientation is that better decision-making requires the involvement of citizens and organizations interested in deliberations on the use of new technologies.[7] It is believed that technological innovations can develop significantly greater participation by citizens and civil society organizations, thereby changing information control from top-down to the bottom-up process that characterizes most Western democratic systems. The implied expectation is that citizens can achieve active commitment characterized by empowerment so new cognitive profiles of citizens and better network access rights ensue. At the same time it is

---

[6] See the Royal Commission on Genetic Modification 2001; Human Genetics Commission 2003; Royal Society Science in Society Programme 2003.

[7] In this area the term 'deliberative' denotes participation processes complementary to representative democracy, where the traditional mechanisms of representation and decision-making do not guarantee all the points of view of those potentially interested are present in the elective assembly. Deliberative procedures are those based on the use, in the decision-making process, of the logic of rational and impartial argument rather than the negotiation of the aggregation of preferences, and they are democratic in that those affected by the consequences of the decisions participate in them. The prospect of more widespread use of these practices, in a way that tries to guarantee the conditions for an open and effective public debate able to produce shared decisions, is a stimulating and significant response to the crisis in the relationship between science, politics and society, referred to earlier in the text.

hoped that decision-makers, experts and the various stakeholders involved will acquire better information and more accurate perceptions of the problems negotiated.

Proposed here is a typology of the capacities for change that these procedures and instruments have generated. But it will not list and classify all experiences of recent years, and it will eschew the pedantry that imposes an unreliable nomenclature (Rowe & Frewer 2005). The typology is intended to show the strengths and weaknesses of attempts to modify relations among the actors considered. It outlines a pathway that begins with information and concludes with forms of participation and reciprocal influence that favour democratic inclusion.

B. Biotechnologies and democratic processes: an interpretive model

1. *Knowing public opinion*

Table 1 depicts the relations among experts, political decision-makers, the general public, and social actors when decisions are taken on biotechnologies. In the first quadrant, actions undertaken are of vertical type and managed by political and scientific institutions through information transfer to a general public, presumed, according to the deficit model, to need more information.[8]

In this diffusive model, the transmission of information takes place in a single direction; from a broadcaster to a passive receiver (Logan 2001). An example of this procedure is suggested by the principles established by the Convention of Aarhus, which underlines the crucial role of information for citizens, especially in the field of environmental legislation (UNECE 1998). On launching the document *Improving the knowledge bases for better policies*", The European Commission emphasised the importance of enhancing the transmission of expertise with regard to the general public, proposing a series of guidelines to foster their effective intervention according to the contexts of action (Commission of the European Union 2002).

This type of provision has favoured the growth of initiatives for the popularization of science in several European countries with the

[8] According to the theorists of this interpretation, the increasingly fierce debates and conflicts on techno-scientific issues are due to the serious state of misinformation in which the public finds itself on these subjects (Wynne 1995).

Tab. 1 Relations among experts, politics and public

Actions	Type of relationship
A. Knowing public opinion B. Evaluating public opinion	*Closure* (one way)
C. Public engagement D. Public participation	*Openness* (two ways)

creation of numerous *Public Understanding of Science* (PUS) programmes (Paisley 1998; Laugksch 2000). Also, the various community directives on biotechnologies later adopted by the member states emphasize the role of information delivered by public authorities to citizens. On the basis of these directives, since the mid-1980s European governments have undertaken a series of information and popularization for the general public, normally managed by the public authorities and also by companies in the sector. Citizens and civil society organizations are treated as passive recipients, to whom information is furnished almost always after the government has made a decision. One exception is the Dutch Informal Consultation Group, which constitutes representatives from industry, environmentalists and consumers, and which has reached an informal agreement on the labelling of products developed by means of genetic engineering, establishing that the companies producing these products should inform consumer associations before placing them on the market (Commandeur et al. 1996).

2. *Evaluating public opinion*

On the same level, the second quadrant consists of initiatives aimed at evaluating public opinion in order to obtain elements useful for political action. In recent years apprehension among politicians has increased with regard to

> the opinions of a complex and finely tuned electorate so that they devote enormous resources to uncovering what that electorate thinks with the concern of having to deal with the consequences. (Crouch 2003: 18)

To be cited in this regard are the public surveys and research carried out in order to gauge the opinions of Europeans concerning biotechnologies (Commission of the European Union 2003). Both quadrants illustrate a top-down model of information transmission, in which the public are objects – rather than subjects – with which to communicate.

Therefore, relational dynamics of this type are marked by one-sided conclusions – not dynamic communication – as demonstrated by the absence of feedback mechanisms, and the fact that the public and scientific institutions typically start such procedures (third quadrant). In this exchange, a product takes the form of a survey, informational materials, events, etc. This emphasis on the product is caused by the intention to fill a gap in public awareness in through means that fail to take into account the receiver's complex involvement.

3. *Public engagement*

The fourth quadrant comprises of the various ways in which attempts are made to familiarize the public with questions covering a wide range of techno-scientific content. In this case, initiatives seek to activate a specific interaction that goes beyond simple information to take cognizance of the positions arising from civil society and activating forms of public discussion. The objective is to enhance the points of view of single and collective civil-society actors with procedures that encourage their evaluation of techno-scientific innovations. Some examples are: public assemblies; hearings on questions of great local interest; surveys that use social research techniques like focus groups. The main objective of all these activities is to give a voice to citizens and groups in civil society through their active involvement, which in turn allows the collection of information, criticisms, suggestions and all considerations deemed relevant to a particular argument. These involvement-based procedures may be activated by various subjects – and not only by public institutions, though promoters are frequently organisations with particular competences with regard to content and its organization. Some examples of these kids of subjects are: the Dutch science shops; agencies which act as mediators among civil society; scientists; and public institutions that promote applied research activities which are normally encouraged by nongovernmental organisations. However, the actions promoted in this area do not have a significant impact on political decisions, even if over the medium- to long-term they help improve relations between society and the scientific world (Banthien/ Jaspers 2003: 22).

This class of initiatives introduces an element that qualifies the relationship between the actors involved by activating cognitive processes in which lay knowledge interacts with that of the expert. Thus, two-way mechanisms are introduced, whereby communication is no longer directed by the public institutions or scientists but is based on issues raised by civil society.[9]

4. *Public participation*

The last quadrant comprises activities which favour the active participation of actors, increasing the value of their contribution to the adoption of decisions on techno-scientific questions. This is the case of the so-called "deliberative arenas" in which face-to-face interaction among political decision-makers, experts and the public permits the exchange of information and suggestions which may impact decision-making processes (Bobbio 2002: 5–29).

The use of the conditional is necessary here because not all initiatives of this type have certain influence over subsequent political decisions. Nevertheless, such initiatives are characterised by genuine dialogue in which reciprocity between the actors is fostered, and through which it is possible for them to change their initial opinions. Accordingly, it is possible to speak of a real transaction of knowledge, opinions, and different (often conflicting) perceptions of the subject being dealt with. It is assumed that knowledge is not a finished product proposed only by certain privileged actors, but the outcome of an intense and continuous process of interaction (Bucchi 1998; Gibbons 1996; Wynne 1991). These epystemic fora are places of greater democratic openness in communication between decision-makers, scientists and the general public, because they allow for active participation through deliberation and mediation procedures, giving voice to minorities.

C. Participative methods and Biotechnologies

To deal with the controversies linked to biotechnological innovations, several procedures have been introduced to involve the actors concerned in debate and decision-making. Since these initiatives are significantly innovative from the point of view of democratic arrangements, it is worth analyzing their implementation and their results in detail.

The consensus conference is perhaps the best-known participation procedure used to address the issue of biotechnologies. This is a

[9] To be mentioned in this regard are the mechanisms of *Public Awareness of Science* described by various authors: Stocklmayer et al. 2001; Clark/Illman 2001: 5–27.

discussion and decision-formation model intended to provide non-experts – normally a group of citizens selected according to various variables, such as gender, age and occupation – with an opportunity to influence decisions on important techno-scientific issues: i.e. highly complex questions at the centre of public debate and the cause of ethical and political conflicts. Owing to these characteristics, consensus conferences have been promoted in association with parliamentary discussions or prior to the enactment of laws. The organizers seek to facilitate debate among various opinions and bodies of knowledge, encouraging a dialectical confrontation based on active participation by social actors that normally do not interact in a single context. The aim is thus to prevent decision-forming based on participation by a limited number of subjects, normally public decision-makers and experts.

Consensus conferences organized according to the model of the Danish Board of Technology, the body that first established it in Europe, typically hold four sessions (see table 2).

During the first session, a panel of about 15 citizens, assembled according to their representativeness of the general public, meets to analyse study materials on the topic in question and formulates questions to pose to experts and stakeholders of different orientation. In this session, which takes place over a weekend, the panel also identifies and selects the experts in view of the next stage. In the second session, the group of experts attends a meeting in the form of a public debate, answering the questions put by the panel of citizens, thereby enriching the discussion of other points of view and knowledge.

During the third session, the panel of citizens draws up a final document which is issued during the final session, normally at a meeting with the press and the public. The entire consensus conference is coordinated by a moderator whose tasks are to facilitate dialogue among the participants, encourage the emergence of different positions, and help the group draft the final document.

Consensus conferences have been used on several occasions in various countries to discuss biotechnologies, mainly in order to provide policy makers with knowledge regarding not only techno-scientific aspects but also regulation, guarantees for citizens, ethical problems and implications regarding relationships with developing countries. The promoters of these deliberative arenas are often institutions not directly concerned with the theme of the conference. Danish and Swiss conferences have been conducted by, for example, independent bodies

Tab. 2 Organisational diagram of a Consensus Conference

Stage	Activity	Subjects
First Session	Study of the documentation, formulation of the questions, selection of the experts	Panel of citizens and a moderator
Second Session	Meeting with the experts, debate	Panel of citizens, moderator, experts, public
Third Session	Preparation of the final document	Panel of citizens, moderator
Fourth Session	Presentation and discussion of the final document.	Panel of citizens, journalists, politicians

connected with the national parliaments whose aims include fostering dialogue between decision-makers, the world of science, and civil society.[10]

Although the results of consensus conferences are not binding on public decision-makers, their weight and the publicity that accompanies them push politicians to express opinions and take account of the results arising from the public meetings (Bereano 1999). The most obvious impact on decision-makers is indubitably the increased number of elements that must be considered when decisions are made. For example, a consensus conference held in the UK in 1994 on the subject of transgenic plants enabled the panel of citizens to express their concerns about the lack of information and the need for guarantees provided by a control system managed by international bodies. In the years that followed, these suggestions were widely taken up by European and national legislative bodies. Another effect revealed by evaluation of the Dutch and British initiatives is that they have enabled democratic discussion which overcomes the limits of representative democracy by allowing the public's greater involvement in the political process (Durant 1994).

Important to note, the final documents of consensus conferences do not necessarily express unanimous agreement; indeed, the final reports

[10] For Denmark the Danish Board of Technology (http://www.tekno.dk) and for Switzerland PTA Suisse (http://www.ta-swiss.ch).

normally represent the differing attitudes within the panel of citizens, thereby offering a wide range of opinions and recommendations to favour broad and detailed examination of problems connected with biotechnologies. Nor are they documents that must necessarily evidence the pro and cons of biotechnological applications. In the case of a Danish consensus conference held in 1992, on the subject of animals modified with genetic engineering techniques, the panel of citizens expressed, for example, concerns regarding their integrity and the risk of unlimited and unmotivated manipulation, together with possible imbalances in the relationship among species as far as the protection of biodiversity is concerned. Particular worries concerning ecological matters were not expressed, however, the assumption being that controlled use may be made of bio-modified animals. Furthermore, several cases have generated documents that question public decision-makers, mentioning critical areas and considerations regarding issues not often addressed in the political-institutional debate.[11]

A variant of the consensus conference is the so-called citizens' jury, also known as a citizens' panel, planning cell or citizens' forum. These juries are means by which decision-making institutions gather informed recommendations on a specific policy or issue from a representative group of citizens, generally 15–20 selected on the basis of variables deemed most relevant to the subject in question. They are assigned the formulation of joint recommendations regarding a pre-established set of problems. The jury is normally assisted by a professional facilitator and has access to a group of experts tasked with representing the main positions on the debated issue. There is often a consultative body with regard to selection of the experts and the questions for discussion. Citizens' juries typically deliberate on three of four predefined options, so that this is a deliberative method normally situated further down the decision-making process.

In Italy, a consensus conference was recently held over two weekends[12] on open-field trials of GMOs. This was an original undertaking: for the first time it enabled comparison between two different participation procedures, involving two panels of citizens in the selection of

---

[11] For a critical analysis of *consensus conferences* see Joss/Durant (1995).

[12] In March 2004, as part of the project "Partecipazione Pubblica e Governance dell'Innovazione", the Region of Lombardy promoted in collaboration with Fondazione Bassetti di Milano and Observa – Science in Society an institutional experiment in the form of a *consensus conference* on biotechnological research issues.

Tab. 3 One consensus conference; two participation procedures

Actors	Procedure 1	Procedure 2
Panel of citizens, experts	Closed door preliminary discussion, selection of the experts	Hearings of six experts, debate
Panel of citizens, experts	Hearings of three experts, debate	Debate with experts and stakeholders
Panel of citizens	Final document preparation	Final document preparation

the experts and in discussion of the topic selected. The use of evaluative instruments (pre-meeting questionnaire, telephone follow-up and analysis of the transcript) revealed significant differences between the results achieved with the two types of meeting (Tab. 3).
Both procedures required the citizens to compile the final document after acquiring expert information and through a process of rational argument[13] so as to define shared arguments while respecting areas of dissent. What differentiated the two variants was the way in which the expert information was introduced into the process, and, as a consequence, the relationship between this information and articulation of the theme – the release of GMOs into the environment – as a specific problem. *Procedure 1* let the citizens:

a) first introduced all the experts;
b) then allowed the citizens to debate the relevant frames to deliberate on the basis of this information.

It was predicted that these different procedures would produce different results in terms of the stability of the panel's positions. Analysis of the results confirmed this hypothesis by illuminating the fact that procedure 1 produced more stable judgments among participants with a greater coherence among opinions, while the participants in procedure 2 were more likely to change their opinions. For that reason these

[13] Deliberation is a decision process with arguments offered by and for participants, which champions rationality and impartiality. It's a process intended to transform preferences rather than aggregate them as in a vote. The implicit consequence is that deliberation brings various frames to the surface so that they can be debated, shared, disproved, etc. – conferring evidence to the ethical structure of the group of decision-makers (Elster 1998: 5).

findings seemingly confirm the hypothesis that different procedures structure participants' openness to expert information in different ways: the early assumption of a position within the group – therefore a role – may induce citizens to adopt a normative attitude in search of confirmation rather than critical evaluation and eventual revision of their positions.

The initiative just described shows that the importance and strength of consensus conferences lie in their organization, which must be designed to guarantee a correct convening procedure, adequate selection of the participants, discussion dynamics conducted effectively in respect to different positions and social roles, as well as the production of a result that can be submitted to the public and to public decision-makers.

Consensus conferences and citizen juries are among the instruments of so-called "deliberative democracy", a view of democratic government which gives particular importance to public debate. The main features of this concept emphasize the "educational" role of rousing greater interest in and awareness of the *res publica* among citizens. According to several theorists, deliberative democracy also promotes a greater sense of community through the mechanisms of comparison and public debate among subjects oriented towards common values and traditions (Barber 1984; Taylor 1989). Other scholars stress the procedural efficacy of deliberative arenas, which, in their opinion, are likely to produce better decisions because they are strongly inclusive of the actors concerned (Benhabib 1996: 70).

Deliberative procedures are such in that they are based on rational argument rather than on negotiation or the aggregation of the preferences; and they are democratic in the sense that those who participate are in theory those potentially exposed to the consequences of a particular decision. The prospect of the increasingly widespread and convinced use of these practices, in a way such that the conditions for open and effective public debate able to produce shared decisions are ensured, represents a potentially stimulating and significant response to the crisis in the relationship between science, politics and society.

With regard to biotechnologies, numerous consensus conferences have been held around the world on both biomedical issues and those concerning agriculture and the agro-food sector.[14] To be noted are the

[14] Since the 1980s, the American Institute of Health has organised more than 100 "consensus development conferences" on technology applied in medicine, on the use

Danish Consensus Conference on gene therapy held in 1995; the Citizens' Conference on genetically modified foodstuffs promoted in France by Prime Minister Lionel Jospin in 1998; the first Citizens' Conference on genetic tests carried out in Germany in 2001; the second Korean Consensus Conference on cloning of 1999 and the first "Consensus Conference on Gene Technology in the Food Chain" held in Australia in 1999.

Judgment on these various initiatives is generally positive, although the way in which they have been implemented and the procedures used to assess their impact on decisions are rather different.

In several cases, consensus conferences have been used as policy instruments, while in other countries they have performed a more general consultative role (Einsiedel/Eastlick 2000). Many scholars recognise that these arenas are valuable opportunities for dialogue and favourable occasions for discussion among stakeholders, whereby knowledge of the topic can be broadened and the most critical areas highlighted.

D. Conclusions

The impossibility of considering biotechnologies as scientific undertakings completely independent of political and democratic concerns requires a revision of several ideas about knowledge through a completely different scientific perspective: that is, the dichotomy of rational and irrational and the ideas of progress and objectivity. When the role of science induces debate on political decisions of strong public impact, it must be rethought and reinterpreted, so that it makes sense in a setting that accepts comparison with standpoints not bound to scientific rationality alone (Jasanoff 2005: 24).

Often, when a debate involves apparently irreconcilable points of view, appeal is made to a third party able to resolve the controversy using objective criteria. But in the case of biotechnologies, it is not possible to identify an authoritative actor entirely extraneous to the interests at stake and with plausible universally applicable criteria. Public institutions, for example – which should protect the rights of citizens – in several cases have made improper use of genetic data banks unknown

of genetic tests and biotechnologies. For a review of Consensus Conferences in the world see: http://www.loka.org/pages/worldpanels.htm.

to the general public.[15] Phenomena of this kind have compelled several scholars to underline the mechanisms of domination which may be concealed behind biotechnologies, grouped together under the heading "bio-power", signifying the disciplining and normalizing of bodies in new forms of subjectivity and "cultural resistance" in a neo-Foucaultian reading of modern power (Haraway 1991). These and other scholars indicate the presence of a new power to intervene in biological life and envisage unthinkable alternatives, as well as a series of new problems which undermine conventional ethical principles, consolidated judicial categories and political decision-making procedures in a democratic and pluralistic society.

From a political point of view countries have seen themselves lose their sovereignty owing to the unforeseen phenomena of economic and financial globalization, the accelerated development of communication, movements of knowledge and work. Supernational mechanisms regarding the environment and trade have progressively restricted the power of local governments, and with it the capacity for dialogue with citizens. This process has provoked crisis in a conception of politics founded upon the centrality of the state in the definition of policies, opening a space increasingly characterised by demands for pluralism and attention to local interests advanced by civil society.

The formal institutional framework reveals numerous shortcomings in aggregating the proposals and concerns of civil society in a process that fosters better understanding of values and preferences (Lanzara 2005: 68).

In light of these considerations, it is possible to list requirements and conditions which may orient efficacious decision-making to foster better democratic procedures.

The complexity of issues associated with biotechnologies has generated contrasts and conflicts which can no longer be neglected by public policy makers. Initiatives for debate and discussion must be considered if the intention is to deal with the inevitable controversies provoked by particularly pervasive techno-scientific innovations. However, this line of action cannot be undertaken only to activate symbolic and formal mechanisms to unite actors with diverse interests in certain issues. Careful assessment must be made as to the nature and the purpose of these public arenas. The adjective normally applied to

[15] In this regard note the American, British and Icelandic cases.

them – deliberative – should be considered in its sense as discussive, comparative, and also as decisional. It is clear that the power assigned to the actors, according to the meanings given to it, is highly differentiated, the consequence being the need for principled commitment to the procedures to which must be made, according to the context, *ad hoc* adjustments. Inappropriate use of these methods, for example for ill-concealed instrumental purposes, may further delegitimize their promoters and the public decision-makers, with the consequent rejection of the procedures themselves (Abels 2002). In short, participative procedures are not neutral instruments; rather, they reflect the power mechanisms that operate in the social, political and economic contexts which influence the choices of the actors. They can neither be adopted as a certain remedies, nor to earn easy consensus, and they are most effective if they are used as complementary instruments to the conventional mechanisms of representative democracy.

Another area of reflection is the action of the public institutions and decision-makers. These actors must carefully evaluate their role in the participative procedure; a role of mediation and control, given that it is based on governance mechanisms whereby the public decision maker is not the primary decision-maker, but rather the main actor in respect to the subject under discussion, meanwhile bearing in mind that participative procedures favour the search for the most urgent questions rather than the formulation of the best answers.

Scientists, companies, civil society organizations and citizens are called upon to be consciously responsible in preventing polarisations that divert attention from the problematic crux of decisions on biotechnologies: the management of uncertainty. Entrenched scientific certainty and precaution do not help in dealing with the inevitable challenges of biotechnologies, which pose new scenarios in regards to the mutation of nature and man. Notwithstanding the reconfiguration of roles, one cannot deny the primary responsibility of political decision-makers.

Not infrequently, dialogue and comparison are only used in situations of strong opposition or open protest: moments when social conflict is so acute and complex in its articulation of interests, values and knowledge that it precludes any approach or constructive comparison between the parties. Participative practices could prevent these situations if they are conducted with a certain continuity, and if they activate inclusive processes before rather than after the end of the decisional process.

With regard to the relationship between decisions and the right to choose, one notes repeated attempts to apply an economic model to questions of strong valorial impact, such as biotechnologies, focused on the preferences as a market mechanism and the relationship between supply and demand. In this sense the opportunity to use particular biotechnological practices or products seems in some way to "off-load" all responsibility onto the citizen-consumer by emphasizing the possibility of choice in a radical liberal vision. With this application placed downstream in the decisional chain of events, limited contribution can be made in the decision making process. What is more is that it excludes the possibility to intervene in decisions regarding (for example) the introduction of a particular biotechnological application.

The challenge to democracy posed by biotechnological innovations highlights a paradox. On one side, the public debate is animated by a strong scientific content, while on the other side,various standpoints open up to criticism of official science. Both sides invest enormous resources in legitimizing their positions and proceed with actions they deem innovative. The two sides do not commit, except in a few cases[16], the same amount of energy and means to promoting public debate that would involve the actors concerned and enable adequate examination of the question of who must decide and on which basis, and above all on how to make decisions motivated by comparisons along with assumptions, methods and values.

If biotechnologies have the power to modify human nature, their management requires new forms of communication which moderate opposing positions in order to achieve useful comparisons, even if the contenders do not wish to change their positions. These forms of communication become more effective the less they impel decision-makers to take sides on alleged techno-scientific certainties, and the less they foster an apocalyptic vision of scientific progress. Instead, decision-makers should pay lively attention to a future of science destined to remain ambiguous, contested and open.

References

Abels, Gabriele (2002): Experts, Citizens and Eurocrats: Towards a Policy Shift in the Governance of Biopolitics in UE. European integration Online Papers (EIoP) Vol. 6, No. 19, 2002. http://www.eiop.or.at/eiop/texte/2002-019a.htm.

[16] See in particular the debate on cloning for therapeutic reasons which developed in the UK in the nineties.

Banthien, Henning, Jaspers, Michael and Renner, Andreas (2003): Governance of the European Research Area, the role of the civil society, Study IFOK Interim Report. Commission of the European Union.
Barber, Samuel (1984): Strong Democracy. Berkeley CA, University of California Press.
Beck, Ulrich (1986): Risikogesellschaft. Auf dem Weg in eine andere Moderne. Surkamp Verlag, Frankfurt am Main. (tr. It. La società del rischio, Roma, Carocci, 2000, p. 264).
Benhabib, Seyla (1996): Toward a deliberative Model of Democratic Legitimacy. In S. Benhabib (ed.) Democracy and Difference, Princeton NJ, Princeton University Press, p. 70.
Bereano, Phil (1999): Report on Danish "Citizen Consensus Conference" on Genetically Engineered Foods, Washington D.C., Loka Insitute. http://www.loka.org/pages/DanishGeneFood.htm.
Bobbio, Luigi (2002): Le arene deliberative. Rivista Italiana di Politiche Pubbliche, No. 3, pp. 5–29.
Bucchi, Massimiano (1998): Science and the media, alternative route in scientific communication. London and New York, Routledge.
Callon, Michel (1999): The Role of Lay People in the Production and Dissemination of Scientific Knowledge, Science, in: Technology and Society 4(1): 81–94.
Clark, Fiona; Illman, Deborah L.: Dimensions of Civic Science. Science Communication, No. 23, pp. 5–27.
Commandeur, Peter; Joly, Pierre-Benoit; Levidow, Les; Tappeser, Beatrix; Terragni, Fabio (1996): Public Debate and Regulation of Biotechnology in Europe", Biotechnology and Development Monitor, No. 26, pp. 2–9.
Commission of the European Union (2001): European Governance: A White Paper.
Commission of the European Union (2002): Communication from the Commission on the collection and use of expertise by the Commission: Principles and Guidelines, "Improving the base for better policies".
Commission of the European Union (2003): Europeans and Biotechnology in 2002, *Eurobarometer 58.0*.
Crouch, Colin (2003): Postdemocrazia, Roma, Laterza.
Dolmetta, Aldo (2001): Trasparenza e labelling (spunti di riflessione). In: Maria Chiara Tallacchini, Robert Doubleday. eds., Politica della scienza e diritto: il rapporto tra istituzioni, esperti e pubblico nelle biotecnologie, Politeia XVII, No. 62, 2001, pp. 77–85.
Durant, John (1994): Preface. In: Final Report of UK National Consensus Conference on Plant Biotechnology, London, National Center for Biotechnology Education.
Durant et al. (1998): Biotechnology in the public sphere. A European sourcebook. Science Museum, London.
Einsiedel, Edna F. and Eastlick, Deborah L. (2000): Consensus Conferences as Deliberative Democracy. Science Communication, No. 4, pp. 323–343.
Elster, Jon (1998): Deliberative democracy. Cambridge, U.K. and New York, Cambridge University Press.
Frewer, Lynn, Howard, Chris and Shepherd, Ronald (1997): Public concerns in the United Kingdom about general and specific applications of genetic engineering, in: *Science, Technology and Human Values*, 22, 98–124.
Gaskell, George and Bauer, Martin (2001): Biotechnology 1996–2000: The years of controversy. Science Museum, London.
Gibbons, Michael (1996): The new production of science and research in contemporary societies, London, Sage.
Haraway, Donna (1991): Cyborg Manifest. Free Association Books, Routledge, London-N.Y.
Il Sole 24 ore 26/09/99: Manifesto per il buon uso delle biotecnologie
Jasanoff, Sheila (1995): *Science at the bar: law, science, and technology in America*, Harvard University Press, Cambridge Ma.

Jasanoff, Sheila (2005): Design of Nature: Science and Democracy in Europe and the United States. Princeton University Press.

Joss, Simon and Durant, John (1995): Public participation in science: The role of consensus conferences in Europe. London, Science Museum.

Laugksch, Rudiger C. (2000): Scientific literacy: a conceptual overview. In: *Science Education*, No. 84, pp. 71–94.

Lanzara, Giovanni (2005): La deliberazione come indagine pubblica. In: Luigi Pellizzoni, La deliberazione pubblica, Roma, Meltemi, p. 68.

Logan, Robert A. (2001): Science Mass Communication, its conceptual history. In: Science Communication, Vol. 23, No. 2, pp. 136–163.

Mayer, Sue, Hill, Julie, Grove-White, Robin and Wynne, Brian (June 1996): Uncertainty, Precaution and Decision Making: The Release of Genetically Modified Organisms into the Environment, ESRC Global Environmental Change Programme, Briefings n. 8.

Office of Science and Technology (July 1998): Memorandum to the Scientific advisory system: genetically modified foods inquiry by the Science and Technology Committee, London, OST.

Paisley, William J. (1998): Scientific literacy and competition for public attention and understanding. In: Science Communication, Vol. 20, No.1, pp. 70–80.

Pellizzoni, Luigi (2005): Discutere l'incerto, in: Luigi PELLIZZONI (a cura di) *La deliberazione pubblica*, Roma, Meltemi, p. 93.

Rowe, Gene and Frewer, Lynn J. (2001): A Typology of Public Engagement Mechanism. Science Technology and Human Values, Vol. 30 No. 2, Spring, pp. 251–290.

Salter, Brian and Frewer, Lynn (2001): *The changing governance of Biotechnology. The politics of public trust*, University of East Anglia, UK.

Stocklmayer, Susan, Gore, Michael and Bryant, Chris (2001): Science Communication in Theory and Practice. Kluwer Academic Publishers.

Taylor, Charles (1989): Cross Purposes: The Liberal Communitarian Debate. In: Rosenblum (ed.) *Liberalism and the Moral Life*, Cambridge MA, Harvard University Press.

UN Economic Commission for Europe (UNECE) (1998). Convention on Access to Information, Public Participation in Decision-Making and Access to Justice in Environmental Matters.

Wynne, Brian (1991): Knowledge in context. Science Technology and Human Values, No. 16, pp. 111–121.

Wynne, Brian (1995): Public Understanding of Science. In: Sheila Jasanoff, Gerard E. Markle, James C. Petersen and Trevor Pinch, eds., *Handbook of Science and Technology Studies*, Sage, Thousand Oaks-London-New Dehli, pp. 361–388.

Wynne, Brian (1999): Knowledge in Context, in: E. SCANLON, E. WHITELEGG and S. YATES (eds.) Communicating Science: Contexts and Channels. Reader 2. Routledge, London.

CHAPTER THREE

DEMOCRATIZING AGRI-BIOTECHNOLOGY? EUROPEAN PUBLIC PARTICIPATION IN AGBIOTECH ASSESSMENT

Les Levidow

Abstract

European decision-making on techno-scientific issues has encountered public suspicion and legitimacy problems. These have resulted from government policies promoting specific technologies as if they were objective imperatives. The consequent difficulties have been diagnosed according to various 'deficit' models, which in turn inform efforts at governing the societal conflict.

Anticipating or responding to European public concerns over agbiotech in particular, state bodies have sponsored participatory exercises in technology assessment (TA). Some participants sought to open up technological decisions vis à vis alternative futures and normative choices, but such efforts were marginalized; the biotechnological innovation trajectory was protected from challenge. Questions about agbiotech *as* control were displaced and channelled into regulatory issues and control measures.

In designing and managing the TA exercises, boundaries were imposed – between biotechnological imperatives versus alternative options, between scientific versus policy issues, and between expert versus lay roles – thus closing down issues. Some participants challenged the boundaries, thus opening up issues for a broader lay expertise. By contesting lay/expert boundaries, participants performed different models of the public. Pervasive tensions have arisen between discussing a 'common' problem – how to make agbiotech safe or acceptable – versus containing conflicts around problem-definitions of societal needs.

To some extent, participatory TA exercises have helped to hold governments accountable for regulatory criteria, but not for innovation choices. These participatory TA exercises generally internalized assumptions about agbiotech as societal progress. Despite aspirations to democratize technological choices, the exercises tended to biotechnologise democracy. The prospects for democratization will depend upon wider, autonomous forms of participation—neither sponsored nor welcomed by state bodies.

Introduction

Public participation in technoscientific issues has recently gained mainstream support in Europe, in response to greater conflict around innovation and regulation of controversial technologies. STS scholars have played key roles in stimulating or organizing such participation. The exercises have attracted diverse views regarding their appropriate design, roles and consequences. And they have attracted various criticisms – e.g. that participants were not representative of the public, or that the government did not make a prior commitment to follow views expressed there, or that technical aspects were separated from other issues.

Those criticisms may be descriptively accurate but imply particular benchmarks, even simplistic models of direct democracy. Together they imply that participants truly representing the public could guide government decisions – as if the government had no agenda of its own, nor a wider accountability to representative democracy. Amidst proposals for participation, there are diverse models of what would count as a democratic assessment of technology (Joss 1998: 4). According to a survey of participatory TA exercises, these rarely have a demonstrable impact on political decision-making (Bütschi and Nentwich 2002). Perhaps such exercises matter in more subtle ways, which therefore need different analytical questions about democratic accountability.

For some analysts of participatory TA, at issue is 'how to make those in charge accountable' and thus 'how to organize effective accountability' for government decisions (Hagendijk and Irwin 2006: 56–57). Some have echoed concerns that participatory methods may 'subvert broader democratic political processes' or that they may not be 'fit for purpose', (Burgess and Chilvers 2006). Participatory TA has been seen as supplementing older political forms of accountability with broader social forms. But this aim leaves open some difficult questions: 'who is holding whom accountable, and by which means?' (Abels 2007: 111).

As a basis to evaluate various participatory methods, criteria for success include the following: the quality of deliberative processes, consensual proposals from the process, influence on policy, etc. (Rowe and Frewer 2004; Rowe et al. 2004). Although those concerns and criteria are valid, they imply that state-sponsored TA exercises could have a clear purpose in promoting technological democracy and citizenship. Why should this be generally true?

As a case study for such analysis, this paper focuses on agricultural biotechnology, a sector which has faced extraordinary public protest in Europe. Agbiotech has attracted diverse forms of public participation, e.g. open mass meetings, protest, boycotts, mass-media stunts and sabotage. Through these means, an emerging citizenry has demanded government accountability for innovation choices. Among the various responses, many state bodies across Europe have sponsored formal participatory exercises, beyond simply access to regulatory procedures. So agbiotech provides a rich, multi-country case study.

This paper discusses the following questions:

How and why did state bodies sponsor participatory TA of agbiotech?

What aims arose in designing, managing and using those exercises?

What was their relevance to democratizing agbiotech?

Democratising technology – or managing conflict?

Participatory technology assessment has been promoted as a means to democratize technology, especially by enhancing the public accountability of innovation trajectories. To do so, participatory design should acknowledge that science and innovation are social, cultural and institutional activities.

> As such, public engagement offers a way to be more accountable for the particular values and interests, which underpin both the governance of science and the general use of science in governance… Public engagement holds greatest value when it occurs 'upstream' – at the earliest stages in the process of research or science-informed policy making… In practice, the relationship between representative democracy and participatory methods becomes most clear and complementary, when engagement is approached as a means to 'open up' the range of possible decisions, rather than as a way to close this down. Choice among the options thereby identified then becomes a clearer matter of democratic accountability (Stirling 2006: 5; cf. Stirling 2005).

Achievement of such accountability depends upon the aims, design and management of the process.

However, public participation in technological issues has had diverse agendas. According to Lars Klüver (2006, cf. 1995), a long-time advocate at the Danish Board of Technology, public participation has recently become mainstreamed, along with changes in its policy role. Originally it was promoted as a vehicle for democratization and citizen empowerment, so that people could challenge policy assumptions and influence decisions. Now public participation goes hand-in-hand with liberalism: politics is seen as a market of opinions, so citizens should be invited into the open market (cf. Popper 1962).

Participation now becomes yet another governance tool among others, e.g. for adjusting, supplementing or enhancing the policy process. Aware that they often lack public confidence, policymakers seek methods of upstream conflict-management. These professional reasons have recently driven interest by mainstream institutions in public participation and will continue to do so, he argues (Klüver 2006).

Upstream conflict-management restricts the role of participants. In the UK, for example, there have been various proposals for 'upstream public engagement' between the public and scientists at an early stage (e.g. HM Treasury/DTI/DfES 2004: 105). Such engagement has been advocated as means to deliberate possible innovation choices and to make them more accountable (e.g. Wilsdon and Willis 2004). By contrast to those ambitious aims:

> [public engagement] is sometimes portrayed as a way of addressing the *impacts* of technology – be they health, social, environmental or ethical – rather than helping to shape the trajectory of technological development. The hope is that engagement can be used to head off controversy... (Wilsdon et al. 2005: 33).

Indeed, conflict-avoidance or conflict-management may be built into the design of public engagement. Rather than evaluate participatory TA according to an ideal model, each case should be seen as an arena for diverse strategies for how to represent agbiotech, the public and the relevant expertise.

Denmark 1987: sustainable agriculture?

The Danish consensus conference has been advocated as a 'counter-technocracy' –a means to challenge expert claims through a deliberative process. The lay panel has no vested interest different than the general public, and its report helps to promote technology assessment (TA) as a broad societal process. It extends a Danish tradition of *folkeoplysnig* – people's enlightenment through an adult education network which builds a reflective, informed citizenry (Joss, 1998: 20).

As its guiding principle, 'a well-functioning democracy requires a well-educated and engaged population'. Successful participation is understood in those terms: as a participant commented, for example, 'We initiated a really good assessment process among the public' (cited in Klüver 1995: 41, 43). In the Danish consensus conference, then, 'interested citizens' personify a political culture in which technological decisions are held accountable to public debate, mediated by Parliament.

Denmark's debate on agricultural biotechnology was initiated in the mid-1980s by environmental NGOs. A series of 'debate booklets' were issued by NOAH, the Danish affiliate of FoE, proposing new legislation to regulate GMO releases. In response to public concerns, a Parliamentary 'green' majority imposed a statutory ban in the 1986 Gene Technology Act; GMO releases would not be permitted unless there was sufficient knowledge about the ecological consequences (Toft 1996). With this wording, the government could be held accountable to demonstrate such knowledge for risk assessment; this burden of evidence meant a *de facto* ban for several years.

Parliament also mandated funds for an information campaign on biotechnology. Some funds were specially earmarked for NGOs, especially NOAH and some trade unions, in order to stimulate further debate on advantages and disadvantages of biotechnology. In these ways, environmental NGOs gained extra resources and political opportunities to frame the issues for further public debate. NOAH organized ten public conferences on the wider environmental consequences, on sustainable agriculture including organic agriculture, on food labelling, on animal welfare and ethics, on the Third World, on seed diversity (including patents), and on biological warfare. These debates were reported through a series of publications and statements from NOAH.[1]

In that context the Danish Board of Technology held its first consensus conference in 1987 on 'Gene Technology in Industry and Agriculture', timed to coincide with Parliamentary debate on the issue

[1] Much information here, supplied by Jesper Toft, is not available in English-language documents.

(Hansen et al. 1992; Klüver 1995: 44). In its report the lay panel took up risk issues as well as ethical ones (Teknologinævnet 1987). Accepting a key recommendation, Parliament voted to exclude animals from the 1987–90 national R&D program for gene technology. The conference eventually had more profound effects on the Danish regulatory regime through wider public debate.

A further information campaign was coordinated by the Board of Technology and Danish Adult Education Association. During 1987–1990 they supported more than 500 local meetings all over the country in order to stimulate debate on human and non-human uses of biotechnology, including concerns about risk and ethics. Environmental NGOs were often invited to speak, as the most visible critical actors on the scene.

The government also funded a subsequent program, organized by trade unions, to stimulate further debate on advantages and disadvantages of agbiotech. Their educational materials posed questions about sustainable agriculture: For example, would genetically modified crops alleviate or aggravate the existing problems of crop monocultures? (Elert 1991: 12). Through that wider debate, the consensus conference indirectly influenced Parliament and thus regulatory policy.

In the EU-wide regulatory procedure, dominant member states implicitly took for granted eco-efficiency benefits of herbicide-tolerant crops, while disregarding the herbicide implications or assuming them to be benign (Levidow et al. 1996, 2000). By contrast to those EU-level assumptions, Danish regulators were held publicly accountable for assessing the broad implications of GM crops for agricultural strategy, herbicide usage and the environment. Such judgments were scrutinized by the Parliament's Environment Committee, often by drawing upon specific questions from NGOs. Under such domestic pressures, Danish representatives in turn proposed that risk assessments evaluate those implications at the EU level (Toft 1996, 2000).

Thus citizen participation enhanced government accountability for regulatory criteria, going beyond optimistic assumptions about environmental benefits. GM crops were subjected to criteria of sustainable agriculture, which in turn were opened up to the lay expertise of agbiotech critics. Environmental NGOs found greater scope to influence regulatory procedures and expertise.

Agri-innovation choices became more contentious in the late 1990s, however; NGOs demanded alternatives to agbiotech and to intensive agricultural methods. In a 1999 consensus conference, the lay panel asserted the need for extra measures – not only for product safety, but also to prevent GM products 'becoming controlled by monopolistic companies', as well as measures to evaluate ethical aspects (Einsiedel 2001). As the conference organizers emphasized, those proposals were expressing citizens' viewpoints, thus providing a basis for dialogue with decision-makers (Teknologinævnet 1999). The panel's proposals challenged the assumptions and limits of the EU legislative framework. Yet public demands for accountability were being channeled into more stringent measures to regulate biophysical risks. This pervasive tension has parallels in later TA exercises.

Germany 1991–92: participation trap

Since the time that the German government promoted agbiotech in the 1980s, this policy provoked widespread protest – e.g., from the Green Party, environmentalist groups and local campaigns. Although critics gained high-profile attention in the mass media and civil society, their views remained marginal to official procedures, unlike German corporatist arrangements for labor issues. Opposition to agbiotech split civil society and the major political parties (Gill 1996).

TA exercise

German public controversy focused on herbicide-tolerant crops, given their potential for spreading that trait and for changing patterns of herbicide usage. To address such conflicts, the government sponsored a TA exercise on GM herbicide-resistant crops in the early 1990s. Funding came from the Ministry of Industry and Research, which was strongly promoting biotechnology. It was initiated and coordinated by the Berlin Wissenschaftszentrum (Science Centre) as an experiment in environmental conflict management. The 50-odd participants had quasi-expert roles; they included overt proponents and opponents of HR crops, as well as representatives of regulatory authorities, agricultural associations, consumer organizations, etc. From the start, conflict erupted over how to define the relevant scientific issues and the expertise needed to evaluate them.

A broad participation was needed to deliberate the arguments arising in the polarized public debate on agbiotech, according to the organizers. The TA was designed to evaluate those arguments for and against herbicide-resistance GM technology, especially its possible consequences – but not alternative options for weed control in agriculture. Thus the procedure was 'a technology-induced TA, not a problem-induced TA' (van den Daele 1995: 74).

Environmental NGOs counterposed the latter approach. They wanted the TA to compare biotechnology products with other potential weed-control methods, as alternative solutions to agricultural problems. However, the NGOs' proposal was rejected by the organizers (Gill 1993). Consequently, the narrow remit set difficult terms for participation by the broadly representative individuals from NGOs – indeed, terms for their expert status.

As the organizers acknowledged, 'The TA implicitly accepted the matter-of-course development of technology as the starting point', as well as possible risks as the main grounds for state restrictions: 'If critics fail to provide evidence of relevant risks, the technology cannot be banned.' So critics held the burden of evidence for any risks. Advocates held the burden to demonstrate benefits, though failure to do so would have no bearing upon regulatory decisions (van den Daele 1995: 75). This framework marginalized alternative agronomic solutions, while reinforcing the dominant system: 'intensive farming as the reference system'. Within that framework, participants themselves defined their controversies as debates about empirical evidence, e.g. regarding the possibility of environmental damage – not about values and goals (ibid: 76, 77).

The organizers aimed to include and deliberate all viewpoints on the risk-benefit issues. By subjecting expert views to scrutiny, the TA could reach conclusions about empirical claims, rather than political or ethical ones. 'This procedure placed participants under massive pressure either to admit consensus or justify dissent', especially through detailed empirical evidence (ibid: 80).

From NGOs' standpoint, the technology-induced TA framework effectively favored experts in specialized technical areas, e.g. gene flow and herbicide effects. In practice, the TA exercise set a lower burden of evidence for demonstrating benefits than for demonstrating risks, in a period before much empirical research had been done on risk scenarios. Consequently, the discussion emphasized environmental benefits, especially the prospects for farmers to use less harmful herbicides and/or lower quantities of them (Gill 1993).

On the basis of the expert reports, the TA symbolically normalized any risks. According to agbiotech proponents, echoing the government's advisory body, any risks from GM herbicide-tolerant crops were similar to those from conventional crop plants and herbicide usage. 'In many areas it was argued that there was no need for political action because the identifiable problems could be dealt with in the established registration procedures.... if one agreed to the "normalization" of the risks' (van den Daele 1995: 82). In this way, the exercise undermined NGO claims about novel or unknown risks; once normalized, any risks would be manageable through regulatory procedures, even contemporary ones.

Science court or parliament?

The technology-induced TA framework posed a dilemma for participation by agbiotech critics. Once inside such an exercise, 'They have to criticize a technology which promises to satisfy some needs which may even be produced by the technology itself...' (Gill 1993: 74). That is, putative benefits satisfy 'needs' which are predefined by biotechnological solutions for intensive monoculture. Thus a technology-induced TA tends to accept and reproduce the social vision built into the technology.

Environmental NGOs and their associated research institutes faced a difficult choice: either play a quasi-expert role within that framework and thus help legitimize it, or else abandon that role and be treated as merely lay voices. After much conflict, they withdrew before the TA exercise could report its conclusions. They gave several reasons for withdrawal, e.g. that their voluntary participation was occupying too much time, especially the task of commenting on long expert reports (van den Daele 1995: 81). According to an NGO expert, 'I had not imagined that you could destroy participation by throwing paper on top of people' (cited in Charles 2001: 107). By withdrawing from the TA, they could devote greater resources to public protest and preserve their credibility with NGO members and activists (Gill 1993: 81–82).

After this withdrawal decision, they were criticized by the WZB coordinator:

> One cannot present one's position in public as scientifically substantiated and then cast fundamental doubt on science as neutral... Participation in the procedure implies the readiness to submit oneself on the empirical issues to the judgment of science (van den Daele 1995: 84; also 1994).

As the WZB coordinator told the story many years later, he had been skeptical of claims that herbicide-tolerant crops had special risks or special benefits, so he saw NGO arguments about risks as a proxy for political ones:

> ... the idea of special risks is not a good argument. We should turn to the issues of democracy and who's going to decide how society develops... Apparently it would have been difficult for them [NGOs] to declare explicitly that the conflict was not about risks, but about social goals and political reforms... (van den Daele, cited in Charles 2001: 107).

However, that distinction was not so clearly drawn by the organizers beforehand; it became more explicit in later retelling the story. According to a social scientist who attended the TA exercise, some NGO participants saw it as analogous to a parliament which could evaluate agbiotech in terms of societal goals. However, van den Daele retrospectively portrayed it as a science court, whose remit the NGOs did not understand or accept; this portrayal offers a *post hoc* legitimation for the failure to integrate them (personal communication, Bernhard Gill 2006).

Moreover, the distinction between a science court and parliament is not so straightforward; neither is the distinction between risk assessment and socio-political goals. At issue was the range of questions to be answered by science, their normative assumptions, and the alternative technological options to be considered as comparators for agri-environmental assessments. Some questions from participants were pre-empted or marginalized by the TA exercise, especially by constructing particular boundaries between expert and lay voices.

Societal futures were reduced to scientific issues, readily assessable by experts in 'the state of the art'. Civil society representatives found themselves in a 'participation trap'; they could either participate within the government's risk-benefit framework for GM crops per se, or else be marginalized. Overall the exercise reinforced the government's policy framework and its public unaccountability. In a similar way, societal conflict over agri-innovation issues was channelled into risk assessment through regulatory procedures. Together these practices extended and reinforced the *Rechtstaat*, at least until government policy began to change in 2002.

France 1998: The Benign Technocratic State

By 1997 French regulatory policy faced a legitimacy crisis. France had led efforts to gain EU-wide approval for GM crops, yet these were now opposed by a broad range of organizations. The Confederation Paysanne, representing farmers who elaborated a peasant identity, opposed agbiotech while counterposing 'quality' alternatives to industrialized agriculture (Heller 2002). An oppositional petition was signed by many prominent scientists, not necessarily anti-agbiotech, but all of them concerned about regulatory failures to develop appropriate ecological expertise and risk research (Marris 2001).

In February 1997 the Prime Minister decided not to authorize commercial cultivation of Ciba-Geigy's Bt 176 GM maize in France, even though French regulators had led EU authorization of the same product. This unstable policy indicated a crisis of official expertise within an elite-technocratic political culture. According to some critics, an official 'objectivity' too narrowly defined the relevant expertise. As an alternative approach, expert procedures would open up a scientific critique of possible options; this space would provide the expertise necessary for decisions (Roqueplo 1996: 67), my paraphrase). By incorporating counter-expertise, regulatory procedures would develop an *expertise contradictoire* (contradictory expertise), which would enhance democratic debate and state accountability for decisions.

In November 1997 the government announced a set of measures, including a plan to sponsor a consensus conference on GMOs, by reference to the Danish Model. This event was later officially called a Citizens' Conference. As an official rationale, this event would provide 'a new way of elaborating decisions' and a means to implement 'participatory democracy', according to the Ministry of Agriculture. Yet the government never clarified the relation between the citizens' conference and its own decision-making procedure (Marris and Joly 1999). This relation was subtly played out within the conference process, especially by defining expert roles.

From the start, the conference was designed to re-assert the benign expertise of the state, especially the Parliament, which saw itself as the only legitimate representative of the Nation. Organization of the citizens' conference was delegated to a Parliamentary unit, Office Parlementaire d'Évaluation des Choix Scientifiques et Technologiques (OPECST), which symbolized a political neutrality separate from the government. OPECST appointed the steering committee, which in turn decided that the panel membership should represent diverse views of ordinary citizens – rather than stakeholders in the debate. It also decided which 'experts' – all of them scientists – would give briefings or testimony to the panel, thus framing the issues in advance (Marris and Joly 1999). The organizers saw those arrangements as necessary 'to prepare a public debate which is not taken over by one side or the other', i.e. to correct or avoid biases in the existing public debate (OPECST 1998a). Implicitly, such biases included anti-agbiotech NGOs on one side and Monsanto on the other side, especially from the perspective of the Left-Green Parliamentary majority.

Held in 1998, the conference included different framings of the policy problem. At the public hearings, the citizens' panel often challenged claims by experts about risks and benefits of GM crops. According to the panel's report, control by multinational companies could threaten farmers' independence. Genetically altered species pose a risk of standardization. And GM rapeseed poses known risks of uncontrolled proliferation, both through pollen and seeds. Nevertheless GM crops could bring economic benefits to European agriculture (OPECST 1998b; Boy et al. 1998). Together these arguments implied the need for national public-sector expertise in agbiotech innovation.

The panel's recommendations focused on institutional arrangements for better managing agricultural biotechnology. Such measures included the following: greater social participation in scientific advice; public-sector research on ecological risks and agbiotech innovation; a system to ensure traceability of food derived from GM crops; and adequate labeling to inform consumer choice. 'Until these conditions are satisfied, part of the panel believes that a moratorium would be advisable' (ibid.). By advocating state funds for agbiotech innovation, the panel accepted the government's problem-definition of a national technological gap whose solution requires public-funded science, presumed to be benign. The panel's concerns about rapeseed complemented the French government's decision to oppose approval of GM herbicide-tolerant rape, on grounds that gene flow could complicate weed control (Marris and Joly 1999).

The panel's conclusions were translated into policy advice by the Parliamentary organizers, as if they were neutral experts in the public good. Moreover, having attended the proceedings, the OPECST President presumed to speak for the panel:

> Taking all these views into account he then himself adopted a position on a number of topics…
> He has identified the issues and looked into peoples' fears and concerns (OPECST 1998b).

This translation can be illustrated by the strategic issue of how to structure expert advice. The panel had proposed that a citizens' commission should be part of the scientific advisory committee. Yet OPECST recommended instead that it be kept separate; this proposal could better perpetuate a neutral image of scientific advice, thus reinforcing a boundary between expert/lay roles.

The panel's advice anticipated the general direction of government policy: more stringent regulatory criteria, risk assessment by a broader scientific expertise, and 'independent' risk research, which was equated with public-sector institutes. It helped to legitimize and reinforce such initiatives, which had not been universally accepted within the government beforehand. In June 1998 the government announced measures along those lines (Marris and Joly 1999). Institutional reforms emphasized expert procedures to minimize the risks and enhance the benefits of a controversial technology.

Despite its limitations, the citizens' conference initiated a new form of active public representation and knowledge-production. Panel members explored techno-scientific and social aspects together from the perspective of ordinary citizens. They sought to inform decision-makers about the views of those who do not normally speak out – and who do not feel represented by political parties, trade unions, or environmental and consumer NGOs. This potential for participatory evaluation, especially for considering alternative options, was limited by the overall structure, especially the small opportunity to interact with designated experts (Joly et al. 2003).

Overall the citizens' conference was used to legitimize state claims to represent the public good, especially through expert roles. OPECST selectively promoted some accounts of agbiotech and its regulation as the expert ones, while explicitly speaking on behalf of citizens. The Agriculture Ministry had claimed to implement 'participatory democracy', yet the exercise extended the French tradition of technocratic governance (Marris and Joly 1999).

Within this framework, expert roles remained the exclusive realm of the state authorities and their officially designated advisors. Ordinary people could question experts and recommend institutional reforms, but Parliamentary experts would officially speak for them. Thus the process reinforced lay/expert boundaries, in the face of public challenges to the official expertise for agbiotech.

UK 2003 Public Dialogue: policing boundaries

From the late 1990s onwards the UK had a widespread public controversy over agbiotech. Protest actions and attacks on field trials gained public support by linking GM crops with various issues – BSE, other food scares, globalization, 'pollution', etc. (Levidow 2000). The government faced an impasse over regulatory decisions, especially the criteria for permitting a GM herbicide-tolerant maize which the EU had approved in 1998. As a key issue, conservation agencies had warned that changes in herbicide usage could harm farmland biodiversity, so the government funded farm-scale trials to monitor such effects.

To address wider issues beyond risk regulation, the government had created the Agricultural and Environment Biotechnology Commission in 2000. Its report, *Crops on Trial*, advised the government to initiate an 'open and inclusive process of decision-making' within a framework that extends to broader questions than herbicide effects. It proposed a 'wider public debate involving a series of regional discussion meetings' (AEBC 2001: 19, 25). The government was persuaded to sponsor this – alongside the intense, sporadic debate which was occurring anyway.

Called 'GM Nation?', the official public debate was carried out in summer 2003. Beforehand the government vaguely promised 'to take public opinion into account as far as possible'. The exercise was intended for the organizers to gauge public opinion, rather than for participants to deliberate a collective view on expert matters (Horlick-Jones et al. 2006). 'GM Nation?' also aimed to elicit views of the ordinary public, rather than organizational representatives – an artificial distinction, given that most civil society organizations and wider social networks had discussed agbiotech in previous years.

An overall Public Dialogue had a tripartite structure which explicitly distinguished between lay and expert issues. 'GM Nation?' was designed mainly for the lay public. An expert panel carried out a Science Review of literature relevant to risk assessment. And a government department carried out a Costs and Benefits Review of GM crop cultivation in the UK.

The Public Dialogue was designed in those three separate parts, with an explicit aim that they would work closely together. The three procedures were kept formally separate, yet the supposedly lay and expert issues became intermingled in practice. The official boundaries were both challenged and policed, thus constructing the participants in contradictory ways.

Representing public views?

'GM Nation?' featured several hundred public meetings open to anyone interested, drawing over 20,000 participants (DTI 2003). When participants in 'GM Nation?' largely expressed critical or skeptical views towards agbiotech, arguments ensued over whether they were 'representative' of the public. According to a pro-agbiotech coalition, the Agriculture and Biotechnology Council, the exercise was hijacked by anti-biotech activists, so the format was not conducive to a balanced deliberation of the issues.

According to academic analyses, however, that criticism frames the public as atomised individuals who have no prior opinion. The exercise predictably drew a specialized public which was largely suspicious or hostile to agbiotech. Participants represented both themselves as individuals and wider epistemic networks. The debates were filling an institutional void, in the absence of any other formal opportunity to deliberate the wider issues (Reynolds and Szerszynski 2006).

The government sponsors had asked the contractors to involve 'people at the grass-roots level whose voice has not been heard'. As the official evaluators noted afterwards, however, it was problematic to distinguish clearly between 'an activist minority' and a 'disengaged, grass-roots minority'. Many participants in 'GM Nation?' were politically engaged in the sense that their beliefs on GM issues formed part of their wider worldview. Yet policymakers tend to construct 'the public' as an even-handed majority – and therefore legitimately entitled to participate in engagement exercises (Horlick-Jones et al. 2004: 135; Horlick-Jones et al. 2006). Indeed, 'grass-roots' conventionally means local organized activists, yet this term was strangely inverted to mean a passive, uninformed public.

As envisaged by the sponsors, separate focus groups would allow the public to frame the issues according to their own concerns, yet special measures were needed to realize the policymakers' model of the public. They saw the open meetings as dominated by anti-biotech activists, unrepresentative of the general public. Politically inactive citizens were seen as truly representative and thus as valid sources of public opinion, by contrast to 'activists'. To exclude the latter individuals from focus groups, candidates underwent surveillance and screening. 'Perhaps paradoxically, the desire to allow the public to frame the discussion in their own terms led the organizers to rely on private and closely monitored forms of social interaction'. According to this ideal model of the focus groups, the organizers would be listening to the *idiotis*, by analogy to ancient Greek citizens too ignorant to fulfill their responsibilities (Lezaun and Soneryd 2006: 22–23). In this way, the more informed, expert citizens would be excluded from representing the public.

'GM Nation?' was intended to canvass all views and concerns about agbiotech, yet there were boundary disputes over issue-framings, admissible arguments and participants' roles. Some used the opportunity as politically engaged actors in their own right, not just as indicators of public opinion. Attending shortly after the US-UK attack on Iraq, some participants drew analogies between government claims about agbiotech and about Weapons of Mass Destruction. They suspected that the government was concealing or distorting information in both cases; they wondered whether it would ignore public opinion towards agbiotech, as in the attack on Iraq. Initially the chair tried to steer the discussion back to agbiotech, on grounds that 'GM Nation?' was not about the Iraq war, though participants still elaborated the analogy. Thus the public consultation had a disjuncture between public politics and government policy as understood by the sponsors of the exercise (Joss 2005b: 181).

Expert/lay roles

For the carefully selected focus groups, the organizers commissioned 'stimulus material', so that participants would have a common knowledge-basis for discussion. The Steering Group asked the contractors to supply 'objective' information. Yet there were grounds to include 'opposing views' because this is often how people encounter information in real life', according to the official evaluators of 'GM Nation?' The ultimate material did include divergent views, but their sources were removed from the workbook for focus groups. Afterwards the official evaluators questioned 'the extent to which information is meaningful if it is decontextualized by stripping it from its source' (Horlick-Jones et al. 2004: 93–94; Walls et al. 2005).

Indeed, people often make judgments on the institutional source of expert views, but they had little basis to do so in the 'GM Nation?' focus groups. Omission of the sources was not simply a design deficiency in the exercise. By default, the issue of expert credibility was diverted and reduced to scientific information about biophysical risk. Participants had little basis to evaluate such information, so the exercise constructed a lay/expert boundary, constraining public roles even more narrowly than in the wider public debate.

Separate from 'GM Nation?', the GM Science Review was officially limited to a panel of experts evaluating scientific information. At the same time, relevant NGOs were consulted about experts who could represent their views on the panel. In this way, panel members were selected along relatively inclusive lines, encompassing a wide range of views about GM crops. As these selection criteria recognized, the public did not regard scientific expertise as a neutral resource (Hansen 2006: 580), so the Panel's public credibility would depend upon a diverse composition. Although the Panel's report identified no specific risks, it emphasized uncertainties and knowledge-gaps important for future risk assessment of GM products (GM Science Review 2003). These uncertainties implied scope for a wider public role in expert judgments.

As a high-profile part of the GM Science Review, the Royal Society announced a meeting to 'examine the scientific basis' of various positions. Opening the event, the chair announced the laudable aim 'to clarify what we know and do not know' about potential effects of GM crops. In the morning, agro-ecological issues were analysed in a rigorous way, especially for their relevance to the prospect that broad-spectrum herbicides may be widely used in the future. But those complexities were ignored when considering GM herbicide-tolerant crops in the afternoon (Levidow 2003). By downplaying expert ignorance, the overall structure did not facilitate a debate about knowledge versus ignorance, nor provide much basis for public involvement.

Moreover, the boundaries of 'science' were policed along pro-biotech lines. Inconvenient issues, findings or views were deemed non-scientific. For example, speakers freely advocated the need for agbiotech to solve global problems, e.g. environmental degradation, the food supply, etc, but the chair cut off anyone who questioned these claims – for going beyond science (ibid.). Thus biotechnological framing assumptions were reinforced as 'science', along with the expert status of their proponents – while skeptics were marginalized as merely expressing lay views on extra-scientific issues.

In sum, the UK Public Dialogue involved a struggle over how to construct the public, especially in relation to expertise. The structure and management imposed boundaries between apolitical grassroots versus activist, as well as between lay versus expert status. Nevertheless participants challenged those boundaries, performed different models of the public and questioned dominant expert assumptions.

Conclusions: Democratizing Agbiotech?

The Introduction posed the following questions:

How and why did state bodies sponsor participatory TA of agbiotech?

What aims arose in designing, managing and using those exercises? What was their relevance to democratizing agbiotech?

Since the 1980s various state bodies in Europe have sponsored a participatory technology assessment (TA) of agbiotech; this can be analyzed as a specific type of arena with diverse forms and contexts. In most national contexts, agbiotech was being officially promoted as an essential source of eco-efficient GM products, whose safety would be validated by experts as the only necessary scrutiny. These neoliberal policy frameworks were increasingly challenged by autonomous citizen initiatives.

In responding to or anticipating public concerns about agbiotech, participatory TA exercises were sponsored with diverse, overlapping, even contradictory aims. From various deficit models of public unease, sponsors and other advocates sought to democratize technology, to educate the public, to counter 'extreme' views, to gauge public attitudes, to guide institutional reforms, and/or to manage societal conflicts. Such aims had a bearing upon the design, management, staging and process of each exercise. Each process manifest diverse accounts of technology, the public, expertise and democracy (cf. Joss 2005a).

In these TA exercises, individuals were pre-selected to participate in a group process, questioning expert claims in order to reach a group view. Participants deliberated the normative, value-laden basis of expert claims, thus developing a lay expertise; they went beyond simply questioning experts (cf. Kerr 1998; Wakeford 1998). By contrast to a negotiation among interest-groups, participants addressed the public good by appealing to common societal interests and problems (cf. Hamlett 2003).

However, dominant problem-definitions incorporated or marginalized critical voices. Some problems were treated as common ones for group deliberation, while others were ignored or marginalized as uncommon ones, inconvenient for a group consensus or for a thinkable government policy. Some participants questioned whether agbiotech would provide a means for sustainable agriculture and a benign control over the agri-food chain; some suggested the need for alternatives. These questions were generally channeled into regulatory criteria and were reduced to control measures.

In such ways, participatory TA exercises biotechnologized democracy. The innovation trajectory was protected as societal progress, partly by diverting any challenge into managerial problems. Discussion generally focused on appropriate regulatory arrangements for agbiotech, represented as a series of potentially beneficial products; at issue was how to minimize risks and maximize benefits. Citizens' roles were modeled according to the biophysical 'risk' frameworks of EU and/or national legislation, thus generating conflict over such roles.

In analogous ways, public participation in EU agbiotech regulatory procedures manifest tensions between the broad comments submitted and the official 'scientific' criteria for relevant evidence (Bora and Hausendorf 2006; Ferretti 2007). By serving a statutory procedure, science closes the factual debate; politics is excluded by pre-determined concepts of risk, nature, citizen, public, etc.

More generally, 'wherever a sharp political controversy appears within the context of a rather narrow legal-procedural framework for citizen participation, we can expect a variety of depoliticized positions with different frames of reference' (Bora 2009). Through such procedures, conflicts over societal futures can be managed 'by re-absorbing discourses of polarity into a system of "legitimate differences" and by defining the locations where differences can be articulated', as anticipated by a critical analysis a decade earlier (Gottweis 1998).

Regardless of other views held by TA participants, any wider deliberation was constrained – by a search for consensus, by the design of each exercise, and by the government policy framework. This overall context limited what could be said with influence on the process, and thus what roles could be credibly performed by participants (cf. Hajer 2005). The process internalized and reinforced policy assumptions about agbiotech as essential progress – albeit perhaps warranting more rigorous, publicly accountable regulation. Through a discursive depoliticization, contentious issues were displaced onto the management problems of an inevitable future, as in neoliberal governance more generally (cf. Goven 2006; Pestre 2008). Consequently, tensions arose between discussing a 'common' problem – how to make agbiotech safe or acceptable – versus encompassing problems of political-economic control, innovation choices and societal futures.

Those tensions took the form of various boundary conflicts, which erupted more starkly in some cases. In the German TA exercise, as an extreme case, the NGO representatives could maintain their official expert status only by accepting a risk-benefit framework. Instead they rejected these terms for participation, demanded a broadly comparative assessment, and thus were relegated to the lay public or irrational objectors. In the 2003 UK Public Dialogue, the official structure nominally separated all relevant issues into three components – public concerns, scientific risk assessment, and economic benefits; accordingly, expert matters were formally separated from other issues for discussion by lay participants. Despite that official tripartite structure, all the issues became mixed in practice; their boundaries were both contested and policed.

In the design and management of the TA exercises, then, boundaries were imposed – between biotechnological imperatives versus alternative options, between scientific versus policy issues, as well as between expert versus lay roles – thus closing down issues. By contesting those boundaries, some participants opened up policy issues and performed different models of the public, implying broader roles for citizens. These performative interactions produced different understandings of the policy problem (cf. Hajer 2005). If analyzed in this way, then public engagement can 'clarify what conflict is really about' (de Marchi 2003).

In each TA exercise, issues were opened up beyond the government policy framework, though they remained more narrow than in the parallel public debate. Ultimately the process reinforced official boundaries between scientific and extra-scientific issues, as well as between expert and lay roles (though these boundaries took different forms across the national cases). Agbiotech was being co-produced along with particular models of expertise, citizenship and their relationship. Institutions were created or adapted in designing and managing each TA process accordingly.

To some extent, state-sponsored participatory TA exercises anticipated, stimulated or reinforced policy changes which enhance the state's accountability for regulatory frameworks. Such outcomes depended upon a longer-term socio-political agency beyond the TA exercise and its panel. However, the TA exercises did not help publics to hold the state accountable for its commitment to agbiotech as an objective imperative.

What does this mean for efforts to democratize technology?

> ... appraisal conducted in 'opening up' mode might be seen as substantively more coherent and normatively more consistent with the prevailing institutions and procedures of representative democracy (Stirling 2005: 229).

> In practice, the relationship between representative democracy and participatory methods becomes most clear and complementary, when engagement is approached as a means to open up the range of possible decisions, rather than as a way to close this down. Choice among the options thereby identified then becomes a clearer matter of democratic accountability (Stirling 2006: 5).

In the state-sponsored cases analyzed here, participatory methods and representative democracy do not seem complementary. Or perhaps they are perversely so. In performing publics, participation symbolically set boundaries on citizen roles and closed down innovation (non) choices. By default, if not by design, such issues were channeled into regulatory arenas, which thereby carried the burden of conflicts over societal futures. Thus state-sponsored participatory TA readily complements neoliberal representative democracy and its unaccountability, while reproducing its contradictions through contested boundaries.

In order to open up societal choices, participatory exercises should:

- Synchronise with key periods of government decision-making.
- Facilitate overlaps between 'lay' and 'expert' roles.
- Examine the assumptions and limits of 'risk' frameworks.
- Encourage scrutiny of 'technical' aspects as value-laden, socio-political issues.
- Explore the societal problems that supposedly need a technological solution, while also considering alternatives, especially as regards who may be empowered or disempowered.

Democratic accountability remains a task for a wider societal contest over normative policy commitments and pre-empted futures. The prospects will depend upon wider, autonomous forms of participation — neither sponsored nor welcomed by state bodies.

Acknowledgements

Helpful editorial comments on previous versions were received from the following colleagues: Gabi Abels, Bernhard Gill, Dominic Glover, Joanna Goven, Christine Hauskeller, Maria Paola Ferretti, Pierre-Benoit Joly, Mercy Kamara, Huei-Chih Niu, Dominique Pestre, Stefan Sperling, Andy Stirling, Zoe Sujon, Jesper Toft, John Walls, Sue Weldon, Bernhard Wieser and Richard Worthington.

Also helpful were comments on related talks at these events:

- Participatory Approaches to Science and Technology (PATH) conference, June 2006, Edinburgh.
- Critical Social Science for/on Contentious Technologies, workshop in November 2006, Egenis Centre, Exeter.
- Critical Issues in Science and Technology Studies, 6th Annual IAS-STS Conference, May 2007, Graz.

- Science and Democracy Network annual meeting, June 2007, Cambridge, UK.
- Reconstruction Agro-Biotechnologies for Development', 3–4 November 2007, Kyoto

A longer version has more case studies and more systematic reference to analytical perspectives (Levidow 2007).

References

Abels, G. (2007): Citizen involvement in public policy-making: does it improve democratic legitimacy and accountability? The case of pTA. *Interdisciplinary Information Sciences* 13(1): 103–16.

AEBC (2001): *Crops on Trial*, www.aebc.gov.uk

Boy, D., Donnet-Kamel, D., and Roqueplo, P. (1998): A Report on the Citizens Conference on Genetically Modified Foods (France, June 21–22, 1998), including the report prepared by the French Lay Panel. http://www.loka.org/pages/Frenchgenefood.htm

Bora, A. (2009): Technoscientific normativity and the 'iron cage' of law. *Science, Technology and Human Values* 34 (Online First, published on March 6, 2009 as doi: 10.1177/0162243908329566)

Bora, A. and Hausendorf, H. (2006): Participatory science governance revisited: normative expectations versus empirical evidence. *Science and Public Policy* 33 (2): 479–488.

Burgess, J. and Chilvers, J. (2006): Upping the *ante*: a conceptual framework for designing and evaluating participatory technology assessment. *Science and Public Policy* 33(10): 713–28.

Bütschi, D. and Nentwich, M. (2002): The role of participatory technology assessment in the policy-making process. In: S.Joss and S.Bellucci, eds, *Participatory Technology Assessment: European Perspectives*. London: Univ. of Westminster Press.

Charles, D. (2001): *Lords of the Harvest: Biotech, Big Money and the Future of Food*. Cambridge, MA: Perseus.

De Marchi, B. (2003): Public participation and risk governance. *Science & Public Policy* 30, 3: 171–76.

DTI. (2003): reports on GM Nation?. London: Dept of Trade & Industry, www.gmnation.org.uk/

EEC (1990): Council Directive 90/220 on the Deliberate Release to the Environment of Genetically Modified Organizms. *Official Journal of the European Communities*, L 117, 8 May: 15–27.

EC (2001): European Parliament and Council Directive 2001/18/EC of 12 March on the deliberate release into the environment of genetically modified organizms and repealing Council Directive 90/220/EEC. *O.J.* L 106: 1–38.

Einsiedel, E.F., Jelsøe, E. and Breck, T. (2001): Publics at the technology table: The consensus conference in Denmark, Canada, and Australia. *Public Understanding of Science* (10): 83–98.

Elert, C. et al. (1991): *Biotechnology at Work in Denmark*. Copenhagen: Danish Board of Technology (Teknologinævnet).

Ferretti, M.P. (2007): What do we expect from public participation? The case of authorising GMO products in the European Union. *Science as Culture* 16(4): 377–96.

Gill, B. (1993): Technology assessment in Germany's biotechnology debate. *Science as Culture*, 4, 1: 69–84.

Gill, B. (1996): Germany: splicing genes, splitting society. *Science & Public Policy* 23 (3): 175–79.
GM Science Review (2003): *First Report: An open review of the science relevant to GM crops and food based on the interests and concerns of the public*. London: GM Science Review Panel. www.gmsciencedebate.org.uk/report/pdf/gmsci-report1-pt1.pdf
Gottweis, H. (1998): *Governing Molecules: The Discursive Politics of Genetic Engineering in Europe and the United States*. Cambridge, MA: MIT Press.
Goven, J. (2006): 'Dialogue, governance and biotechnology: acknowledging the context of the conversation. *Integrated Assessment Journal* 6, 2: 99–116.
Hagendijk, R. and Irwin, A. (2006): Public deliberation and governance: engaging with science and technology in contemporary Europe. *Minerva* 44(2): 167–84.
Hajer, M. (2005): Setting the stage: a dramaturgy of policy deliberation. *Administration & Society* 36(6): 624–47.
Hamlett, P. (2003): Technology theory and deliberative theory. *Science, Technology and Human Values* 28(1): 122–40.
Hansen, L. et al. (1992): Consensus Conferences. Copenhagen: Danish Board of Technology.
Hansen, J. (2006): Operationalising the public in participatory technology assessment. *Science and Public Policy* 33(8): 571–584.
Heller, C. (2002): From scientific risk to *paysan savoir-faire*: peasant expertise in the French and global debate over GM crops. *Science as Culture*, 11, 1: 5–37.
HM Treasury/DTI/DfES (2004): *Science and Innovation Investment Framework 2004–2014*. London: HM Treasury.
Horlick-Jones, T. et al. (2004): *A Deliberative Future? An Independent Evaluation of the GM Nation? Public Debate about the Possible Commercialization of Transgenic Crops in Britain, 2003*. Understanding Risk Working Paper 04-02, Norwich: University of East Anglia.
Horlick-Jones, T., Walls, J., Rowe, G., Pidgeon, N., Poortinga W. and O'Riordan, T. (2006): On evaluating the GM Nation? Public debate about the commercialization of transgenic crops in Britain. *New Genetics and Society* 25(3): 265–88.
Joly, P.-B., Marris, C. and Hermitte, M.A. (2003): A la recherche d'une 'démocratie technique'. Enseignements de la conférence citoyenne sur les OGM en France. *Natures, Sciences et Sociétés* 11(1): 3–15.
Joss, S. (1998): 'The Danish consensus conferences as model of participatory technology assessment. *Science & Public Policy* 25 (1): 2–22.
Joss, S. (2005a): Lost in translation? Challenges for participatory governance of science and technology. In: H. Torgersen and A. Bogner, eds, *Wozu Experten/Why Experts?*, pp. 197–219. Wiesbaden: Verlag für Sozialwissenschaften.
Joss, S. (2005b): Between policy and politics. In: S.Maasen and P.Weingart (editors), *Democratization of Expertise? Exploring Novel Forms of Scientific Advice in Political Decision-Making*, pp.171–88, Dordrecht: Springer, Sociology of the Sciences Yearbook.
Kerr, A., Cunningham-Burley, S. and Amos, A. (1998): The new genetics and health: mobilizing lay expertise. *Public Understanding of Science* 7: 41–60.
Klüver, L. (1995): Consensus conferences at the Danish Board of Technology. In: S. Joss and J. Durant (editors), *Public Participation in Science: the Role of Consensus Conferences in Europe*, pp.41–49. London: Science Museum.
Klüver, L. (2006): New trends in public participation. PATH conference, http://www.macaulay.ac.uk/pathconference
Levidow, L. (1998): Democratizing technology – or technologizing democracy? Regulating agricultural biotechnology in Europe. *Technology in Society* 20, 2: 211–26.
Levidow, L. (2000): Pollution metaphors in the UK biotechnology controversy. *Science as Culture* 9(3): 325–51.

Levidow, L. (2003): Policing the Scientific Debate on GM Crops: the Royal Society meeting of 11th Feb 2003. http://www.gmsciencedebate.org.uk/topics/forum/0070.htm

Levidow, L. (2007): European public participation as risk governance: enhancing democratic accountability for agbiotech policy?. *East Asian Science, Technology and Society (EASTS): an International Journal* 1(1): 19–50 http://www.springerlink.com/content/7wv9764lw42r7867/fulltext.pdf

Levidow, L., Carr, S., von Schomberg, R. and Wield, D. (1996): Regulating agricultural biotechnology in Europe: harmonization difficulties, opportunities, dilemmas. *Science & Public Policy* 23(3): 135–57.

Levidow, L., Carr, S. and Wield, D. (2000): Genetically modified crops in the European Union: regulatory conflicts as precautionary opportunities. *Journal of Risk Research* 3(3): 189–208.

Lezaun, J. and Soneryd, L. (2006): *Government by Elicitation: Engaging Stakeholders or Listening to the Idiots?*. London: LSE CARR Discussion Paper no.34, www.lse.ac.uk/Depts/carr

Marris, C. and Joly, P-B. (1999): Between consensus and citizens: public participation in technology assessment in France. *Science Studies*, 12, 2: 3–32.

Marris, C. (2001): Swings and roundabouts: French public policy on agricultural GMOs since 1996. *Politeia* 60: 22–37.

OPECST (1998a): Letter from Steering Committee to participants in the preparatory weekends, 16 April.

OPECST (1998b): Conférence de Citoyens Sur l'Utilization des Organizmes Génétiquement Modifiés en Agriculture et dans l'Alimentation. Paris: L'Office Parlementaire d'Évaluation des Choix Scientifiques et Technologiques (OPECST), Assemblée Nationale. www.senat.fr/opecst/

Pestre, D. (2008): Participation, governance and politics today. *Science as Culture*, forthcoming.

Popper, K.R. (1962): *The Open Society and Its Enemies*. vol. 1. London: Routledge.

Reynolds, L. and Szerszynski, B. (2006): Representing GM Nation. PATH conference, proceedings at http://www.macaulay.ac.uk/pathconference

Roqueplo, P. (1996): *Entre savoir et decision, l'expertise scientifique*. Paris: INRA.

Roy, A. and Joly, P-B. (2000) France: broadening precautionary expertise?. *Journal of Risk Research* 3(3): 247–54.

Rowe, G. and Frewer, L. (2004): Evaluating public-participation exercises: a research agenda. *Science, Technology and Human Values* 29(4): 512–57.

Rowe, G., Marsh, R. and Frewer, L. (2004): Evaluation of a deliberative conference. *Science, Technology and Human Values* 29(1): 88–121.

Stirling, A. (2005): Opening up or closing down? Analysis, participation and power in the social appraisal of technology. In: M.Leach, I.Scoones and B.Wynne (editors), *Science and Citizens:Globalization and the Challenge of Engagement*, pp. 218–31. Zed, London.

Stirling, A. (2006): From science and society to science in society: Towards a framework for 'co-operative research. Report of a European Commission workshop, 24–25 November 2005, www.cipast.org, http://eurosfaire.prd.fr/7pc/bibliotheque/consulter.php?id=308

Teknologinævnet (1987): *Genteknologi i industri og landbrug*. Teknologinævnets Rapporter 1987/2 og 1987/4.

Teknologinævnet (1999): Final document of the consensus conference on genetically-modified foods. Copenhagen: Danish Board of Technology, www.tekno.dk

Toft, J. (1996): Denmark: seeking a broad-based consensus on gene technology. *Science & Public Policy* 23, 3: 171–74.

Toft, J. (2000): Denmark, potential polarization or consensus?. *Journal of Risk Research* 3, 3: 227–36.

van den Daele, W. (1994): *Technology Assessment as a Political Experiment*. Berlin: Wissenschaftszentrum.

van den Daele, W. (1995): Technology assessment as a political experiment. In: R. von Schomberg (editor), *Contested Technology: Ethics, Risk and Public Debate*, pp.63–89. Tilburg: International Centre for Human and Public Affairs

Wakeford, T. (editor) (1998): *Citizen Foresight: A Tool to Enhance Democratic Policy-Making, Part 1: The Future of Food and Agriculture*. London Centre for Governance Innovation and Science and the Genetics Forum, http://www.ncl.ac.uk/peals/assets/publications/Citizenforesight.pdf

Walls, J., Horlick-Jones, T., Niewöhner, J. and O'Riordan, T. (2005): The meta-governance of risk and new technologies: GM crops and mobile telephones. *Jnl of Risk Research* 8: 635–61.

Wilsdon, J. and Willis, R. (2004): *See-through Science: Why public engagement needs to move upstream*. London: Demos, www.demos.co.uk

Wilsdon, J., Wynne, B. and Stilgoe, J. (2005): *The Public Value of Science: or how to ensure that science really matters*. London: Demos, www.demos.co.uk

PART II

PARTICIPATION IN THE GOVERNANCE OF AGRO-BIOTECHNOLOGY

CHAPTER FOUR

MAKING SENSE OF PARTICIPATION: HERRSCHAFT AND PARTICIPATORY PROCEDURES IN ADMINISTRATIVE DECISION-MAKING

Peter Münte

A. Introduction

This chapter has two objectives. The first one is to summarize the results of a case study on participation in administrative decision-making on the release of genetically modified organisms. The study evolved from a research project on social positioning within communication between government officials and citizens in different legally driven participation procedures.[1] Similar to previous research, this study unveils a process of communication that—subject to rather high expectations of policy-makers on participatory instruments in general, and in the specific field of regulating genetic engineering in particular—can only be identified as failure.[2]

The second aim of this chapter is to provide a specific analytical perspective on our case. Focus is on those tasks referring to the specific problems from the release of genetically modified plants with respect to the more fundamental issue of maintaining and forming public order, and on two completely different ways how public authorities deal with these tasks.

The fulfilment of these tasks regarding decisions on new and disputed technologies (on the level of administrative decision-making), requires to deal with various issues, such as establishing knowledge

[1] For the theoretical and methodological framework see: Bora/Hausendorf (2006) and Hausendorf/Bora (2006).

For an overview on the various regulatory regimes taken into account in the mentioned research project: Bora (2006). See also: Jülich (1998).

[2] For this previous research, see: Bora (1999). These results are restricted to a special field of administrative decision-making, which is linked to a rather specific technological conflict. There are of course other administrative procedures with such a participatory component. To them, our results do not necessarily apply. For some examples, see: Schmitt Glaeser (1984).

fundamental for decision-making, and dealing with conflicts. This chapter will prove that how these tasks are fulfilled depends on a general attitude on what "good" public order consists of, or, in a more analytical term: an interpretational pattern.[3] Of course, answers to this question are at discussion. Which specific goods should be protected, and how, is not the only question at issue. Also disputed is the form and structure of individual contributions made by different actors in the overall process of creating public order, as by politicians, administrators, citizens, organisations of civil society, experts, etc. Thus, a general model of the relationships between those actors and their individual contributions to public order itself, is an essential aspect for interpretation of what "good" public order should consist of. In that respect, this chapter is about deviating concepts of how to create public order.

For our case we can distinguish two forms of contribution by public authorities: To carry out a legally driven procedure, and to deal with objections and conflicts in an "informal" manner. With respect to the first form, the authorities are responsible for a procedure that is meant by the lawgiver as a special contribution to public order. For the second, the authorities contribute to public order by assuming the responsibility to deal adequately with the public, and to respond to public clamour.

It will be argued that it is the second contribution form, and not the first one that provides appropriate response to citizens' objections. With respect to the developed argumentation in this chapter, it is important to note that this response does not at all refer to concepts of participation, or cooperation.

Such results call for explanation: Why is there something as participation in administrative decision-making in the particular field of deliberate release of genetically modified organisms, if—according to our results—the former is more or less condemned to failure?

At first glance, quite simple and common answers give the impression that the idea of participation was inadequately transferred. As proved hereinafter, this idea—as it seems to be devised on the abstract thinking level of policy-making—indeed cannot be realised *within* the administrative procedure. The conjecture argues that the participation-in-administrative-procedure-solution only works theoretically, i.e. on

[3] For the interpretational pattern approach, in German: "Deutungsmusteransatz", see: Oeverman (2001); Oevermann (2001a).

the level policy-making discourse. In this respect, a primary thesis of this chapter states that the discourse in which participation and cooperation are key concepts, is uncoupled from the concrete level of interaction and its specific problems.

The failure of this specific form of participation does not imply that participation in the regulative process of genetic engineering is meant to fail in general. There might be more flexible and more sophisticated participatory settings that could accompany the administrative procedure and prove effective, one way or another.[4]

Nevertheless, our case study demonstrates that there *are* other ways of dealing with the difficulties surrounding the release of genetically modified plants; ways that are not at all related to the ideas of participation or cooperation. Thus, in my opinion this study suggests to raise another question: from the standpoint of a sociologist, in the first place do not ask, how could participation be implemented, but why do people think that some forms of participation or cooperation should be part of the solution!

With reference to the above question it is assumed that the discourse, which provides the "participatory solution", is based on a specific interpretational pattern. This pattern channels the perception of social reality and its problems, and pre-structures the reflections on how to deal with them appropriately. Thus, the basic idea of this chapter is to demonstrate that certain ways of dealing with problems our case study proved to be existent, are completely out of policy-makers' sight, due to the fact that this interpretational pattern is deeply rooted in their conviction. Adherence to this pattern itself is a social phenomenon, which requires separate explanation.

The reconstruction of this interpretational pattern and its occurrence in political thinking went of course far beyond our research.[5] Nevertheless, this chapter should at least give a first clue of how diverse the two approaches are to fulfil the task of maintaining and forming public order. It will be argued that the first approach follows a rather traditional rôle of public authorities as part of *Herrschaft* and being particularly responsible to contribute to public order. Whereas, the second is to be interpreted as an expression of technocratic thinking, aiming at a rational organisation of society, which would supersedes such

[4] See again: Bora (1999).

[5] This question has proved to be central in an ongoing research project under the title, "Politikberatung als diskursive Politikgestaltung".

"traditional" social relationships as *Herrschaft*. In my opinion, this idea seems to be core of the interpretational pattern underlying the idea of participation.

I will first present key results from our case study, with focus on the communication between public authority and citizens within the permitting procedure. Then a broader perspective on this case will be developed as a complex and organised process of dealing with the problems that emerge with respect to the application of new and argumentative technologies.

B. The Case Study

1. *Research Design*

Subject of our research were field trials with genetically modified plants, which took place in Germany in the early 2000s.[6]

The case was documented by means of regular contacts to central actors in the field via e-mail and telephone; several visits to the local site; ethnographic field notes; interviews with the applicant, officers from public authorities, and local people; a survey of local and national newspapers; insight into official files; collection of documents as flyers; an audio-recording of a local public hearing. We inquired as to what did the people expect to happen when the intended release would be made public; how the release became a public issue; how the conflict evolved and who was involved in this conflict.

But the focus of our research was on the procedure itself. At the centre of our study of the procedure was the sequential analysis of the following documents, and then of the sequence of these documents as those very files constitute the communication between the approving authority and the public on the formal stage of administrative procedure. The documents are: the announcements of the

[6] For a more extensive account of this case study see: Münte/Bora (2004). See also: Bora et al. (2004).

The research summarized there was carried out from 2001 to 2004 in two closely related research projects at the Institut für Wissenschafts- und Technikforschung at the Universität Bielefeld. A great part of the analyses were carried out in the meetings of a work group by: Alfons Bora, Ingrid Furchner, Heiko Hausendorf, Marc Mölders, Peter Münte, Irena Rathert, and Tatjana Zimenkova. The basis of this interdisciplinary work group of sociologists and linguists, was the detailed, extensive and sequential analysis of "natural" data. These analyses, as they were worked out by Ingrid Furchner and Peter Münte, were the basis for the above-mentioned research reports.

authorising body, the objections of citizens, and the approving letter of the authorising body.

In this respect we asked the following basic questions: How was the permitting procedure opened up to the public? How was the possibility to contribute to the procedure interpreted by concerned people, and how was it used by them? How did the approving authority deal with these contributions? We also asked: Which type of communication between authority and citizens took place in this sequence of documents, and how were the positions of public authority and citizens as contributors to this communication process constituted?

2. *Opening up the Procedure for Public Participation*

The procedure was opened up by the authorising body, the *Robert Koch Institut* (RKI) by two public announcements of the application: one in the *Bundesanzeiger*, the official announcing paper of Germany, and one in the local press.[7] That the application is announced in the local press implies that it might be of special importance to local people. The text of the announcement establishes it as a formal act to be carried out in a legally prescribed procedure. Its language is technical and rather implicit. It contains a short description of the intended project. For to understand this description some scientific knowledge is required. The announcement also refers to additional documents concerning the field trial that are open to public inspection, which in fact turned out to be just the application itself. At the end of the text, the possibility to submit objections is mentioned. Raising objections is also framed as a formal act. Reference is made to a time limit for objecting and a formal decision on the objections then submitted. The text leaves no doubt that submitting an objection is a formal step in the decision-making procedure.

These announcements are the only official undertakings to inform the public, and to submit objections is the only officially communicated opportunity for citizens to converse with the approving authority. Submitting objections is referred to as a formal act in a procedure prescribed and regulated by law. Yet, no advice on the formal criteria that objections must meet in order to be taken seriously in the application process is provided in the text. Accordingly, the approving

[7] For a short account of the procedure and the involved authorities, see: Bora et al. (2004).

authority seems to accept that citizens might use this possibility in quite different ways. If they are familiar with such procedures, their objections might address questions relevant in the procedure. But it seems quite probable that many citizens, especially if they are not informed about such procedures, might simply communicate to the authorities their thoughts on the project.

Three weeks after the official announcement, the first newspaper article on the planned release was published. With this article, the release became a public theme. At the end of the article its author refers to the possibility of submitting objections. In this connection the people are called on to go into the matter, and the possibility to object is presented as an important opportunity to influence administrative decision-making. The readers are also told that the objections have to be "well-founded", and that the number of people that contribute matters. Thus, in this article, the opportunity to contribute to the procedure, which the approving authority formally provided, is presented as an important tool for the local people to bring in their interests and viewpoints.

3. *Citizens' Contributions*

How did citizens make use of the possibility to submit objections?[8] First of all, many different things are done with these "objections": People state to be prepared to negotiate—especially, if they have an official function in the municipality—; they ask for more information or discussion; they lament not having been informed early enough; they criticise the public authorities and the applicant; they claim to give advisory opinions and expert statements, or to interpose their veto; they ask questions; they request the responsible authorities to explain their general reasons for approving certain techniques of genetic engineering; they state to be against the release of genetically modified organisms.

Thus, what the people are doing often does not match the officially required format of "objection". Some "objectors" are using the opportunity to submit objections simply as a tool to communicate with the responsible authority. Some are pretending to perform institutional

[8] There had been about 1250 objections submitted. But this relatively high number of objections is due to the fact that some objections contained signature lists. Counted as documents, 16 different objections were submitted.

acts that cannot be performed in the given context, e.g. interposing a veto. There are also "objectors" that are anxious to give their written communication a somehow official or scientific appearance, something that is not required for raising an objection.

As a result of our analysis—and with some idealisation—we distinguished two major groups of objections. On one side we had objectors that presented themselves as members of a local community that is affected by the intended field trial. They tend to dramatise apparent problems concerning safety measures and focus on possible harmful consequences of these trials for the region. They did not discuss the trials as intended by the applicant: From the applicant's point of view, the field trial is simply a scientific experiment, which is good for nothing but signifying scientific progress and bears some vague prospect for future applications. To the local people the central question was, whether the region needs such trials. Thus established, as a criterion for local support the field trials should bear some benefit for the region.

It is quite interesting to note that the negative consequences feared by these objectors in many cases are not directly linked to the assumed risks of genetic engineering, but to the already bad reputation of the region that should not be tainted further by being associated with such field trials.

An other important theme of these objectors, is that they have not been informed about the intended field trials. It seems odd to find such a complaint in an objection that is reacting to an official announcement, or respectively, to the reporting in the local press. But this complaint refers to an implicit concept of an adequate form of information supply: the authorities and the applicant should have entered into direct communication with the local people or their political representatives, and there should have been room for a local decision-making process based on sufficient information.

Respect for the people in the region is a fundamental issue for these objectors. It is related to how they are informed, if their viewpoints are recognized, and how their specific problems are taken into account. Thus, one important reason for rejecting the intended field trials simply was: the feeling that the local concerns were not adequately considered in administrative decision-making, or by the applicant, a university institute which is in no way related to the region.

Objectors of this kind are different in character as on occasion of the planned release they are spontaneously reacting as members of a local community that is affected by the field trials. In their response, they reveal their identity as members of a local community and they claim the existence of this community by facing a decision making process that is, in their view, ignoring the concerns of this community.

A second group of objectors can be identified, whose objections seem to be primarily motivated by opposition to genetic engineering as such. For them, the case subject to decision is just an instance of deliberate release of genetically modified organisms in general. Their objections seem primarily motivated by their alignment with a position in the overall debate on genetic engineering, or, more specifically on the release of genetically modified organisms. For them, the planned release is also a welcome opportunity to display their identity as "critical citizens", picking holes into the arguments of the applicant, the above-mentioned university institute representing "official science".

They are somehow familiar with administrative procedures and its specific requirements. They address aspects of the planned field trials relevant in the permitting procedure. Some of them are pretending to give advisory opinions, or to display expertise on the subject of decision-making, though often not very convincingly. They focus on the possible harms of the field trials, and refer to biological processes that are suspected to bear harmful consequences. The planned project is described in rather alarming terms, suggesting that something dangerous is going on.

Risk arguments play an important role. Some of these objectors reject the planned project because 100% security is not guaranteed, thereby presupposing that this level of security is requested for approval. One of them quotes a statement made by the applicant to the effect of no risks for humans or the environment were to be expected, and then uses it to argue that the applicant itself admits that such risks cannot be entirely excluded. The cited statement was of course simply meant to indicate that the requirements for permission are *fulfilled*. Nevertheless, by using the expression "is not to be expected" instead of the stronger one "can be excluded", the applicants' statement as the objectors realises is implicitly conceding that it is just highly probable, not certain. This pragmatic implication is used by the objector to turn the applicant's "pro" statement into an argument "contra" permission. Another argument is that the knowledge available about the consequences of such a release is insufficient for adequate risk assessment.

The point is, that all these arguments do not really contribute to the knowledge fundamental to the decision, which is to be made. There is not so much of a dispute on the scientific justification of specific knowledge claims. What is disputed is the *epistemic status*, that is required for accepting scientifically justified knowledge claims as a basis for decision-making with respect to such a controversial technology as genetic engineering or the release of genetically modified organisms.

Such an "epistemologisation" of the conflict can be interpreted as strategic: Since the opponents cannot compete with the applicant and the authorities with respect to their obviously superior scientific expertise, they can question whether the knowledge the applicant and the authorities claim to possess should be accepted as a basis for decision-making, or whether possible risks can be definitely excluded. But these epistemic arguments also indicate, that what is accepted as sound knowledge and as a basis for decision-making, in the case of a controversial technology, or if interests are affected, is a function of ones position in the conflict.

The arguments proposed by this type of objectors nevertheless, are somehow related to what is defined as relevant in the procedure: it's one of the main purposes of the procedure to assess the risks of the intended project. But at the same time, these arguments completely miss the point. It is up to the public authority to decide whether there is a sufficient knowledge base, and "absolute safety" is not and cannot be requested by law as a prerequisite for permission.

Yet even if irrelevant within the administrative procedure, these arguments might have side effects. Such arguments are part of a discourse about genetic engineering as a technology that—according to the view of the opponents—is connected with special risks that require special, in the end unattainable security measures. If such a discourse successfully establishes the view on genetic engineering as a "high-risk technology", the public authorities might fail to establish a generally accepted knowledge base for its decision-making.

4. *The Authority's Response*

How does the responsible public authority deal with the submitted objections in the final letter of notification? First of all, the official letter does not address the objectors or the public; it is addressed to the applicant, and replies to the initial application of the applicant submitted to the responsible authority in order to obtain permission for the intended field trial. Instead, for the public, there was simply an announcement in the *Bundesanzeiger* and the local press, stating that the responsible authority has approved the project.

The main section of the official letter comprises a detailed explanatory statement in which the project is discussed under legal as well as scientific aspects. This extensive discussion indicates that the decision must meet legally defined requirements that can be enforced by legal action.

From a careful textual interpretation of the official letter, we can learn a lot about the type of administrative action articulated in the document. First of all, administrative decision-making of this type is part of state action, or, to put it in the more traditional terms of classic sociological thinking: a specific part of *Herrschaft*. As such, it leads to decisions superior to those of the governed people, and can be imposed on them by the power of the state. Endowed with governmental power, the administration is authorized to perform an official approbation required by law. In the modern democratic state, the people themselves empower the state to do so. The decisions made by public authorities can only be appealed against with reference to those laws the executive authorities are bound to observe, or to execute.

Part of this kind of administrative action is also to explicate the legal basis of its decision-making. The authority refers to the intentions of the legislator as they are interpreted by actual jurisprudence and jurisdiction. Such an explication is a genuine jurisprudential operation that can only be performed by a trained jurist. The relevant legal regulations do not determine administrative action; to refer to an ongoing process of interpreting the law is part of the administrative decision-making process itself.

Also part of this type of administrative action is to assess whether legally recognized goods might be affected by the intended project. Such an assessment, according to the *Gentechnikgesetz*, has to refer to the actual state of science and technology. Therefore, the type of administrative action underlying the official letter is also based on profound scientific knowledge. One purpose of the explanatory part of the official letter is to link the scientific and legal aspects of the intended project, in order to assess its risks with respect to legally protected goods.

It is interesting that the approving authority that has to decide according to the actual state of science and technology, in the official letter takes the scientific description of the project supplied by the applicant for granted. This practise implies that the account of the applicant, the university institute mentioned, conforms to the actual state of science and technology. In this respect the communication between applicant and public authorities is framed by a universal scientific discourse, in which both sides, applicant and authorities likewise are supposed to be competent. Nevertheless, by adopting the account of the applicant, in the course of administrative decision-making, the status of the scientific statements of the applicant is changing: these statements are now not only accepted as scientific knowledge, but also as a sound basis of the decision-making of public authorities.[9]

The duties and responsibilities of the approving authority comprises also to weight up between benefits of the planned project, and its harmful effects—if the authority is coming to the conclusion that there are such effects. In the case we studied, the authority came to the conclusion that such effects can be excluded. The authority also has the power to impose licensing requirements, which in our case has been done.

Administrative action in the case studied here is a rather complex activity: It is based on jurisdictional as well as scientific knowledge related to genetic engineering. Nevertheless, from a sociological point of view, it is not a jurisdictional or scientific action, but a governmental activity, or *Herrschaftshandeln*. The public authority, based on the competent application of specific knowledge, has to perform sovereign acts: permitting a project for which official approbation is required; making a short-term determination of the state of science and technology with respect to this project; weighing harmful effects against benefits, if necessary; and imposing licensing requirements in conjunction with the permission.

With respect to the authority's discussion of the objections, it is interesting that the official statement on the requirements for approval is strictly separated from the discussion of the objections. This composition suggests that the public authorities are in the possession of all relevant information for decision-making. Accordingly, administrative decision-making is presented to the reader as a self-contained process.

---

[9] It is important to note, that these two things are quite different. The aim of modern science is to produce good and universally acceptable hypotheses on a rather restrictive, but shared data basis. Such a hypothesis, even if universally accepted in the scientific community at a particular time, might be quite different from what should be called "reliable knowledge" with respect to practical purposes. The question, for example, of how far pollen can be spread in single cases, might be of minor importance with respect to scientific questions. However, it is of great importance with respect to the question of to whom the release of genetically modified plants might be harmful.

This is astonishing, because the official letter even enjoins some additional safety restrictions that can be clearly related to concerns posed in the objections. The applicant is, for example, instructed to cover the fields with a net in order to prevent the leaves of the transgenic plants to be blown over. The problem that the leaves might be blown over before their collection and disposal was brought up in the objections. Nevertheless, the text of the official letter fails to say whether or not the objections had any influence on the authority's decision-making.

In fact, the authority is not just omitting this opportunity to acknowledge the objections as being relevant to its decision-making. At the very beginning of the acknowledgement of the objections they are altogether rejected. This is striking, because as we have already seen, these "objections" are a rather heterogeneous collection of criticism, suggestions, statements, and questions. As such a collection of different things they cannot be simply rejected. What is crucial here seems to be the specific interpretation of objection: as a legally relevant request not to approve the application. According to this interpretation, all objections have to be rejected, if the application is approved.

A completely different way to deal with the objections would be to acknowledge them as welcome contributions that might help the authorities to make better decisions. Such a function of the objections is explicitly mentioned in a later passage of the official letter. There, being a stimulus for the administration is referred to as one of the official functions of objections. However, this function is just mentioned; it is not formative for the overall style of the final letter and its way of dealing with the objections in general.

Let us take a closer look on how the authority discussed the objections. First of all, the authority did not discuss the objections one by one as statements that have been made by individual objectors, or by people who have signed such an objection. It discusses a list of arguments, presupposing that this list contains all the arguments proposed.

Such a decomposition of the objections into single arguments has the effect that everything that is not expressed explicitly in form of an argument is omitted—and that is quite a lot. If, as in one case, the authors of an objection simply state that *as farmers* they too are against the planned field trial, the authority does not consider this objection at all, since it contains no argument that could be transferred to the list of arguments to be discussed. Thus, the official letter does not contain a comprehensive discussion of the objections submitted; it addresses specific aspects of these objections: only the explicit arguments against the project.

But even with respect to the enumerated arguments, there can be serious differences between those discussed by the authority and those originally proposed by the objectors. Dissolving these arguments from their original context and transferring them into the list of arguments for discussion can change their meaning. The authority, for example, discusses the argument that the public was not involved in decision-making and that it is impossible for citizens and their representatives to get scientifically sound answers or to scrutinise the risks before the close of period for objections.

To this, the authority replies that all legal requirements with respect to public participation are fulfilled and that it is up to the people to address their questions to the applicant or the approving authority. Yet if we look at the argument in its original context, it is quite clear that the objector is referring to a local public that should have the opportunity for opinion building. While the authority refers to *individuals* longing for *more detailed information*, the objector bears in mind the *local community as a whole* that should have the opportunity to develop a *well-founded standpoint*.

The complaints about the reliability of the applicant are another example. In answering such a complaint, the authority simply refers to the result of its own formal assessment as to the reliability of the applicant (a requirement of the procedure as a whole). These results had been outlined at the very beginning of the explanatory part of the final letter.

But the objectors' complaint was about something else: It is about the applicant's dealing with the matter, i.e. without respect for the sensitivities of the local people. The objectors question the applicant's reliability in a specific sense: For them, the essential question is not the scientific or technical expertise of the applicant. What matters is a trustful relationship between applicant and local people.

Of further interest is how the authority discusses the objection's arguments. One way of dealing with them is simply to state their irrelevance in regard to the legal basis of the permitting procedure, because they are not referring to the legally recognised goods as defined in the *Gentechnikgesetz*. Answering, for example, the argument that the planned project might contribute to the already bad image of the region, the authority states that the image of the region is not a legally protected good, according to the *Gentechnikgesetz*.

This argument shows that the seemingly comprehensive abstract goods defined in the law as "life and health of humans, animals, plants", "environment", and "material goods", do not include those goods that matter with respect to the identity of the local people as members of a local community. The goods protected by the law are defined in both abstract and general terms as property, health, or environmental issues. However, the goods of worth in human life cannot be reduced to such universal goods as life and health of individuals, property, and the protection of an environment worth living in. There are also goods related to the identity of particular individuals or communities within a broader legally constituted community. Nevertheless, only goods legally recognised matter in the administrative procedure.

There are also arguments that are treated as relevant with respect to the legal basis of the permitting procedure, for example, all those that claim that the intended release might have harmful effects on the environment, especially by transferring modified genes to other organisms. Here, the authority's answers refer to its own risk assessment, concluding that such effects are not to be expected. With respect to the risk argument that such effects cannot be excluded with absolute certainty, the authority declares that such certainty is not required by law as a prerequisite for approval. In this respect the arguments are once again rejected as irrelevant.

But this way of dealing with the objections—rejecting them as irrelevant with respect to the legally recognised goods, or as unjustified with respect to the authorities own competent judgement—is not kept up consequently. In the conclusive letter we also find hints at a dialogue with objectors. In some passages, the authority addresses concerns of objectors, even if they are outside the scope of problems that matter for the permitting procedure.

An outstanding example is the way the authority addresses the question of a non-local organisation whose objection concerns the problems connected with the application of antibiotic resistance genes in transgenic organisms. The authors of this objection attempt to start a dialogue with the approving authority on its general licensing policy. The authority replies by explaining its general standpoint on the application of antibiotic resistance genes.

This stands out for two reasons: First, this explanation is not necessary for justifying the authorisation. It is just an answer to a question the authors of the objection are interested in. Secondly, since the official letter is addressed to the applicant, this "dialogue" between authority and objectors is somehow misplaced.

We also find passages in which the authority even sympathizes with the concerns of objectors, or is trying to clear up misunderstandings. Even the tone in the authority's responses to specific arguments in the list takes on that of the authors of the respective objections.

All in all, four different types of effects on the final letter caused by the objections can be observed. First, there are objections that are simply rejected as irrelevant with respect to the legally recognised goods, or the legal requirements that matter in the procedure. In the final letter's response to the objections, the approving authority makes explicit the specific criteria which objections must meet in order to be considered in the decision-making process. (In fact, the authority itself has given way to objections that later had to be rejected as irrelevant, by not communicating these criteria more explicitly when the procedure was opened up for contributions from the public).

Second, there are arguments that do address relevant themes according to the legal basis of the procedure, but still fail to contribute to the decision-making process in a productive way with respect to the specific aims of the procedure. Objectors claim there might be harmful effects on the environment, but in doing so they are not enriching the factual basis of decision-making or introducing new arguments. They simply refer to renowned phenomena that are supposed by the objectors to imply unacceptable risks, and by the authority to be unproblematic.

Third, there are more practical arguments dealing with simple safety measures, such as provisions to prevent leaves to be blown away, or the elimination of the roots of the transgenic plants after the field trials are finished. Here, the objections actually seemed to have some effect on the decision-making, because additional—and quite expensive—safety measures have been imposed on the applicant which are clearly related to the concerns posed by local people in their objections. Thus, at least in this case, it cannot be stated that the objections had no effect on the decision-making at all. However, it is not explicitly expressed in the conclusive letter that the objections had any influence on the decision-making process. (Moreover, in our interview with an administrative officer of the approving authority, we were told that the public contributions in relation to the release of genetically modified organisms do not, in practise, affect the authority's decision).

Fourth, in some passages the authority is engaged in a kind of "hidden dialogue" with the objectors, in answering questions and clearing up misunderstandings.

Now, our case study was not just covering what was going on within the procedure. Yet with respect to the many local activities reacting to the planned field trails only one episode should be mentioned, because it is of great concern for the following argument.

At a certain point in the emerging local conflict, and completely independent from the participation procedure (which was in the focus of our research), an officer from a *Landesbehörde* took responsibility to address the local protest. The respective authority represented the federal state in which the field trial should take place. (Its rôle in the procedure is to evaluate the case, and control the release).

Hearing about the local protest, a representative of the federal state travelled several times to the local site, trying to mediate in the conflict between the applicant and the municipality on whose land the release should take place. He also forced the mayor to call a meeting of the inhabitants. On the occasion of this meeting, he informed the public about the project and answered questions. Acting from behind the curtains, he pushed the two conflicting parties, applicant and municipality, to find a solution. As far as we can judge, this informal conflict management—at least on level of local politics— was successful. A compromise between the community and the applicant was found. This conflict management of course touched only one aspect of the complex conflict. Nevertheless, by calling a local meeting a forum was created, wherein a representative of a public authority was dealing with the different types of objections to the project.

C. An Overall View on the Case

1. *The Model of Analysis*

The focus of the case-study just sketched was on the communication within the procedure, and the reconstruction of an emerging dynamism of interaction. For a "full understanding" of this case we have to expand our focus, because the complex reality of interaction sketched above depends on achievements made elsewhere.

This is of course a basic problem we face when asking for the "social possibility" of a social event. Every course of interaction we study constitutes a social reality of its own. But it is based on achievements made apart: individual experience, community building, developing ideas, forming institutions, producing artefacts, shaping the environment in which people live and act, etc. And it leads to achievements accessing further action in many different ways. The overall complexity of this process is of course beyond any research.

In the present case the problem is more specific. We should be particularly interested in those achievements entering the course of action we studied, that are constitutive for the formal frame of this process of communication as a formal procedure with defined steps, that have to be run through, as well as formal slots for specific contributions which have a defined status in the overall procedure.

To make this frame a social reality, is a task of interaction itself. This frame must be set in the course of interaction under reference to former achievements constitutionally important for such a reality as a formal procedure. In this respect, this frame differs from the formal patterns we find in "organisations", which define concrete operating sequences and schedules of responsibilities, and are to be observed by the members of an organisation. In our case, the public authority has to depict its performance as subject to a legal framework. This, of course, is the major reason why the executive public authority is dealing with the citizens' contributions in a rather unproductive way: often merely by stating that from a legal standpoint the contributions miss the point.

It was quite clear from the launch of our project that participation, as part of the legal regulation of genetic engineering, was to be interpreted as an attempt to deal with the two-pronged problem of on one hand meeting the general request for technological progress, and on the other, dealing the fierce conflicts about genetic engineering. One of the aims of the project was to compare the rather ambitious expectation of policy-makers on participation as an answer to its reality in practise.[10]

However, according to the specific methodological perspective on our case, which should be employed here, we have to ask more basic questions: Which tasks are to be fulfilled in administrative decision-making on the release of genetically modified organisms? How are these tasks interpreted? Which interpretation is leading to the participatory solution? Which alternatives to this solution might be available? – Of primary interest are, of course, those tasks that emerge in the overall process of constituting social reality from a basic sociological point of view. The tasks in question can be specified as those referring to the problems that emerge from deliberate release with respect to the fundamental problem of creating, maintaining and forming public order.

[10] See: Bora/Hausendorf (2006a).

If we look on our case from such a methodological viewpoint, it turns out to be a complex sequence, much more comprehensive than the sequence we have analysed above. In order to comprise this sequence as a subject of research, we would first of all have to look at the discussions followed by the legal texts regulating the release of genetically modified organisms.[11] Here we would have to reconstruct the formation of a general political understanding of the problems that policy-makers face, as well as the prevailing interpretational resources that help them to make up such an understanding and to form ideas of how these problems might be solved in a socially appropriate and practically effective manner. We would have to look at the emergence of the idea of participation-in-the-administrative-procedure in an environment of a general interpretation of how society should be, and a widely accepted knowledge of how things work. We would have to analyse it as part of an emerging collective understanding of a specific aspect of the social world, which at some point leads to decisions, that make participation a part of the solution of its problems.

At one of these points, the general idea of participation is somehow cast into a legal text. This, of course, is also a complex process. Most notably, the idea of participation we can find in policy-makers' discourse is not transferred verbatim into law. Law-making is a complex political process characterised by compromise between competing interests and viewpoints, and accompanied by jurisdictional considerations.[12]

Then, the participative procedure as prescribed by law on a very abstract level, has to be fleshed out by an appointed administrative body into a practical procedure, and put into action under specific conditions in concrete cases. In putting the procedure into action, a communicative interaction emerges, which, according to the "intentions" of the lawmaker, should somehow contribute to public order.

---

[11] This would be a long story, with respect to the discussions on the regulation of genetic engineering we would have to start with the conference of Asilomar in 1975, where 140 leading scientist from 14 countries voted for a moratorium on specific experiments in the field of genetic engineering. The discussions on participation reach back to the late 60s, early 70s.

[12] For these kinds of considerations, see: "Bericht des Ausschusses für Forschung, Technologie und Technikfolgenabschätzung (20. Ausschuß) ", in: Deutscher Bundestag, 12. Wahlperiode, Drucksache 12/7095, p. 32 ff. In the 1990s, due to attempts make administrative decision-making more effective, we also find tendencies toward the restriction of participation, leading to such laws as the Verkehrswegeplanungsbeschleunigungsgesetz, Investitionserleichterungs- und Wohnbaulandgesetz und Planungsvereinfachungsgesetz.

Thus looking at the "whole case", we face a serious methodological problem, especially serious for studies based on the sequential analysis of records of defined sequences of social process.

The case-study summarised in the first part of this chapter is based on the analysis of the written documents of the participative component in the permitting procedure. But if we want to analyse the "whole sequence", it is difficult to specify where we would have to search for documents of this sequence—if this sequence is documented satisfactorily at all. In that respect, the methodological approach described above is not a mere analysis of a continuous and documented sequence of actions, but of a *Bildungsprozeß* that proves its existence by actions dispersed in time and space.[13]

Not surprisingly, the reconstruction of such a complex process was far beyond the scope of research carried out in our project, and is far beyond of what could be covered herein. Accordingly, the following aims to give a more solid idea of how participation is meant by policy-makers to contribute to the process of constituting public order. This does not imply that there could not be competing tendencies within the scope of policy-making, and the goal here could not be to give a historically accurate picture of how the idea of participation appeared (with respect to administrative decision-making) and found its way into the regulation of genetic engineering. What follows shall therefore give a rough idea of an answer to the above question by illuminating a general interpretational pattern, which is assumed to underlie the discourse on participation in policy-making in one version or another since the late 1960s.

In this regard, we will focus on a specific aspect of the process of creating, maintaining and forming public order: the relationship between public authorities and citizens. We will ask what kind of relationship—according to essential statements by policy-makers—should be established by participation, and how should it contribute to which aspect of public order. Then, the respective model of the relationship between authorities and citizens will be compared with those established in the course of the participation procedure itself.

---

[13] Here, an important difference can be seen between the type of sequential analysis practiced in Conversational Analysis or Ethnomethodology, and that which we can find in what is called in the German-speaking social sciences "Objektive Hermeneutik", for which methodological approach the reconstruction of Bildungsprozesse is of great importance. For this approach: Oevermann (2000); Wernet (2000).

For a comparison between different approaches in sequential analysis, see: Maiwald (2005).

By comparing these models, we can more precisely determine in which respects the administrative procedure fails to meet with the expectations of policy-makers. Even more importantly, we can show that the model we find within the policy-makers' discourse seems to be aiming at a far-reaching readjustment of the relationship between public authorities and citizens, whereas in practise the administrative procedure follows fairly traditional patterns.

2. *The Implicit Model of the Relationship between Public Authorities and Citizens on the Level of Actual Policy-making Discourses and its Inadequacy with Respect to the Citizens' Objections Reconstructed in our Case*

There are some important international declarations and agreements giving an impression of the importance of the idea of participation in policy-making.[14] Of great significance in this respect is principle 10 of the *Rio Declaration on Environment and Development at the 1992 United Nations Conference on Environment and Development* (UNCED).[15] An elaboration of this principle is *The United Nations Economic Commission for Europe (UNECE) Convention on Access to Information, Public Participation in Decision-Making and Access to Justice in Environmental Matters*, in short: Åhus-convention, which was adopted in 1998 and entered into force in 2001.[16] This agreement

[14] These declarations and agreements of course succeed the Gentechnikgesetz. The legal regulation of genetic engineering in Germany dates back to 1990, when the Gentechnikgesetz—following the 1986 OECD Recombinant Safety Considerations, and EU-directions 90/219/EWG, 90/220/EWG—came into force. Nevertheless, the documents affirm the idea of participation in the administrative procedure with respect to the regulation of genetic engineering, and we find here a in my opinion quite good and explicit example in regard to the type of reasoning on participation in policy making. Moreover, these agreements are of general importance because they influence the actual legislation, especially in Europe. I take it for granted that these documents represent a general trend, and that their spirit on a basic level, of which we take interest here, is not different from what is underlying the earlier efforts to strengthen the rôle of the public in administrative decision-making.

[15] This principle reads as follows: "Environmental issues are best handled with the participation of all concerned citizens, at the relevant level. At the national level, each individual shall have appropriate access to information concerning the environment that is held by public authorities, including information on hazardous materials and activities in their communities, and the opportunity to participate in decision-making processes. States shall facilitate and encourage public awareness and participation by making information widely available. Effective access to judicial and administrative proceedings, including redress and remedy, shall be provided." See: http://www.un.org/documents/ga/conf151/aconf15126-1annex1.htm.

[16] See: http://www.unece.org/env/pp/documents/cep43e.pdf.

obliges the European Union to approximate national law according to the contents of the convention.

These documents are part of international efforts for the protection of environment. Participation is looked upon as an important means to this general goal as a national objective. The Åhus-convention states "that every person has the right to live in an environment adequate to his or her health and well-being, and the duty, both individually and in association with others, to protect and improve the environment for the benefit of present and future generations," "that, to be able to assert this right and observe this duty, citizens must have access to information, be entitled to participate in decision-making and have access to justice in environmental matters, and acknowledging in this regard that citizens may need assistance in order to exercise their rights," and "that, in the field of the environment, improved access to information and public participation in decision-making enhance the quality and the implementation of decisions, contribute to public awareness of environmental issues, give the public the opportunity to express its concerns and enable public authorities to take due account of such concerns." Also mentioned is the general aim "to further the accountability of and transparency in decision-making and to strengthen public support for decisions on the environment".

The case of release of genetically modified organisms is explicitly mentioned in this connection: The parties to the convention recognise, we are told, "the concern of the public about the deliberate release of genetically modified organisms into the environment and the need for increased transparency and greater public participation in decision-making in this field." And with respect to the participation in permitting procedures, it is stated in article 6: "Procedures for public participation shall allow the public to submit, in writing or, as appropriate, at a public hearing or inquiry with the applicant, any comments, information, analyses or opinions that it considers relevant to the proposed activity."[17]

[17] See: The United Nations Economic Commission for Europe (UNECE) Convention on Access to Information, Public Participation in Decision-Making and Access to Justice in Environmental Matters, http://www.unece.org/env/pp/documents/ cep43e.pdf.

For further official documents that are interesting in this respect, see: Directive 2003/4/EC of the European Parliament and of the Council of 28 January 2003 on public access to environmental information and repealing Council Directive 90/313/EEC; Directive 2003/35/EC of the European Parliament and of the Council of 26 May 2003

Thus, we find here a quite explicit example of the type of political reasoning that can lead to the decision to open up the permitting procedure for the release of genetically modified organisms to public participation.

It is important that participation is considered a general solution that applies to all fields of regulation related to the protection of environment. In this respect, three principal intentions are connected with the idea of participation: By public participation, the quality of decision-making in relation to environmental issues should be improved; environmental awareness of citizens be raised; and support of decisions affecting the environment be strengthened.[18]

How exactly this model should work on the level of interaction is left unclear. But it requires some kind of cooperation between authorities and citizens (as individuals or in associations) that should lead to an improvement of the decision-making process with respect to general national objectives as environmental protection. Thus, the basic idea is that public participation is a means to realise general and legally recognised goods. According to this model, both the contributions of the administration and those of the citizens would have to be oriented to the protection to these goods. There might be differences or even conflicts about how these goods should be protected, but the general assumption seems to be that the dominant mode of interaction is cooperation for common, general objectives.

The rôle of the authority according to this model would be to organise a decision-making process that assesses the risks for the legally recognised goods on the basis of its own expertise and the contributions of concerned citizens. The rôle of the citizens would be to contribute to this decision-making process according to the legal specifications and

providing for public participation in respect of the drawing up of certain plans and programmes relating to the environment and amending with regard to public participation and access to justice Council Directives 85/337/EEC and 96/61/EC; see also: "Gesetz über die Öffentlichkeitsbeteiligung in Umweltangelegenheiten nach der EU-Richtlinie 2003/35/EG (Öffentlichkeitsbeteiligungsgesetz)", in: Bundesgesetzblatt Jahrgang 2006 Teil I Nr. 58.

[18] These intentions at the first sight do not really fit together. A public strongly committed to environmental matters seems to be one of the preconditions, if decision-making of public authorities should be improved by participation in regard to the general aim of environmental protection. It seems not very coherent, if in one and the same document it is also stated that participation should contribute to an education of the public with respect to environmental matters. These intentions can be considered as coherent, of course, if we assume that the public has to be educated first in order to play then its expected rôle in the aimed-at model.

in due consideration of what might be useful knowledge in the decision-making process.

To put it in more analytical terms: the basic idea of this model is a far-reaching revision of the relationship between public authorities and citizens in respect to the question of how the common good is to be achieved. The "traditional" model of the relationship of public authorities and citizens is based on the assumption, that the former ones are representing the public good, whereas the later ones are acting in pursuit of private interests. This interpretational scheme, which is essential for the "old" understanding of the state, seems to have lost ground dramatically in the last decades. It was competing with a culturally powerful subversive interpretational scheme that simply inverted the distribution of rôles: authorities as the government or official science are represented as falling short in the realisation of the common good, whereas the rôle of a "critical public" is to force these authorities to realise it.[19] In the aforementioned documents, we find a rather harmonistic and establishment-related version of this new interpretational pattern based on the idea of a cooperative realisation of the common good.[20]

It is quite obvious that to satisfy the requirements of such a cooperative realisation of the common good would be rather hard for ordinary citizens, or even voluntary associations.

If we look at the results of our case-study, some local environmental organisations indeed attempt to assume rôles that meet with the requirements of the model just sketched, but as we have also learned, the manner in which they perform these rôles is neither constant, nor exceptionally convincing.

According to this model, as mentioned before, it would be quite reasonable for the approving authority to actively search cooperation with non-governmental organisations that satisfy the specific requirements for the type of cooperation that is expected from this model.

In our case, the realisation of such a model was doomed to fail for two reasons: The approving authority, as we have seen, does not act according to this model at all, and the major concerns of the objectors do not conform to those considered relevant according to this model.

---

[19] And if the majority of public fails to be as "critical" as required, it has to be educated to be so.

[20] For the change in the understanding of authorities' and citizens' relationship in jurisdictional discourse, see: Schmitt Glaeser (1984).

Articulating these concerns cannot improve the permitting procedure with respect to the protection of the legally recognised goods.

The first group of objectors we distinguished in our case-study, claims respect for the local community. This encompasses many different aspect: The project has to be explained to the local people, the disadvantages for the region have to be taken into account in the decision-making process, the project must also prove beneficial for the region in order to be accepted, the decision cannot be made without consideration of the history of this particular region, etc. Thus, even if in their contributions the local people call attention to what appears to them as lack of safety, the major concern is about goods that are related to their local identity and have no legal status.

Objectors that belong to the second group we distinguished, also call attention to in their view apparent safety deficits. Moreover, they try to demonstrate competence and to give critical expert statements that should influence the authority's decision-making. However, it is quite obvious that these "critical objectors" are not particularly familiar with the case or the specific requirements of this type of decision-making.

Nevertheless, with regard to this group of objectors too, the crucial motive for objecting is not to improve that kind of decision-making the approving authority is engaged with. Quite to the contrary, arguments about potential risks that they propose are intended to undermine the kind of expertise-based decision-making process that the public authorities are conducting. At first glance, these arguments might fit into the framework of the permitting procedure. But in actuality, they are an expression of a fundamental rejection of genetic engineering as a technology—or at least of the release of genetically modified plants.

The objectives of the decision-making authorities and this type of objector might be identical: to protect life and health of people, animals, and plants, and the environment as such. Nevertheless, the authority's risk assessment is based on stating the actual state of science and technology, which is considered sufficient for decision-making. The essential presupposition here is that genetic engineering, or the use of transgenic plants, is part of the realm of "normal" human activities that are to be assessed on the basis of knowledge attainable for humans.

The objectors do not share this premise. For them there is as of yet no sufficient scientific basis to assess the risks, because there are so many things left unknown about the possible consequences of the application of this new technology genetic engineering. But more importantly, in their view the use of transgenic plants is special. For them, the possible negative consequences of the release of transgenic organisms are not considered as within the scope of incidents humans are able to live and/or deal with. The question is if any kind of attainable knowledge will ever meet the expectations of a convinced opponent to this technology. Accordingly, this type of objector demands that possible risks are excluded with absolute certainty; something no scientist can ever guarantee, as one objector writes. The contested question is: Are the possible, or even unknown (!) negative consequences to be considered acceptable, or are they to be considered as unacceptable? To answer is of course a matter of belief, not of knowledge.

In summary: Both groups are not primarily interested in such an improvement of the decision-making process that, according to the discussed model of participation, is expected (by policy-makers) to come from their contributions. Thus, these contributions, as they are, cannot be part of an improved process of decision-making oriented by the broad regulatory objectives defined by law, and based on the kind of risk-assessment required by law. Moreover, being part of such a process does not resolve any conflicts. In fact, they are reproduced within this process.

3. *The Implicit Model of the Relationship between Public Authorities and Citizens in the Realisation of Participation by the Administrative Body and its Failure to Meet with the Requirements of the Policy-makers' Model*

The implicit model of the administrative procedure, as it can be extrapolated on the basis of how the approving authority opens up the procedure to public participation as well as its dominant response to the objections submitted, is completely different from the model we found in the policy-makers' discourse (examples of which were presented in the previous section). Specific to the administrative model is that the approving authority is refraining from any activity to clear up the rôle of the citizens' contributions in the procedure, or from animating the public to get involved therein respectively. It is left to individual citizens to take this opportunity in the manner they consider appropriate. Only at the end of the procedure, in the acknowledgement of the objections, does the authority explicitly outline the fairly strict criteria that the objections must satisfy in order to be relevant in the procedure.

This model of participation conforms to models we can find in the jurisprudential literature that came to be when the introduction of participatory elements in administrative decision-making requested interpretation from a jurisprudential point of view. Here as prominent function of participation is discussed that third parties are granted the possibility to protect their legally recognised rights early in the procedure. In this respect, the purpose of participation according to jurisprudential interpretations is completely different from that which underlies the policy-maker model: it is not to improve the decision-making process with respect to general objectives as protection of the environment by active involvement of the public, but to grant the protection of individual rights. Consequently, it is up to concerned parties to use this opportunity to protect their rights. If people submit contributions that are irrelevant according to the specific requirements of the procedure, it's their problem.

Nor is the common good realised by a cooperative endeavour, but by the authorities under consideration of the citizens' contributions. The rôle of the authority is to take into account relevant objections in respect to the legal basis of the procedure, and to make a decision reconciling the different interests, if possible. The idea is to make a "good" decision, which for example, cannot be made a subject of appeal later on.[21]

---

[21] The discussion of participation in the administrative procedure in jurisprudential literature is of course much broader: There, we can find a quite formal discussion of functions attributed to participation in administrative decision-making. In this context, the following functions are discussed: (i) transfer of relevant information from the public authorities to the public, and conversely from informed citizens to the authorities, as well as to the applicant and, (ii) pacification by making decision-making transparent to the public, or by the correction of public misjudgements, (iii) control of the administration by a critical public, in addition to administrative control within the administration, (iv) economisation of the whole process of decision-making by giving authorities and applicant the possibility to react to possible objections early on in order to avoid later legal actions, and by forcing citizens to submit their objections during the administrative permitting procedure if later legal action should not be precluded, (v) protection of individual rights early on in the administrative procedure, not just in a lawsuit succeeding the administrative decision, when a fait accompli might be created already.

Clear from the above listing, there can be specific procedural arguments for participation. Participation can lead to an improvement of decision-making with respect to the requirements of the administrative procedure itself, for example by getting procedurally relevant information from concerned citizens, or avoiding later legal action by taking into account their interests. There are also arguments more related to governmental responsibilities, as pacification of conflicts between applicant and third parties, or the correction of public misunderstandings. And there are legal arguments concerning the protection of individual rights as a value in itself. From a jurisprudential

There are also objections that somehow conform to this model of participation. Objectors argue that their rights are affected by the planned release—but without substantiating them, so their objections are rejected. In fact, if the risks associated with the release of transgenic organism can only be judged on the basis of scientific expertise, and if the possible harms of such a release are not related to particular interest, but related to such general goods as life and health of people, animals, and plants, and the environment in general, it is hard to understand how citizens should defend their rights by public participation.[22] The conclusion—according to the "old way of thinking"—seems to be quite obvious: It is the task of the public authorities to provide protection of these general goods.

If we—for the sake of the argument—assume that the first model was the motivation to provide public participation in the process of law-making in our case, the way participation is practiced by the approving authority is far from the intention of the law maker. Thus, we would have to ascertain a serious gap between intention and realisation.

The intention, of course, is articulated within a relatively abstract vein of governmental activities, where a search for general solutions of general problems takes place. These activities lead to official declarations of intent and to actual laws. The approving authorities that are to implement these new solutions are doing this in a way that conforms more to the "liberal" model wherein third parties are granted an opportunity to protect their rights early on in the procedure. Thus, a simple explanation for this gap would be that the means of implementation do not match the subject of implementation.

---

point of view one might also ask whether participation with respect to one of these functions is demanded under constitutional law, in other words: if there might be specific jurisprudential arguments for public participation in the administrative procedure. One can argue, for example, that it is part of the constitutional duties of the state to secure that citizens are enabled to effectively protect their constitutionally guarantied rights. Thereby, at least for those whose constitutional rights might be affected by the decision, participation in the administrative procedure can be interpreted as constitutionally demanded. In more detail, see: Huth (2001); Luckes (1977)

[22] It should be noted here that a cross-breeding with transgenic organisms—a harm that is quite obvious to the concerned parties as organic farmer for example—isn't considered a loss according to German jurisdiction, see: OVG Berlin, Genehmigung gentechnischer Freisetzungsversuche NVwZ 1999 Heft 1, 99 f.

This lack of coherence on the level of governmental action, between the discourse of policy-makers, and the thinking of administrative bodies, is important to note. Regulation by law in the sense of "governing administrative action by law", would presuppose a shared understanding between policy-makers and administrative bodies of the "real" intentions of the respective laws.

Nevertheless, as we have already seen, we are not only facing a problem of implementation. The intended model itself is incompatible with the types of spontaneous citizen contributions articulated in the participative procedure. In this respect, the idea of participation-in-the-administrative-procedure turns out to be a mere paper solution. It cannot be transferred to the level of interaction, because citizens—at least in our case—do not act according to the policy-makers' model.

4. *The Non-participatory Model of the Relationship between Public Authorities and Citizens that Emerges in the Case*

With respect to the citizens' contributions and some respective reactions from the authority, a third model can be extrapolated: Especially objections of concerned locals are simply aiming at a dialogue *about* the decision making process. Thus, in these cases the implicit model of the relationship of public authorities and citizens is not a model of participation in the procedure. Quite to the contrary, such a dialogue could unfold just outside the procedure and its rather restricted thematic focus.

It is informative that even in the fairly restricted context of the permitting procedure, the approving authority feels sometimes impelled to response to the objections, not just on the level of performing the procedure by rejecting them as irrelevant or unjustified, but by entering into a discussion about the decision to make.

Thereby, not just the mode of communication, but the rôle of the authority also is changing. The authority is not acting in the performance of the procedure; it addresses public concerns by explaining its decision, giving information, and clearing up misunderstandings. To put it in more sociological terms: the purpose of these activities is simply to contribute to a public order of peaceful cohabitation of enlightened citizens, for which the approving authority, as a part of the state, is bearing special responsibility.

With respect to this goal, it is obviously inadequate to deal with contributions of concerned citizens who demand dialogue solely as objections in the permitting procedure. Likewise, it is obvious that the final letter of the approving authority is not at all an appropriate occasion to enter into a dialogue with the citizens.

At this point we can begin to "speculate" about what might actually be appropriate means of dealing with citizen's objections and of reacting to citizens' complaints. The authority might not only enter into a dialogue with concerned citizens; it can also organise a forum where such a dialogue can really take place. But, as our case-study indicates, much more would be required than a mere unrestricted dialogue. Central questions the authorities could ask themselves with respect to their possible contributions to the creation of public order are: How should the local public be informed at the beginning of the project? And, how could the authorities contribute to a resolution of the conflict between the applicant and the local people?

In the case studied, the approving authority simply publishes a quite formal announcement, and does not react at all to fierce local protest or the emerging conflict between the applicant and the local people. It is completely absent from the local site. It carries out the permitting procedure and drafts the final letter; it is in this context that the public authority deals with the objections, files them and processes them in an official document almost nobody will ever read. And, the complete procedure takes place far away from the potential site, in an office somewhere in Berlin.

According to a model of administrative action in which power and its resources are used more extensively to contribute to public order, direct addressing of local protests and more dedicated support of public peace would be required. Now, that this is exactly what the representative of one of the above-mentioned public authority, the *Landesbehörde*, tried to do. Having been informed of the local protest, he travelled several times to the local site. This episode shows that the responsibilities of a public authority entrusted with granting the permission of a controversial project (e.g. the release of genetically modified plants) bears room for interpretation, and involves much more than carrying out a procedure.

Keeping public peace and order by employing the powers and resources of a public authority may take on various meanings with respect to our case. In relation to the concerns of local people with stake in the autonomy of their local community, the responsible authorities could be challenged to take into consideration all those goods, which are not legally recognised but important to the people who live where the field trials are to take place. Regarding the conflict between applicant and municipality, the authority can act as a mediator for reconciliation—actually successful in our case. Concerning the technological conflict about genetic engineering and the release of genetically modified organisms, all the responsible authorities can do, is to make explicit that the basic decisions about the technology at issue and its application have already been made, and that the decisions are not subject to revision via the current decision-making process. But even then, the administration and the representatives of the political sphere are in the position to organise a forum with these questions at discussion.

D. Conclusions

In the first part of the case study sketched above, the communication within the participatory component of the permitting procedure was analysed as a "communicative collision" between the public authority obliged to contribute to a legally constituted public order, and citizens who want to discuss or negotiate the subject with authorities, or otherwise "deconstruct" the knowledge base of the authority's decision-making.[23] These parties act on the basis of different understandings of citizens' participation in the administrative procedure. The result is a rather fruitless sequence of framing and reframing activities.[24]

In broadening our focus in the second part of the case-study, an even more incoherent course of communication became visible. Starting with what we assumed to be the policy-makers discourse on participation and the basic interpretational pattern which lead to the idea of participation-in-the-administrative-procedure, it turns out that *all* parties involved in the *whole* process act on the basis of completely different interpretations of citizen participation. It is already on the framing level of the administrative participation procedure that a process of diverse sense-giving activities is started. During this process, interpretations vastly different from the original idea of how participation should function are employed, consequently, no common ground of understanding is available.

[23] For the concept of such collisions, see again: Bora (1999).
[24] For this concept, see: Furchner/Münte (2006).

But more importantly, our enlarged focus on the general question of how authorities contribute to public order enabled us to distinguish two completely different models of performance. According to the first model, the problems and the conflicts due to the application of new technologies as for the release of genetically modified organisms should be dealt with in a participative procedure based on the cooperation between authorities and citizens, and aiming at general regulatory goals. According to the second model, such problems and conflicts are solved by exercise of governmental powers and resources.

Of course not all problems that should be solved according to the first model can be solved according to the second. Yet by using the second model, at least some of the problems can be sufficiently addressed, whereas the first model—at least in our case—fails completely.

It is illuminating to compare these two models from the point of view of a rather traditional sociology of *Herrschaft*. Important to mention is that in the first model, the authority's power (at least on the level of administrative decision-making) is diminished by public participation—what the authorities in former times should have done themselves, is now to be accomplished in cooperation with civil society. In the second model, quite the reverse, the power of the authorities would be strengthened, by using their governmental powers and resources in a more comprehensive manner.

But it seems to me, what matters here is not just the question of weakening or strengthening the rôle of public authorities, but the more fundamental question of *Herrschaft* itself in modern societies.

This matter becomes clearer if we look at the more promising conceptions of participation now discussed under the notion of governance.[25] That participation in the administrative procedure fails, does not mean that more successful participatory approaches could not exist. The track that would have to be followed in this respect is quite clear: participation would have to be practised in settings that establish some kind of cooperation between applicant, experts, citizens, representatives of civil society, politicians, and administrators, *outside* the administrative procedure; settings that are based on case-specific considerations; settings that are controlled by new professionals as process and conflict managers.[26]

[25] For these discussions, see: Amin (1997).
[26] See also: Bora (1999).

But in one important respect, these more flexible and sophisticated settings resemble the participation-in-the-administrative-procedure-solution. The fundamental idea of governance is about organised networks and social process, in which different actors, as administrators, politicians, citizens, representatives of civil society, etc., cooperate in order to realise certain general desired goals. The difference is that the respective settings are not established as part of an administrative decision-making procedure—and they prove effective, one way or another.

From a sociological point of view, it is important to note, that *Herrschaft* as a social relationship between those who act in power and those who act from the position of being governed, vanishes in such a setting. This type of setting is created by authorities—advised by experts on communication—searching for a special kind of solution for the problems they believe they face. The respective solution is a type of meta-solution, an organised process, which is characterised by rational communication based on argumentation and negotiation, as well as a strong collectivist attitude. Therein, participants should work together—often supervised by a process manager—in order to find the best solution for the problem in question.

Hence, in this setting the public authorities act in two positions: first as organisers of processes of rational problem solving, and second, as collaborators in the problem solving processes. In the field of action created this way, no social relationship as *Herrschaft* no longer exists. In this new world of universal cooperation (and without opposition), there are only "actors", who, on the basis of different kinds of knowledge, viewpoints and interests, contribute to the best possible solution, to which they are committed since they themselves took part in the cooperative process in which the solution was generated. *Herrschaft* is replaced by a sort of collective rationality.[27] Thus, in these settings, the interpretational pattern underlying the discourse on participation in policy-making—according to which the basic relationship between public authorities and citizens must be readjusted—considers institutional expression much more suitable than the participation-in-the-administrative-procedure-solution.

---

[27] The idea of such collective rational procedures is quite old. A famous and outstanding author in the German tradition of this kind of thinking is of course Habermas, see for example: Habermas (1988); Habermas (1992).

For a discussion that is less theoretical and more related to practice, see: Köberle et al. (1997).

Against this background, it is plausible to surmise that a fundamental motive in the search for participatory settings is utopian. To vanquish *Herrschaft* as a basic social fact of complex societies, and to replace it by rational problem solving was of course always a core element of technocratic thinking.

References

Amin, Ash (ed.) (1997): Beyond Market and Hierarchy: Interactive Governance and Social Complexity. Cheltenham: Elgar.

Bora, Alfons (1999): Differenzierung und Inklusion: Partizipative Öffentlichkeit im Rechtssystem moderner Gesellschaften, Baden-Baden: Nomos.

Bora, Alfons, Furchner, Ingrid, Hausendorf, Heiko and Münte, Peter (2004): PARADYS: Final Report Germany. In Bora, Alfons and Hausendorf, Heiko, Paradys: Participation and the Dynamics of Social Positioning – Final Report to the European Commission, Bielefeld and Bayreuth, pp. 309–356.

Bora, Alfons and Hausendorf, Heiko (2006): Communicating citizenship and social positioning: Theoretical concepts. In: Hausendorf, Heiko and Bora, Alfons (Eds.): Analysing Citizenship Talk: Social Positioning in political and legal decision-making processes. Amsterdam and Philadelphia: Benjamins, pp. 23–49.

Bora, Alfons (2006): Licensing plant GMOs: A brief overview of European regulatory conditions for the deliberate release of genetically modified plants. In: Hausendorf, Heiko and Bora, Alfons (Eds.): Analysing Citizenship Talk: Social Positioning in political and legal decision-making processes. Amsterdam and Philadelphia: Benjamins, pp. 50–60.

Bora Alfons and Hausendorf, Heiko (2006a): Participatory science governance revisited: Normative expectations versus empirical evidence. In: Science and Public Policy 33, 7, pp. 478–488.

Furchner, Ingrid and Münte, Peter (2006): Opening up the public space: On the framing and re-framing of a discussion meeting about GMO field trials. In: Hausendorf, Heiko; Bora, Alfons (Eds.): Analysing Citizenship Talk: Social Positioning in political and legal decision-making processes. Amsterdam and Philadelphia: Benjamins, pp. 199–222.

Habermas, Jürgen (1988): Theorie des kommunikativen Handelns, 2 Bd. – 1. Handlungsrationalität und gesellschaftliche Rationalisierung, 2. Zur Kritik der funktionalistischen Vernunft, Frankfurt am Main: Suhrkamp.

Habermas, Jürgen (1992): Faktizität und Geltung: Beiträge zur Diskurstheorie des Rechts und des demokratischen Rechtsstaats, Frankfurt am Main: Suhrkamp.

Hausendorf, Heiko and Bora, Alfons (2006): Reconstructing social positioning in discourse: Methodological basics and their implementation from a conversation analysis perspective. In: Hausendorf, Heiko and Bora, Alfons (Eds.): Analysing Citizenship Talk: Social Positioning in political and legal decision-making processes. Amsterdam and Philadelphia: Benjamins, pp. 85–97.

Huth, Rebecka (2001): Gentechnik und Umweltrechtskodifikation: Ein Vergleich des Gentechnikgesetzes mit dem Novellierungsvorschlag der Unabhängigen Sachverständigenkommission zum Umweltgesetzbuch, Baden-Baden: Nomos.

Jülich, Ralf (1998): Öffentlichkeitsbeteiligung in gentechnikrechtlichen Zulassungsverfahren im internationalen Vergleich: Die Ausgestaltung von Informations- und Partizipationsrechten in den EU-Mitgliedsstaaten, der Schweiz und Norwegen. Berlin: WZB, Forschungsschwerpunkt Technik, Arbeit, Umwelt.

Köberle, Sabine, Gloede, Fritz and Hennen, Leonhard (Eds) (1997): Diskursive Verständigung? Mediation und Partizipation in Technikkontroversen. Baden-Baden: Nomos.

Luckes, Rudolf (ed.) (1977): *Fünftes Deutsches Atomrechts-Symposium*, 8. bis 10. Dezember 1976 in Münster: Referate und Diskussionsberichte, Köln.

Maiwald, Kai-Olaf (2005): Competence and Praxis: Sequential Analysis in German Sociology. In: Forum: Qualitative Sozialforschung 6 (2005), 3.

Münte, Peter and Bora, Alfons (2004): Strukturprobleme der Kommunikation zwischen Genehmigungsbehörde und Bürgern im Verwaltungsverfahren. Rechtspolitische Empfehlungen für das BMBF auf der Grundlage einer Untersuchung der Kommunikationsstrukturen im gentechnischen Anhörungsverfahren – Abschlußbericht des IWT im Rahmen des Projektteils "Dialog" des Projektverbundes "Kommunikationsmanagement in der Biologischen Sicherheitsforschung" im BMBF-Förderschwerpunkt "Sicherheitsforschung und Monitoring", Bielefeld.

Oevermann, Ulrich (2000): Die Methode der Fallrekonstruktion in der Grundlagenforschung sowie der klinischen und pädagogischen Praxis. In: Kraimer, Klaus (ed.), Die Fallrekonstruktion: Sinnverstehen in der sozialwissenschaftlichen Forschung, Frankfurt am Main: Suhrkamp, pp. 58–156.

Oeverman, Ulrich (2001): Zur Analyse der Struktur sozialer Deutungsmuster (1973). In: Sozialer Sinn 1, pp. 3–33.

Oevermann, Ulrich (2001a): Die Struktur sozialer Deutungsmuster – Versuch einer Aktualisierung. In: Sozialer Sinn 1, pp. 35–82.

Schmitt Glaeser, Walter: Die Position der Bürger als Beteiligte im Entscheidungsverfahren gestaltender Verwaltung, In Lerche, Peter, Schmitt Glaeser, Walter, and Schmidt-Assmann Eberhard, Verfahren als staats- und verwaltungsrechtliche Kategorie, Heidelberg: v. Decker & Müller, pp. 37–93.

Wernet, Andreas (2000): Einführung in die Interpretationstechnik der Objektiven Hermeneutik. Opladen: Leske + Budrich.

CHAPTER FIVE

LAW AND PARTICIPATION

Matthias Baier

A. Problem focus

The issue of participation is of interest to scholars in law because of its relation to new forms of governance and regulation (Black 2000, 2001; de Burca and Scott 2006). Empirical studies of participation in biotechnology licensing show however that such procedures "itself may cause serious trouble when it is embedded in a formal procedure with a relatively strong legal framework." (Bora & Hausendorf 2006: 478) Taking this as an example, the main problem discussed in this paper is that the legal system might be dysfunctional to various political participatory ambitions. Participation implies inclusion, but we see examples of exclusion that originate from the internal operations of the legal system. Considering the many instances of participatory instruments embedded in legal frameworks in many sectors of society, for instance environmental matters, it is important to ask what kind of problems the law might cause and the reasons behind these problems. With environmental law and regulation of genetically modified organisms (GMOs) as an example, this essay analyses the paradoxical tendencies of the legal system to exclude citizens even when regulations have the purpose of including citizens. The scientific residence of this essay is sociology of law.

B. Public participation[1] in environmental law

Environmental law is a good example of an area where there has been a political need for public engagement. Fiorino (1990) has provided an overview of such mechanisms with respect to environmental risk. According to him, there are at least five types of such mechanisms:

[1] Rowe & Frewer (2005) have argued that the concept of public engagement include public participation, public communication and public consultation. However, here the concept public participation will be used as the general term.

public hearings (workshops, seminars etc.), initiatives (enabling citizens to place issues on the ballot for voter approval), public surveys, negotiated rule-making ('decentralised' rule-making with the authority) and citizen's review panels ('jury like model'). There are numerous examples of these types and different ways to institutionalise them. The mechanism chosen in each case is considerably dependant not only upon the matter in question and the political ambitions, but also the regulative culture. The mechanisms can be more or less made legal, i.e. brought into the legal system or the administrative system. In an overview in Abels & Bora (2004), one type is labelled 'Legal public hearing', but it is rather a question of how much these mechanisms depend on the legal-administrative system. Of special interest in this essay are those instances when the participatory mechanisms are brought into the legal system and when a normative conflict arises as a consequence.

If we look to Sweden and the Nordic countries (with a fairly similar, Nordic legal tradition), there are several examples of studies made in order to investigate the effects of different participatory regulations. In environmental law, there is, for example, the Institute of Environmental Impact Assessment (EIA) which provides for ordinary or extended consultations with concerned citizens, depending on the matter. These consultations are directed both to those who are particularly affected by a project in a specific sense, as well to those who are affected in a more general sense. The scope of the consultations is dependant upon the severity of the project. Other examples include regulations to ensure the right to information, or access to justice. The subsequent questions are: how do these participatory mechanisms work, and, are they effective?

When five large Nordic development projects were assessed, the over all conclusion was that "in three of these cases the EIA process seems to have had limited influence on planning and decision-making. In one case the EIA process clearly had an impact and in one the role is unclear." (Hilding-Rydevik 2001: 223) Reference to international work indicates the same results (Petts 1999). A socio-legal study made on the consultations within the EIA process on a large infrastructure project concludes that "the law has not been an active, living part of the process." (Wickenberg 2003: 113, translated here)

Another comprehensive study with focus on the deliberative aspects in the process came to similar conclusions. Linda Soneryd investigated the deliberative aspects of the EIA's planning of an airport. The author found similar results when it comes to legal aspects of these processes and noted that some local residents hired a lawyer who could speak for them. Soneryd concludes that the general exclusion mechanisms identified are the ways of thinking and talking about the environment, as well as institutional constraints due to the dominant role of the developer and the administrators. She also notes that

> deliberations are more effective when they are unplugged, that is outside and relatively autonomous in relation to the decision-making structure than when they are plugged-in to formalised decision-making structures. Soneryd (2002: 60)

Another observation is that there might be a contrast between public involvement at the initial planning of a project, when location and other features of the project are roughly decided, and in the later stages.

Having indicated that participatory regulations are not always effective and can even be dysfunctional, the next section will investigate this problem. It is of course possible to undertake such an investigation from different standpoints; see Skillington (1997) for an example with a focus on framing strategies. This essay focuses on the role of the legal system. Up to now, law is treated as a black box; law is an institution having certain effects on society. In the case of participation it is assumed that formalising participation legally or bringing in participatory mechanisms in existing legal institutions can imply normative conflicts. Such a conclusion is common in the field of law and society or law and sociology. But what are these conflicts, what is their nature? To answer this question, it is necessary to scientifically examine the legal system. Therefore we need an example which can provide the effects of the participatory regulation as well as the internal operations of the law. The Swedish GMO licensing procedure will serve as this example. Data about the regulation, as well as its operations, come from Baier et al. (2004).

C. The Swedish legal-administrative system concerning GMOs

1. *The Swedish GMO regulation*[2]

Starting with the over all picture, the legal domicile of the GMO regulation is within the Environmental Code (EC), which is in turn located

[2] For an overview of the European regulations, see e.g. Sand (2001).

in the public administration sector of the legal system. The ambition of the comprehensive environmental code has been to gather all environmental regulation under one framework. The reason for this location is that due to the nature of environmental problems, it is not considered possible to regulate them within private law. Environmental conflicts are today considered to be a political problem that can not be left to the market to handle, thus the regulation of GMOs is often located within the public law sector. However, this does not mean that other parts of the legal system are left out. The Environmental Code is mostly directed towards public institutions, although some parts or some elements address anyone who is about to take actions that could effect the environment. Deliberate release of a GMO is therefore a matter for the public institutions.

The Environmental Code is very comprehensive, and chapter 13 of the EC is devoted to GMOs. Besides chapter 13, there is an ordinance (SFS 2002:1086) with detailed regulations on the deliberative release of GMOs. In the sector of plants, the deciding authority is the Swedish Board of Agriculture (SBA). The board is in control of the procedure from application to decision. In sum, an application for the deliberative release of a GMO is sent to the SBA, which then refers it to two other governmental agencies (the Swedish Environmental Protection Agency and the Swedish Gene Technology Advisory Board) and eight other referrals. After the consultations, the SBA decides upon the case. According to the law, the SBA is supposed to evaluate the application from a risk perspective and from an ethical perspective.

In order to get an idea of the law, the sections in the GMO-chapter will be accounted for here with translations that are not official, but nonetheless reflect the content of the sections with respect to the purposes of this contribution.

1.1. *Field of application*

§ 1. The provisions in this chapter shall be applied with regard to contained use and deliberate release of a GMO. They shall also be applied when products containing GMOs are released onto the market.

The purpose of the regulation is, in addition to chapter one, section one [sustainable development]; to ensure that certain ethical considerations are taken at actions stated in section one.

§ 2. The government may issue regulations regarding exceptions from this chapter with concern to such organisms developed by methods proven to be of no risk to public health or to the environment.

1.2. *Definitions*
§ 3. Organism…
§ 4. Genetically modified organism…
§ 5. Contained use…
§ 6. Deliberate release…
§ 7. Release onto market…

1.3. *Demand for investigation for risk assessment*
§ 8. Contained use and deliberate release of a GMO shall be preceded by an investigation. It shall provide a sufficient assessment of the effects the organisms may have on public health and the environment. The investigation shall be made according to science and experience. Such an investigation shall also be done before a product containing GMOs is released onto the market.

§ 9. The government or the authority the government chooses, may issue regulations about such an investigation in § 8.

1.4. *Ethical considerations and precautionary measures*
§ 10. Certain ethical considerations shall be taken a propos contained use and deliberate release of a GMO and when a product containing GMOs is released onto the market.

§ 11. The government or the authority that the government chooses may issue special regulations regarding precautionary measures.

1.5. *Demand for permit and duty to report*
§ 12. A permit is needed when releasing deliberately or when releasing a product onto the market that contains GMOs.

§ 13. A permit may be granted only if the activity is ethically justifiable.

§ 14. The government or the authority that the government chooses may issue regulations regarding demands for protection of public health and the environment in order to obtain a permit according to §12.

§ 15. The government or the permitting authority may issue regulations about exceptions from the request for a permit according to § 12.

§ 16. The government or the authority of government choice may issue regulations regarding the request for a permit or the reporting of contained use if needed for public health or environmental reasons.

§ 17. Application for a permit and reporting is completed at the authority the government decides.

Questions concerning permits shall be decided upon within the time limit the government allots.

A permit is valid for five years, unless the permit states otherwise.

1.6. *Labelling*

§ 18. The government or the authority that the government chooses may decide that anyone releasing a product containing GMOs onto the market must label it.

1.7. *Gene technology advisory board*

§ 19. A special board, the Gene Technology Advisory Board, shall monitor the development of the gene technology, monitor the ethical issues at hand, and provide advice for the application for the gene technology.

The government issues regulations concerning the duties of the Gene Technology Advisory Board and for the composition and procedures of the board.

2. *Legal rationalities*

Since the problem of law's exclusionary effects seems to be general, we shall look into the law's general manner of operation instead of looking into single statutes. And since this essay is about participation, it is appropriate to employ a perspective that can comprehend the law's capacity in this respect. The notion of 'reflexive law' developed by Günther Teubner (1983) entails the participative aspects of law. The concept of reflexive law is part of a discussion on the law's capacity to function in or adapt to a changing society wherein complexity is one of several key factors. The discussion assumes a development where the crisis of one legal rationality – formal law – is followed by another legal rationality - substantial law, which, due to another crisis might in turn be followed by a third legal rationality – reflexive law. Irrespective of the developmental aspect, these three rationalities of law are useful in analysing the legal design of modern law.

One reason for the conceptual model developed by Günther Teubner is its combination of internal as well as external aspects of law. To fully understand the law's interaction with other aspects of social life, one requires both the juridical internal perspective and the external social perspective. Teubner's socio-legal perspective is in principle a framework, within which it is possible to further develop and study law and social life. Although the main issue for Teubner is the development of legal rationalities, a diachronic perspective, I believe that this framework can also be used synchronically. Later, this point will be developed using Kaarlo Tuori's theory of a multi-layered perspective on law (critical legal positivism).

Teubner's analysis includes three dimensions: the justification of law, the external functions of law, and the internal structures of law. It is not suggested that a regulation or a program belongs solely to one type of legal rationality; rather it is an empirical question of how each regulation is designed with elements from these different rationalities. It is also an empirical question as to how a regulation actually operates due to its context, its legal design, etc. The perspective presented by Teubner is not primarily a method on how to identify these different rationalities, but rather a development of theoretical concepts. To use this perspective empirically, some sort of method must be developed.

With reference to the Swedish discussion and notion of framework law, Håkan Hydén (1984) has elaborated on the discussion about legal rationality and law's internal operations. Framework law is, in Sweden, a technique for legislation. It is impossible to give an unambiguous definition of this concept; however, one can say that the basic end of framework law is to allocate competence and procedures to administrative bodies in order to realize the overall goal. Compared to legislation with particular rights or duties for a certain addressee, framework law lacks to some extent, clear substantial content that can be directly executed. One typical characteristic is that framework law often opens with a presentation of goals and guidelines rather than substantive rights, e.g. 'sustainable development' or 'good health for all the people'. In many respects, this type of legal rationality corresponds to Teubner's concept of substantive law.

Consequently, framework law often also contains extensive rules assigning rights and duties for bodies to supplement, interpret or else give substance to the overall goal. Moreover, framework law contains rules stating how the other rules shall be interpreted. It is not typically possible to assess the law unless the law has been applied for some time and to a certain extent. It is frequently impossible to assess the outcome of the law with traditional legal methods; social sciences methods are often required. We can discuss a deliberate vagueness in the law, which will be clarified gradually (still in a different way when compared with general clauses). Framework law is thus the legal design often employed to invoke substantive and reflexive elements in the law mentioned above.

When analysing framework law, Hydén starts by defining the tasks certain element of a regulation has. This corresponds to Teubner's internal structures of law. Within a regulation, certain tasks must be assigned: what will be done, who will act and how. These tasks are accompanied with three different kinds of rules assigning competence, procedure and substance (action). A regulation can be designed very differently with respect to these kinds of rules, but it is not possible to configure a law arbitrarily considering the composition of these rules: the choices do matter. It should, however, be pointed out that within the method of legal interpretation lies the ability to find key elements in a regulation; elements that are essential if the law is to operate at all. Historically, laws have been designed differently and hence with different operations and functions. Looking into, for example, traditional contract law, we see a focus on substantive rules addressed to actors in the field, and adjudicative power lies almost exclusively in the courts. Welfare regulations are often configured with focus on programmes where the substantive rules expressing rights and duties are complemented by rules expressing values, as well as rules that balance different interests or navigate means-ends. Extra legal bodies in the welfare system are often vested with the power to 'apply' the law. The role of the courts is thus reduced to securing procedure. This historical development is the key issue in Teubner's different rationalities of law.

The balancing of different interests indicates inter-system conflicts that need to be solved. Since the conflict does not occur within one system, a system specific rule can not be used or developed. Instead, the balancing of interests is often negotiated by representatives of different interests. In Sweden, several boards and special courts with permanent or co-opted representatives for different interests have been set up to solve conflicts in the fields of labour, consumer market relations, technology, etc. (Today in Sweden almost every field or branch has an ethical committee there to solve problems emanating from the system and the consumers, caretakers, users and alike. This development might indicate a problem for the law in handling these types of conflicts, Hoff (2003).

Different rationalities often employ different techniques when it comes to legal operations. The formal legal rationality primarily operates with legal syllogisms. When it comes to the application of law, this operation is completed ex post. Legal operations working with the

	Legal actor	Rules	Decision method	Time	Addressee	Initiation of law
Formal law	Jurist	Rights and duties	Legal syllogism	Ex post	Citizen	Citizen
Substantive law	Professions, Representatives	Goals, programmes	Planning, means-ends	Ex ante	Authorities → 'users'	Authorities or 'users'
Reflexive law	Jurists, representatives	Procedural	Balancing of interests	Ex existere	Users, bodies	Stakeholder

balancing of interests or means-ends rules operate ex ante. These differing temporal perspectives have consequences for legal rationality. In order to summarise this, the legal rationalities are presented together along with key attributes, in a matrix.

3. *Analysis of GMO regulation*

Placing the GMO regulation within the Environmental Code gives it a focus on substantial values like safety, public health and the environment. The code is at the same time based on other market-oriented values like development, free trade, etc. The overall goal of the EC is to balance these two set of values in the case of conflict. The code therefore consists of a variety of regulatory means, depending upon the character of the possibly harmful activity. These regulatory means are basically traditional; permits, reporting, licensing, supervision, etc. Few areas or activities are, in general, forbidden. But it is clear that the EC aims at changing or modifying the conditions and structures of the market in some respects, especially concerning requests for permits, as in the GMO case. Instead of forbidding certain activities, the law is proactive and attempts to achieve a market solution exclusive of externalities.

In regard to chapter 13, devoted to GMOs, it is clear that the structure is similar to that of the Environmental Code. Despite the fact that permits are required by law, the decision of whether or not a permit is granted will be decided by the SBA. This chapter empowers the SBA to decide whether a company or an institution may use its property for scientific testing. Therefore, there is a demand for thorough investigation both when applying for a permit and deliberating an application.

One reason for this investigation is of course to avoid negative environmental consequences. Safety for the environment and other moral and ethical values are of importance. Thus, the code and the GMO regulation would be to a great extent characterised as substantive law, according to Teubner's terminology. Its legal design is also typical for Swedish substantive law: a framework law guided by some abstract ideals; jurisdiction delegated to authorities; means-ends and balancing of interests deemed legal operators. Risk analysis, scientific investigation, precautionary steps, etc, are in this case the means to achieve sustainable development and safety.

Almost all of the substantive rules in the chapter concern the permit. One reason is that from a formal point of view, the chapter infringes upon the right to carry out research, as well as the right to use one's property the way one wants. It is also an indirect infringement on one's right to operate independently in the market. Normally, activities carried out within a plant or on a property which cause a loss to someone through injuries or damages will be legally handled ex post; damages must have occurred. These rights are now limited *ex ante* through the general request for permits. The application procedure therefore represents an exercise of public authority – but only in the field of market relations (i.e. not the field of welfare, etc). Therefore, public interest in the rule of law is very strong. For those reasons, unambiguous, predictable rules which are applied equally are of great importance. This is probably one reason for the 90 day time-limit. The reason for this limitation is the (above mentioned) ambition to achieve sustainable development and simultaneously take ethical issues into account. Yet another reason is the consequences of an "accidental" GMO release might cause damages which market mechanisms alone cannot smooth over. Accordingly, this regulation might secure the market as well as limit it.

But changing the conditions of the market requires special legal format, since it entails infringements of civil rights. These aspects of the EC and GMO regulation may be viewed upon in a more 'formal' manner. The law's operations need to change from a primarily programmatic operation to one that is more rule-oriented, so legality and the rule of law can be maintained in each and every case.

The EC contains some general rules deeming certain kinds of actions criminal. Aside from the more general criminal actions, there are two specific sections in chapter 13, violations of which are also criminal (section eight and eleven). When determining if an activity is harmful to the environment and whether or not it is criminal according to the rules in the EC, modus operandi follows criminal procedure; this is also enumerated in the EC. Thus, ordinary courts rule on a crime in the EC according to principles in penal law. Typically, criminal law belongs to the formal rationality of the law.

There exists, then, a demand for the ethical justification of a decision, suggesting the legal-administrative system is capable of making an ethical assessment of the GMO-technology in general – and of the application in question. There are, however, no rules at all (whatsoever) guiding the SBA for decision-making for this issue. Normally, open-ended rules like this are not coupled with a strong legal operator, as in our case, because it becomes impossible for the SBA to avoid the issue. Furthermore, open-ended rules of this nature are as a rule complemented by guidelines, further instructions, and rulings from appeal courts and alike. The ordinance 2002:1086 complementing chapter 13 is void of the ethical aspect. In general, such an open-ended rule is considered problematic; not just as law, but also as pivotal part of the licensing procedure. In this sense, the SBA has a dilemma. One way out is to refer this question to the Gene Technology Advisory Board, the over-all bearer of responsibility for ethical questions, although, GTAB has no direct responsibility for the licensing procedure. Hence, it is unclear as to how to comprehend this ethical aspect of the regulation.

On this analytical level are strong indications of the nature of the regulation's rationality: the legal design indicated is substantive, with some formal elements. What remains unclear is whether or not there are reflexive elements in the regulation. The SBA refers the application to several more institutions and authorities other than the SBA and SEPA. For a long time, seven referrals were used. Apart from the investigation made by the applicant company, the application was assessed by the SBA, the SEPA, GTAB and five more institutions. Moving to the referral component of administrative activity, we get other suggestions for its legal design.

Taking a closer look at these institutions, we see that all of them are experts in the sense that there are people within the organisation or institution that can understand the complex issues in an application. That said, though, several of these referrals are more than an expert organisation: Swedish farmers and Ecological farmers represent one or more interests, and if nature can be considered an interest, the Swedish Society for Nature Conservation represents an interest. Aside from representing an interest, several of the referrals do represent or encompass an ethical standpoint. For instance, the three universities represent a general position on research and ethics.

Thus, it is possible to view the regulation in a more open, contextual manner. We then see not only the possibility of the deciding body to incorporate several other ethical viewpoints, but also an opportunity for the SBA to free itself from the question. It is stipulated that the SBA shall consult GTAB and SEPA, but the decision to consult other institutions and organisations is made by the SBA. Looking further into the referral component of the regulation, it is important to describe the role played by the Gene Technology Advisory Board. The board is composed by seven members of parliament, seven experts, and one chairman with judicial competence. Besides "consulting" on referred applications, the board arranges hearings, conferences and the like. It also produces minutes from conferences and hearings, reports and investigations. To some extent the board initiates a public discussion, albeit the majority of the discussion is directed toward actors in the field. Participants from the industry, science, experts, and administrations are participating in the discussions and hearings. Hence, one can see elements of reflexive law in the regulation, especially since GTAB is set up to somehow balance politics, technology and ethics. Ethical discourse is therefore likely within this part of the regulation.

Having reached a conclusion, some last remarks should be made. There are formal aspects of the law, there are substantive elements of the law, and there are possible reflexive elements of the law. What should be noted is the legal modus operandi for the SBA is single applications. This means that the decision-making procedure focuses on one application, upon which the overall structure of the procedure is dependant. Accordingly, comments, objections, assessments, etc must be made with reference to the application in question. Another demand is the time frame for the decision, which is set to 90 days. Considering the dynamics of the application process, the time allotted to reflect and deliberate appears rather modest. The discussions surrounding an application and decision in the context of GTAB, however, seem to be of another kind; opinions on a single case provoke deeper discussions on ethical principles. This is of course a different design compared to, for example, the use of hearings on general themes. What is important is the stress in making a decision tailored to the procedure involved in a single case. A discussion regarding a question in general is often quite different when compared to the same question discussed under legal statutes and with the demand to judge the case and come to a verdict.

So far it is possible to give an account for the legal rationalities of the Swedish GMO regulation. It is primarily substantive but with reflexive and formal elements in it. We can thus talk about a legal hybrid when it comes to legal rationalities. According to the matrix, some of the aspects do not work together and we can - prima facie - expect normative conflicts when such a regulation is operating. Will the fact that there are several rationalities within one regulation result in a conflict that has to be solved, or can these rationalities exist side by side? If there is a normative conflict, according to which kind of meta-rationality will it be solved?

D. Inclusion and exclusion

Having presented the Swedish GMO regulation and analysed its legal design formally, the next step is to account for how the law operates with respect to participatory aspects. The main purpose is to decipher how the law attempts to solve the inherent normative conflict of the GMO regulation. Data from the licensing procedure on GMOs were analysed with methods of conversation analyses in order to describe the impact of participatory decision-making on the construction of citizenship, see Baier et al (2004).

The Swedish data showed that there were two kinds of citizenship: one which was centred on the legal procedure and hence was labelled the "procedural" citizenship, and another, "public" citizenship, which was centred on a Greenpeace campaign. The two citizenships were a result from including and excluding dynamics between social positions within the decision-making procedure. In the following, a brief account of those social positions and their dynamics will be presented. The presentation is alphabetical.

'Activist' is the position that resulted from the communication concerning the Greenpeace demonstration. This position is strategic in the sense that it is meant to initiate debate and further communication. Greenpeace, who is the only actor taking this position, later takes the position of Environmentalist during the course of events.

'Administrator' is the position that is centred on the application procedure. As with Activist, there is only one actor taking this position, the

SBA. This position is not surprisingly centred on procedures, decisions, bureaucracy etc.

'Applicant' is the position taken by the applying company, also the only actor. It is centred on technology, economy etc.

'Debating Company' is a position found in relation to the actions Greenpeace took in order to initiate public debate on GMOs. This position is in many respects like Applicant, but still different because the audience is very different; communication with the Administrator is different than with then Activist/General public.

'Environmentalist' is the position that is largely based on the substance of the communication, i.e. environmental values shape this social position. This position is taken by several actors at different occasions.

'Expert' is the position expressing knowledge and making scientific claims. It is assumed by several actors.

'Informing Company', like Debating Company, is a position similar to Applicant, but still dissimilar due to its focus on a local public and due to its dynamics with the Administrator.

'Judge' is the position taken by the SBA and all referrals. It is largely concerning judgments and normative communication and might be seen as corresponding to the more 'legal' component of the legal-administrative complex.

'General public' is accounted for as a category, but not as social position, mainly because it is not a social category in our data. It is, however, part of many social positions, as a relevant actor without being an actor. But the General public can of course be viewed as the totality of citizens, 'people' in general, etc.

1. *Social positions' relations to GMO regulation*

It is obvious that many of the social positions found in the Swedish data have connections to the legal administrative context - direct or indirect. This is not surprising since the data is made up by an application to the SBA and material relating to and resulting from this application. The purpose now is to look closer into the positions and their dynamics in order to see if the different rationalities accounted for in the previous chapter result in certain social position and certain dynamics. Now I will account for the positions from the three different rationalities, beginning with the more formal parts, via the substantive elements to the reflexive parts.

The fact that the GMO issue is regulated by law and not solved within other subsystems and that competence is vested in the SBA to administrate the issue, have obvious bearings on the position Administrator; it is a direct result from the regulation. This position is however not entirely 'legally' defined; rather bureaucratic which of course part of the law is. So, the position of 'Administrator' works in the legal domain with which we are dealing. In all probability, the social position resulting from criminal or civil procedure would be different from this one. However the Administrator could not possibly be very different from the one we found in our material; the exercise of public authority must be communicated in certain way to be legal as well as legitimate.

The position of 'Judge' is most directly related to the formal legal operations. Every referral except for those from GTAB or SEPA is free to argue in whatever manner chosen. The letters of communication following an application normally ask for risk identification; however, ethical considerations are never requested (confirmed with an SBA official). Furthermore, when a referral refrains from communicating the analysis in a legal mode (approval or disapproval), the SBA asks the referral to communicate in binary, legal terms. For the SBA, this means that referring to values incorporated in the regulation is not enough; they must be judged outside of administrative borders, yet within the legal system in communicative terms. It is possible to interpret different reasons for Judge as a position, as well as the dynamics surrounding it. One may understand it as the opening of the law to a broader part of society. This interpretation is typical for framework law and semi-officials often take part in shaping the law. The professional limits of law are transgressed, and jurisdiction over the communication is broadened. An alternate interpretation (or, the other side of the coin) is simply the reduction of complexity. The regulations have not only exposed the legal decision to values other than those which dominate market relations but also opened the law up to almost any value-judgement by virtue of the demand for ethical justification. The environmentally significant values and other possible values connected to the ethical demand might open the decision to almost any argument especially since there are few guidelines of how to balance all these values. Securing the autonomy of the legal system is done by stressing the normative aspect of the decision, since a decision must be reached regarding the case in question. This deliberation on the communication is most likely made with reference to the simultaneous demand for legality and some sort of rule of law concerning the applicant.

The position of 'Applicant' is to some extent a direct result of the dynamics in the legal system. Due to the regulation, it is necessary for a company or an institution to adhere to the legal communication both with reference to the legal requirements and the legal communication. Applicant's argumentation must not just present the facts and risk assessment, but also an assumed claim that the activity itself is legally permissible. By adhering to the legal requirements (both the regulation and the conditions in the permit) and the legal communication a permit may be acquired. One important point is that the requirements are not just fulfilled, they are also legally defined.

The position of 'Expert' is related to the legally requirements based on the environmental character of the regulation. Since one purpose of the regulation is to assess the environmental consequences of certain projects, knowledge on facts as well as systems in nature is crucial; therefore, admittance into the communication presupposes this specialized knowledge. Other 'opinions' must be illustrated in other ways. The only part of the regulation that might open up or presuppose other kinds of knowledge is the ethical justification. This is a difference between the knowledge of natural systems and that of common sense. Clearly, the kinds of communications that constitute the Expert position are directly related to the substantive elements of the regulation.

The position of 'Environmentalist' is also a direct result of the substantive elements in the law. The main differences between the Expert and the Environmentalist are the overall evaluation of existing expert knowledge, and the consequential normative standpoints, as in the precautionary principle.

The position of 'Activist' is not really effected by the regulation since it is communicated outside the administration of the case; in fact, this communicative format is the purpose of the position. Discussions with representatives of Greenpeace confirm the view that being inside the "system" also means communicating differently and achieving different goals. This is also later confirmed when Greenpeace takes the position of Environmentalist. This is probably done in order to legitimize argumentation from Greenpeace's point of view. The 'Debating Company' is accordingly not related to the regulation. Self-image in regards to legality is therefore interpreted as a general difference between illegal activists and legal (i.e. legitimate) companies simply obeying the law.

2. *Conclusion*

The general conclusion obtained from the Baier et al (2004) study was that there are two types of citizenship - one procedural and one public - and the mediating social position between the two is the Environmentalist. A closer examination of the data reveals that certain social positions are connected to certain legal rationalities, as described above. Arranging the legal rationalities in formal rationality (via substantial rationality) to reflexive rationality, illustrates as follows: those social positions central to the legal decision are also 'close' to the formal rationality; likewise, social positions peripheral to the legal decision are closer bound to reflexive rationality. In between lies the social position Environmentalist, bound to substantial rationality. Selection of social positions for the GMO regulation process clearly results from legal rationalities. Put simply, those social positions 'necessary' for the legal decision are included, while social positions not 'necessary' for the decision are excluded.

Since there is an evident selective effect, there is also a strong indication of how the normative conflict is solved. It seems as there is a prioritization-hierarchy of the different rationalities. The subsequent question is why the law solves the normative conflict in this way; is there a meta-rationality that guides such a normative conflict?

E. Analysis

If we look at the Swedish GMO regulation, there are several aspects that point to participatory ambitions. One is that there is an extensive consultation process including not only experts and interests, but a special body (GTAB), the sole task of which involves initiating and housing discussions on the gene technology at hand. Another aspect of participation is the demand for ethical justification. In our social positions, we can see that the Environmentalist can to some extent encompass ethical standpoints. But if we take the ethical demands in the regulation seriously, everyone can argue for or against an application with very different arguments. In that regard, this legal rule is very special and most likely one of a kind in the Swedish legal system.

According to the law, the applications for a permit could result in very interesting and broad discussions among many different people. Today there is also a possibility to comment on applications along the procedure through the SBA web page. But so far this potential has not been met. However, if we examine the more than 100 decisions made by the SBA concerning GMO applications, some further conclusions can be postulated. First, the ethical part of the law was brought up in the decisions (it had to be, due to its strong position in the chapter), but for a long time the SBA used the same formula just stating that the "activity is ethically justifiable". Especially in comparison with the amount of the risk assessment (accounted for on several pages), the SBA did not discuss the ethical part of the permit at all. So, the participatory mechanism that comes with the demand for ethical justification did not have that kind of effect. But how is it possible for the legal system to evade these potentially participatory mechanisms, and for what reason?

It is clear that the law prioritizes the formal rationality of law in the decision-making process. The application procedure starts using formal law, later moves to a more substantive level, and at the end comes back to the formal level. The procedure is initiated by the applicant; without an application, the SBA would not act (GTAB probably would not act either without a request). The application is very often complemented after an initial revue by the SBA, after which it is matched with the formal requirements of the law and in the ordinance 2002:1086, wherein there are numerous detailed prescriptions on what an application must include. The initial process is thus a matter between the applicant and the SBA. After this, the SBA sends out a suggestion for consultations. The last step is the 'actual' decision, when the SBA has to consider all relevant information and subsume it under the formal requirements of the law. This last step is a matter for the SBA alone.

The procedure starts from a demand for permit, which is a way to anticipate possible future claims on the applicant. The procedure ends with a decision whether the applicant can use the property for the purpose of deliberate release of a GMO. In between lies the process where the initial possible future claim has to be analysed. The consultation process serves the purpose of anticipating future damages and thus future claims, be that of civil or criminal character. This process is very thorough since a permit almost totally precludes future claims. The licensing procedure can thus be viewed as a substitute for an otherwise civil matter concerning property. The ethical demands do not, however, fit in to this logic.

When the 'actual' formal decision is made, it must be legitimate from different points of view. According to Teubner (1983:257), different rationalities justify themselves differently. Formal law is justified through the establishment and reproduction of the market, i.e. private autonomy. Substantive law is justified through the compensation of market inadequacies. Reflexive law is justified through coordination of social coordination. This means that there are demands for legitimacy on the regulation in general, but also on the decision in particular. When looking into these decisions, there are strong indications that the SBA is becoming more and more aware of this problem. The decisions are normally quite extensive when it comes to the procedural aspects. The legal requirements are accounted for, the consultation process is accounted for, the precautionary means are accounted for and the way the SBA comes to a decision is accounted for. A relatively small part of the decision actually concerns the technical aspects. The decision is thus communicatively oriented to the general public or the political system; substantive and procedural legitimacy is fulfilled.

But how is the legitimacy of the formal aspects of the law fulfilled? The answer to this question lies in the SBA's 'choice' to not use all the participatory potential in the regulation, the selective effects. This choice is also a way to solve the 'conflict' between different rationalities in the regulation. It is even possible to look upon the regulation as a 'protection' against legitimate critique from anyone. This is the case when comments on the cases through the SBA home page are considered to be of general interest and thus left aside, since to comment on a specific case requires definite expert knowledge. Another example concerns the ethical justification, already mentioned above: one official at the SBA confirms that the missive is very short and does not explicitly ask for opinions on the ethical issues.

Different forms of legitimacy of the procedure, a procedure that is after all regarded as a civil matter, and - as will be discussed further - coherence of the legal system, are matters that direct the analysis to the legal system. This requires an opening of the "black box" of law.

1. *Opening the black box*

Kaarlo Tuori has presented a theory of modern law that was at its first appearance geared towards a multi-layered view on modern law (Tuori 1997). Later, this theory has been labelled critical legal positivism (Tuori 2002). According to the author, the theory deals with the nature of modern, positive law, its legitimacy, and its limits. The two main concepts in this field he is trying to resolve are the Kelsian 'grundnorm' and Hart's rule of recognition. Tuori's goal is to find a realm of legitimacy that is 'beyond' positive law but still not located within different natural law theories. Of importance in this article is not this perspective, but rather how to understand the scope of law and the internal conditions of law – and thus laws external functions and effects; a theory that can help us understand the selective effects of law and the meta-rationality that solves normative conflicts in regulation, like that of GMOs.

Tuori proposes that law consists of three layers: the surface level of law, the legal culture, and the deep structure of law. The surface level of law consists of legal regulations like individual statutes or decrees, court decisions in individual cases and dogmatic legal works. This level is characterised by Tuori as an "ongoing discussion where the legislator, the judges and the legal scholars all make their interventions" (1997: 433). The legal culture is as a level an expert culture with a certain autonomy differentiated from the common legal culture of ordinary citizens. The expert legal culture consists of substantial universal doctrines in different fields of law comprised by general principles and basic concepts. Here we also find argumentative pattern, norms of interpretation and (norm) conflict-solving norms. These doctrines and 'meta norms' are not to be found in statute books. The last level, the deep structure, is the most static level dividing legal history into epochs (traditional law, modern law, liberal law, social law etc.). In this vein, we also find the basic type of rationality manifested by the law, for instance Weber's formal rationality. Here Tuori also places the fundamental normative principles of the given type of law, e.g. basic rights and principles of the rule of law or Rechtstaat.

Thereafter, Tuori proposes six types of relations between these levels. Sedimentation is the relation between legal practices on the surface level and the legal culture and the deep structure. Human rights is one example that through the different constitutional assemblies along the years, together with legal dogmatics, theorists, and philosophers have sedimented into the foundation of modern law. Constitution is the 'bottom-up relations' between the deep structure, the legal culture and the surface level. According to Tuori, these relations

> supply the necessary conceptual, normative and methodological tools without which it would be impossible for the legislator to legislate, for the judge to judge or for the legal scholar to arrive at their norm and interpretation standpoints. (1997: 438)

The surface level then 'pays back' to the deeper levels with concretisation, which is the third relation. While the deeper levels constitute the surface level, there are also limitations. Decisions can neither be made without the deeper levels, nor beyond these levels. For instance, new laws have to be interpreted by judges and legal scholars. The purposive rational way in which modern law is enacted, has to be filtered through practices obeying a different logic. This process does not restrict itself to formal aspects, but Tuori even talks about a "normative censorship" (1997: 340). The last two relations – criticism and justification – concerns the more theoretical aspects of Tuori's theory, that of law's legitimacy.

The normative conflict described as a conflict between different, competing legal rationalities will now be interpreted from this theory of the legal system's internal organisation. Teubner's legal rationalities are induced historically. This means that formal rationality precedes substantial rationality which in turn precedes reflexive rationality. According to Tuori, such a development would result in strong sedimentation and constitution processes between different layers, preferably the legal culture and the deep structure. Put simply, substantial rationality has to, if possible, fit in to the normative structure of the formal rationality, and reflexive rationality has to fit into the normative structure of the former two. This is a matter of internal coherence of the legal system. These processes are however complex and different "solutions" for how to arrange such sedimentation and constitution arise. For instance, Renner (1949) has pointed to the ability of legal institutions to change functions over time. And surely, different legal rationalities can exist side by side inasmuch as the sedimentation and constitution processes have taken place. But, as we can see in GMO regulation, normative conflicts sometimes still arise.

GMO regulation is a balance between different values including the ones typical for the market, private autonomy, free trade, etc. This part of the law is not just the oldest one, but has also deep roots in the legal system in general. A political, instrumental regulation of the market will thus always be carefully judged against this part of the law. Those market principles that are affected are deeply rooted in the law and exist regardless of positive law; they exist in the legal culture and the deep structure of law.[3] According to Tuori's theory, principles of sustainable development and other substantial values will always be balanced

[3] Swedish law had no principle of ownership protected in the constitution until some ten years ago. This fact did not, however, mean the principle of ownership did not exist; it was protected by the courts as a civil right.

against these parts of the law regardless of the normative content in the positive law. The Environmental Code provides for the solution of such a conflict (the first chapter) and this way the potential conflict between different values can be normatively solved – there is a balance formula.

Although the law often is conceived of as a system for justice, modern positive law does not handle ethical discourses. Demands for ethical justification in a broad sense are therefore not compatible with the law. In the last years, the SBA has tried to relate to the ethical demands in the decisions, but they are always interpreted as belonging to the substantive rationality, i.e. as being a matter of efficiency of the market. There is thus a substantive problem for the legal system involved in these kinds of regulations, and an interpretation of the regulation is made in order to avoid a normative conflict. Tuori stresses that there is a normative constitution, i.e. the legal culture and the deep structure of the law, which "provide[s] the principles which form the normative basis for new laws" (Tuori 1997: 439).

Another aspect of the legal system is the modus operandi of the law. The central parts of the law are very much built upon the idea of two parties having a conflict; the two-party axiom. This axiom is most likely based on a millennium long standardisation of typical conflicts. This axiom serves as a model for many other relations: creditor – debtor, buyer – seller, landlord – tenant, and plaintiff – respondent etc. Even when many actors are involved, like in company law, the law uses singular phenomena, e.g. the idea of a 'shareholder'. This two-party axiom is also used when solving conflicts. The conflict solving triad is based on the two parties as well as an independent judge, mediator, arbitrator and the like (Shapiro 1981). I would say that this modus operandi belongs to the deep structure of law and that parts of the reflexive rationality constitute a normative conflict to this normative structure.

GMO regulation poses the opportunity for a vague definition of who can present arguments for or against an application, especially in regards to the possibility of commenting on the application through the SBA web page. This avenue into the procedure is even more important since the procedure itself is in progress; the case has not been decided. Significantly, the law itself decides whether someone has the right to make a legal claim. It is thus a decisive question whether you have a right to 'express yourself' according to different participatory regulations, or the right to make a legal claim according to the deep structure of law. The difference is fundamental.

The law needs to be able to distinguish between any claim and a legal claim because of the subsequent problems with for instance the legal force of the decisions. What a decision comprises from a legal point of view is very important and who can appeal a decision is also of great importance. The necessity of an entrepreneur (or anyone who wants to make an investment or anyone who wants to invest resources in general) to know who has the possibility to take legal action is fundamental; it is a question of the 'rules of the game'. If you as a neighbour 'express yourself' on the SBA homepage about an application from an ethical standpoint, does this also mean that you have exhausted your right to take legal action in the case? This principle is called "res judicata", and is a principle that precludes further legal claims. The circles of those with the ability to take legal action must be strictly controlled by the legal system.

Another important aspect for a legal actor is the right to have your case decided upon, which pressures the law to make a decision albeit a lack of knowledge. The law can not refrain from deciding upon a legally valid claim. A strong principle here is that if an action is not considered illegal, it is legal. The right to assert such a claim in a court is guaranteed in article 6 of the Convention for the Protection of Human Rights and Fundamental Freedoms. The right to have your application tried within 90 days emanates from this principle. The consultation cannot therefore last for too long a time. The interest to have the case decided is strong, perhaps even stronger than the interest to include arguments in the decision process.

2. *Concluding remarks*

From a participatory standpoint, the legal system is very selective. Being a party of a legal conflict, the law is very including. Everyone has the right to present his or her case in a trial where certain procedures should guarantee one's civil rights: Namely, the right to a trial, the right to bring in evidence, the right to argue, and often the right to bring legal expertise etc. The trial itself should guarantee a "fair" handling of the issue. Every argument should be taken into consideration, and accordingly, the legal system is inclusive. At the same time, not everyone has access to the legal system. The norms setting up limits on participation are important for the law since this exclusion is a prerequisite for the inclusion. A "high" level of inclusion necessarily means exclusion.

Having analysed this case, is seems clear that the law solves the normative conflict of the substantive rationality easier than the normative conflict of the reflexive rationality. As proposed here, participatory elements of the regulation are less coherent within the deep structure of the law than with substantive elements. This potential normative conflict will most likely be resolved by the legal system through an ever stronger selection.

References

Abels, Gabriele and Bora, Alfons (2004): *Demokratische Technikbewertung*. Bielefeld, Transcript.

Baier, Matthias, Holsanova, Jana, Hydén, Håkan and Rahm, Henrik (2004): *Sweden*. in Bora & Hausendorf (2004).

Black, Julia (2000): Proceduralization regulation: part I. *Oxford journal of legal studies,* 20 (4) 597–614.

Black, Julia (2001): Proceduralization regulation: part II. *Oxford journal of legal studies,* 21 (1) 33–58.

Bora, Alfons and Hausendorf, Heiko (2006): Participatory science governance revisited: normative expectations versus empirical evidence. *Science and public policy* 33(7): 478–488.

Bora, Alfons and Hausendorf, Heiko (2004): PARADYS. *Participation and the dynamics of social positioning*. Final report to the European Commission.

Born, Asmund. (1988): *Refleksiv ret*. Köbenhavn, Nyt fra samfunsvidenskaberne.

De Búrca, G. and Scott, Joanne (red.) (2006). *Law and new governance in the EU and the US*. Oxford: Hart.

Fiorono, D. J. (1990): Citizen participation and environmental risk. A survey of institutional mechanisms. *Science, technology & human values*. 15(2): 226–243.

Habermas, Jürgen (1996): *Between facts and norms : contributions to a discourse theory of law and democracy*. Cambridge, MA: MIT Press.

Henecke, Birgitta (2006): *Plan & protest : en sociologisk studie av kontroverser, demokrati och makt i den fysiska planeringen*. Lund, Sociologiska institutionen Lunds universitet.

Hilding-Rydevik, Tuija. (2001): *EIA, large development projects and decision-making in the Nordic countries*. Stockholm.

Hoff, David. (2003): *Varför etiska kommittéer?* Lund, Sociologiska institutionen.

Hydén, Håkan (1984): *Ram eller lag? : om ramlagstiftning och samhällsorganisation*. Stockholm, Liber/Allmänna förl.

Hydén, Håkan, Wickenberg, P., et al. (2000): *Miljöledning i citytunnelprojektet : MiC-projektet, delrapport 1 : bakgrud och samråd*. Lund, Sociology of Law Lund Univ.

Löfstedt, R., Boholm, Å., et al. (2004): *Facility citing risk, power and identity in land use planning*. London; Sterling, VA, Earthscan.

Minow, M. (1990): *Making all the difference : inclusion, exclusion, and American law*. Ithaca, Cornell University Press.

Peczenik, A. and Aarnio, A. (1997): *Justice, morality and society: a tribute to Aleksander Peczenik on the occasion of his 60th birthday 16 November 1997*. Lund, Juristförl. : Akademibokh. distributör.

Petts, J. (1999): *Handbook of environmental impact assessment: Impact and limitations*. Oxford, Blackwell Science.

Renner, K. and Kahn-Freund, O. (1949): *The institutions of private law and their social functions*. London.

Rowe, G. and Frewer. L. J. (2005): A typology of public engagement mechanisms. *Science, technology & human values*. 30(2): 251–290.

Sand, I.-J. (2001): The legal regulation of the environment and new technologies - in view of changing relations between law, politics and science. *Zeitschrift für Rechtssoziologie* 22(2) 169–206.

Shapiro, M. (1981): *Courts : a comparative and political analysis*. Chicago, U.P.

Skillington, T. (1997): Politics and the struggle to define: A discourse of the framing strategies of competing actors in 'new' participatory forum. *British Journal of Sociology* 48(3) 453–513.

Soneryd, L. (2002): *Environmental conflicts and deliberative solutions? : A case study of public participation in EIA in Sweden*. Örebro, Univ.

Teubner, G. (1993): *Law as an autopoietic system*. Oxford: Blackwell.

Tuori, K. (1997): Towards a multi-layered view of modern law. In Peczenik, A. and A. Aarnio (1997)

Tuori, K. (2002): *Critical legal positivism*. Aldershot, Ashgate.

Weber, M. and J. Winckelmann (1976). *Wirtschaft und Gesellschaft : Grundriss der verstehenden Soziologie*. Tübingen.

Wickenberg, P. (2003): *Brunnarna i Holma : samrådens konkreta genomförande 2000–2002 för Citytunnelprojektet i Malmö*. Lund, Sociology of Law Lund Univ.

CHAPTER SIX

CONFLICTING FORMS OF CITIZENSHIP? REFERRALS AND THE PRINCIPLE OF TRANSPARENCY IN SWEDEN

Henrik Rahm

A. Introduction

> It's a bit VAGUE and the ISSue is not so much the actual FOOD itself but what happens AFTER i mean th: there's so much ELSE from it.

This is an utterance in English translation from an interview with a Swede in a café. The issue at hand is the view on deliberate release of GMO crops. This utterance shows an attitude of ambiguity and uncertainty which is reflected in the debate in Europe on GMO plants. The above utterance and the GMO debate in Europe provide the background for my interest in democracy and citizenship under different conditions. The questions discussed in this article are as follows: How should democratic processes on important issues be constructed? How can optimal citizen influence be achieved? The focus of this article is on the Swedish GMO discourse from a discourse-analytical perspective, specifically the more limited discourse anchored around an application for restricted and controlled field trials (so called "deliberate release") with GMO canola in Sweden. This discourse includes utterances from the applicant, authorities, interest organisations and individual Swedish citizens. The methodological point of departure is critical discourse analysis.

The aim is to uncover and analyse the relations between the authorities and the referrals and their view on citizen participation in the discussions concerning GMO crops. The focus is on one hand the actors' views on the referring process, and on the other hand their opinions about citizen participation in the decision making process.

This article consists of a description of the investigated data, followed by a section on theoretical and methodological points of departure. The empirical section opens with a description of the discursive practice on applying for field trials with GMO plants in Sweden. Eight subsections follow, dealing with different actors in and aspects of the GMO discourse. Finally, the analyses are summarised and discussed.

B. Data

The data primarily consists of texts regarding an application for the deliberate release of GMO rapeseed (canola) in 2002 in southern Sweden. These documents encompass the correspondence between the applicant and the Swedish Board of Agriculture (SBA), as well as reactions to the application from the organisations functioning as referrals. An important part of the data is interviews conducted with some of the main actors in the Swedish GMO discourse: the SBA; the applying company (henceforth referred to under the code name Crops Ltd); the Swedish Environmental Protection Agency (SEPA); Ecological Farmers and Swedish Society for Nature Conservation (SSNC). Interviews have been conducted with these actors but also with individual citizens. The transcriptions of the interviews come to 367 minutes. These interviews, along with utterances by Swedish citizens sent to the SBA in applications for deliberate release of GMO crops and plants are analysed. The interviews are of course in Swedish, but rendered in English translation. The capital letters signify stressed words or parts of words.

C. Points of Departure

The theoretical basis for this article is Norman Fairclough's Halliday-inspired Critical Discourse Analysis (Fairclough 1992, 1995, 2003). This model consists of three analytical frames. The most encompassing is called the social practice, and aims to contextualise in a broad sense the notions used in sociology, such as hegemony, power and ideology. Fairclough is well aware of the strain put on the analyst, especially when s/he is not a scholar of sociology. However, being a linguist himself, he strongly suggests that all scholars should take the social practice seriously, because without a social dimension discourse analyses would not work. That said, the emphasis of the social practice in analyses is not the same for a linguist (like myself) as for a sociologist.

The second frame is the discursive practice, encompassing descriptions of institutions, the prerequisites of the discourse and intertextual relations. The third frame is the textual practice, which deals with lexical relations, grammatical structures, textual structures and cohesion. The challenge is therefore to make use of all three frames in the analysis.

Fairclough connects the frames to three analytical phases: description, interpretation and explanation. The descriptive phase of course primarily deals with the textual level, while the interpretive and explanatory phases involve the other frames as well, with an emphasis on social and sociological concepts as tools of explanation.

This general CDA framework needs to be applied to the field of research on citizenship. In 2006 Fairclough et al used such an application by analysing instantiations, expressions and relations of citizenships in a public meeting organised by a Parish council of an English village in 2001. The research begins by addressing the two main issues with studying citizenship. One issue is defining the forms and expressions of citizenships in advance; the other is the assumption of being totally free from opinions on what citizenship is in a certain context. The solution offered is that "the research must involve recognising and researching the dialectic between pre-constructions of citizenship and the performance of citizenship within everyday practice" (Fairclough et al. 2006: 102). The research should be conducted through three different lenses: discourses, genres, and styles/voices. Discourses are defined as "ways of representing the world from particular perspectives"; genres as "ways of acting and interacting with other people, in speech or writing" and styles/voices as "ways of identifying, constructing and enunciating the self, including both social and institutional identities" (Fairclough et al. 2006: 104). Making use of these three research lenses is a path "for setting up dialogue between analysts of text and talk (conversation, interaction) and sociological, political etc theorists and analysts" (Fairclough et al. 2006: 105).

Notions regarding intertextuality are central for the analyses conducted on British citizenship. Since these are also key concepts for my investigation, I will elaborate briefly on them below.

Intertextuality is connected to discourse since both notions are connected to the construction of texts. Intertextuality was coined by Julia Kristeva in 1969 in order to create a summarizing term for Mikail Bakhtin's view on the function of language and literature. When the works of Kristeva and Bakthin were translated in the 1980's, intertextuality found its way as an analytical concept into several disciplines. Fairclough (1992) discusses intertextuality through two other terms, manifest intertextuality and interdiscursivity. Manifest intertextuality is the inclusion of a text or part of a text in another, in the forms of direct and indirect speech, quotes, briefs and reported parts and texts. Interdiscursivity is a vaguer and less concrete form of intertextuality, recognised by elements of structure, style, tone, and accent, as well as conventions and norms from other discourses. Analysing the interplay between discourses in texts is of course more complicated, requiring a larger degree of interpretation compared with analysing manifest intertextuality. Nonetheless, this type of intertextual analyses are most important in order to understand, e.g. why a certain actor sometimes employs an informal or popular voice and other times a formal or bureaucratic voice.

The knowledge basis on the GMO discourse in Sweden emanates from a European research project in which I was one of the researchers (Baier et al. 2004).

Methodologically I will start with the discursive practice, mainly as a description. In this section I also deal with the referring procedure as a possible way of acting out citizenship. In other words, it is a preconstructed citizenship from my point of view as a Swedish researcher but also as a Swedish citizen. Then the analyses will follow, inspired by the described method for a Critical Discourse Analysis on citizenship: according to discourses, genres and styles. The analyses will be performed on the discursive practice, the textual practice and to a certain extent on the social practice. A key notion is intertextuality.

The key methodological questions are: How are the GMO discourse related to power structures, traditions of citizenship and ideologies? Which bureaucratic structures underlie the GMO application? How are GMO regulations interpreted? Who decides on the agenda? What discursive arguments regarding the interpretation of citizenship and participation can be observed?

D. The discursive practice: Applying for deliberate release of GMO crops

How is the discursive practice of the research object constructed? The starting point for the research is a description of the discursive practice: What are the relations between the main actors? How does the application procedure work? These questions are the topics of this background section. I intend to describe the main actors involved and the application procedure in order to establish an understanding for the continued analysis.

Fundamental for comprehension is a familiarity with the principle of transparency. This principle is the cornerstone for the work of the

Swedish authorities, and stipulates that all texts produced by and submitted to the authorities are open to the public. Accordingly, any citizen asking for a certain text from an authority must be granted access. The only exceptions are classified material (i.e. certain files regarding defense and security) and working materials before the final version of an authority file, e.g. a decision.

The principle of transparency is employed in application procedures with the Swedish Board of Agriculture (SBA) for deliberate release of GMO plants. (See however below in *subsection* 1. *The application and the applicant* where representatives for the applying company imply an application with classified parts.) Therefore, the applications as well as all related documents in the SBA's archives are public. When the SBA considers a GMO application, it consults other expert authorities and organisations. According to the ordinance of GMOs, the SBA should always refer the application to the Gene Technology Advisory Board (GTAB). Also, when the conditions of its release are new or when the organism itself is new, SBA is supposed to consult with GTAB as well as the Swedish Environmental Protection Agency (SEPA). Besides this, the SBA refers the application to other authorities and organisations. This latter group of referrals is not however regulated by law. These organisations are selected as referrals "if they can contribute with information about GMO," as an SBA official puts in an oral interview.

An application for the deliberate release of new types of GMO plants must be decided within 90 days. In order to adhere to the tight schedule, the application must be thoroughly prepared by the applicant according to a detailed application matrix before reached in to the SBA. An extensive procedure process is employed if the GMO is new; if there is no previous knowledge about the release; or if the physical conditions in the release are different from previous trials. The first step of the procedure, called co-consultation, is as described above, a special form of referral procedure with GTAB and SEPA. The application is also submitted to the National Chemicals Inspectorate, the Swedish University of Agricultural Sciences, Lund University, the Federation of Swedish Farmers, the Swedish Society for Nature Conservation and the Swedish Ecological Farmers Association. After responses from referral organisations and amendments to the applications (if requested by the SBA), the SBA decides upon the application. In some cases, when the applicant company plans to repeat the field trials of preceding year with the same GMO and only requests prolongation, the application process is simplified. This procedure is actually common with five-year applications.

To what kind of apprehension of citizenship does this contribute? One interpretation (in the terms of Fairclough et al. 2006, a pre-construction of citizenship) is that the combination of the principle of transparency and the system of referrals form a represented citizenship. The opinions of the citizens seem to come to expression via organisations. But is this the whole truth? And how do the deciding authority, the applicant, and the referral organisations view citizen participation? These questions will be dealt with in the following section, with an emphasis of the views expressed by representatives for Crops Limited and the SBA, respectively.

E. Analyses of the GMO discourse: texts and actors

In this section some of the key actors mentioned above are analysed. The texts examined are both written (from a file at the SBA or from media) and oral (from interviews with the actors). The first subsection deals with the application and the applicant, henceforth mentioned under the code name Crops Ltd.

1. *The application and the applicant*

The relevant form of application is texts anchored around a bureaucratic procedure, characterised by strict genre expectations both on form and content. The applicant is supposed to write the application according to an extremely detailed, hierarchically organised application matrix with some eighty headlines on different hierarchical levels. The topics considered relevant by the deciding authority are the application, bio-technical issues, and risk. The applicant in the investigated canola case, Crops Ltd, fails to address its motivations for applying for the permit. The driving force for a private company is of course to develop products in order to make profit, rather than formulating and discussing the GMO method versus non-GMO methods for cultivating (which could be the case if the applicant is a university department). Analyses of intertextuality and tacit text patterns are therefore quite enlightening. Other applications for deliberate release also follow the matrix mentioned above. Furthermore, each application is written with previous applications as text model. It is a clear example of manifest intertextuality, both between the headlines in application matrix and the actual application and between phrases in previous applications and the actual application. As a consequence, there is an interdiscursal similarity in style and wording between the applications.

The text pattern is not only explicit but also implicit. The implication lies in what is de-emphasised; the fact that the applicant only superficially deals with the ethical aspects of the application despite its centrality in Swedish GMO regulations. The tacit text pattern is likewise pertinent to other applications because the SBA has made this interpretation of how the ethical aspects of GMO should be treated.

In May 2002, an interview is conducted with two representatives of Crops Ltd. The representatives are asked to describe the application procedure. In this description they mention that Crops Limited requested classification taken from certain parts in another recent application. An ongoing patent registration for the actual GMO plant spurred this request, which the SBA granted. Yet following the classification, representatives describe its disadvantages as a major hindrance:

> when you classify stuff it only causes a lot of misery un/unnecessary questions and unnecessary newspaper articles and that unnecessary quandary on the whole so that (-) we will release it as soon as we EVER can

Here, a colloquial discourse is used. The style and the words (e.g. *stuff*) are informal and its take on publicity is clearly negative. The key adjective is unnecessary, indicating that there is a certain amount of publicity which you have to take, but that all publicity above that level should be avoided. This seems to lead to the conclusion that publicity and citizen participation have to be accepted and tolerated; but at the same time they cause problems for the applicant.

The view on public participation in the GMO discourse is obvious in the beginning of the interview when a representative compares their experience with the GMO debate in Germany: "there has been a LOT of FUZZ in Germany on field trials" There is a clear connection to a colloquial discourse in an informal style when characterising the commitment of German citizens as "a lot of fuzz". However, the representative changes focus and style when elaborating on the theme:

> so I mean t/to describe it as m (-) a a (–) LESS extent in the discussions is is (-) is (-) I mean underSTATEment (-) I mean (-) somehow there has been LITTLE discussion on things that's the way it is in Sweden [Researcher: yes (-) certainly] ENGland and Germany and France have had EXTREmely [Researcher: yes] and extremely larger [Researcher: certainly] discussion (-)

This utterance can be seen as an attempt to draw back the previous utterance or at least the simplified and patronizing view on participation in the process. It is also a shift to an explanatory discourse without judgments, perhaps modeling after an academic discourse.

When asked about the application procedure, the representatives declare their view of GMO production as principally similar to traditional plant breeding. In spite of the fact that traditional plant breeding does not require any permission from the authorities, they do not object to the applications needed for GMO plants. In fact, they characterise the application as a "smooth procedure" with efficient and informal communication with the SBA. The representative is confident in the good bureaucracy where the main actors are the applicant and the authority together constructing an application discourse. As a consequence of this, the researchers ask the representatives if there is any need for an application at all:

> NO (-) i don't think so (–) eh::: (-) because eh:: <PAUSE> the techNIQUE itSELF (–) the techNIQUE itSELF is (-) i mean th-th-the (-) technique itself is not DANgerous and eh: i (-) s::ee them just like the potatoes that WE'RE working with that (—) i-it maybe sh:: (-) i mean (–) shouldn't be so necessary to to regulate in that way (4: m) (–) but (–) the technique itSELF is it's well a very POWERful technique (–) and (–) very NEW techni (-) you know in a hisTORICAL perspective it's w (-) it's still a very NEW technique (4: m) (–) and (–) so i think it's absolutely NECessary that there is some impartial (–) auTHORity (-) that that follows UP (-) and examines and eh:: (–) th: eh:: th-that gives (–) PERmits in these contexts (-) i-i-it would be eh:: (—) eh:: (PAUSE) well (–) i-i-i think so definitely (4: m) (-) so i DON'T think it's unnecessary (4: no okay) (SILENCE)

A possible interpretation of the many hesitations and the vague content of the answer is that the applicant does not want any changes in the application, since the detailed bureaucratic procedure gives legality, legitimacy and a minimal public interest in GMO questions. Actually, the representative of Crops Ltd presents conflicting views on the application procedure, by saying first that "the technique itself is not dangerous" and later saying that "it's absolutely necessary that there is some impartial authority". Some questions that arise are: What is the motivation for the application procedure if the technique is harmless? What is the use of the bureaucratic application procedure in that case?

The next section deals with the administrative and decisive authority, the SBA.

2. *Swedish Board of Agriculture – administrating and deciding*

For the SBA as an administrative authority, the focus of the application matrix is on GMO technology for the actual plant, not on questions of ethics. Consequently, the SBA has an interest in condensing each utterance from the referrals into an approval or disapproval. If a referral is not absolutely clear on this point, an SBA official makes a phone call to get a definitive approval or disapproval. Notes on phone calls of this kind exist in the public SBA files for all applications. The notes merely include the fact that an SBA official has made a phone call in order to get a clear-cut answer from the referral which has produced an answer which can not be interpreted a clear yes or no. The fact that the authority only accepts approvals or disapprovals is definitely worth mentioning. Interestingly, the referrals' criticisms are framed in the permit with this remark: "These referrals disapprove of the application because they dissociate in general to herbicide tolerant plants". However, the referrals generally approving are not framed by the SBA. Their positions are presented as independent and impartial conclusions. The conclusion is that the SBA creates an agenda for control and legitimacy of GMO's via the bureaucratic processes (see above) by focusing on GMO technology. In turn, the organisation almost totally omits questions of ethics apart from internal debates among SBA officials, which are not even visible in the conclusions and decision.

To illuminate this concept to the general public and Swedish citizens, an extract from an oral interview is rendered below. An official at the SBA, interviewed in September 2002, is questioned about publicity practices regarding information about an intended deliberate release which would be published before the SBA's decision:

> no we haven't disCUSSED that in much DEtail yet what we should DO we have conFINED ourselves to (-) FIRST of all that it won't be RELevant till the end of the year so we're pushing it ahead of us a bit (laughs) (Researcher: mm) and then that we the FIRST thing we do is to publish it on the NET and in SOME way make it visible maybe ADvertise it the first time or times eh::: but then TO and a little more circulation for comment but then to leave it at THAT at the BEGINNING (Researcher: mm) and postpone the decision about whether we'll do MORE then (Researchers: mm)

The conclusion to be made is that the SBA has little desire to invoke the interest of the general public as the answer circles around waiting and postponing decisions. The SBA seems to be satisfied with the bureaucratic procedure of referrals, which could be seen as indirect utterances of the general public or rather of certain interest groups (e.g. Ecological Farmers) or certain authorities (e.g. university representatives).

However, this is a simplification. Since March 2003 (i.e. after the canola case analysed in this article) the SBA has opened up for comments from individual citizens. It is possible to sign up for a mailing list on GMO applications and thus receive regular, guaranteed information on ongoing applications. This action has been made according to the EU directive 2001/18/EG which states that the general public should be given a possibility to express its opinions. The citizens on the mailing list are notified about upcoming applications and thus given a possibility to comment.

The mailing list has not been promoted by the authorities, which is one important reason why it consists of some 10 persons. There were a few comments from single citizens on the applications in 2004, but in 2005 there were not any utterances from citizens at all. Here we observe that the SBA accounts for opinions from the referrals and from the general public in different ways. In regard to comments by single citizens, the SBA starts by referring to the legal demand of the EU directive of including the utterances of the general public. Then the organisation states that none of the opinions deal with risk assessment: "The SBA did not receive any opinions that influence the risk assessment in the case. However, the SBA has received opinions of a more general character." The opinions from 2004 by four citizens, in the words of the SBA, are not included as judgments of the application, since they were not about the specific GMO technology in the application. Most utterances from individuals are disregarded because they reflect "a general repudiation" on GMOs. Finally, it is important to bear in mind that no other measures (e.g. information campaigns) have been undertaken by the Swedish authorities in order to evoke increased interest and commitment among Swedish citizens in the GMO topic, which could naturally lead to an increased participation of single citizens in the public GMO discourse.

Below, in section 5. *Greenpeace – the activist neglecting the procedure* the actions of Greenpeace on the canola case are analysed. The SBA representative is questioned on his view of the opinion work of Greenpeace:

> Researcher: How do you LOOK upon the fact that Greenpeace has created so much advertenCY (-) around eh: this CASE what efFECTS does this have for your WORK on the WHOLE SBA representative: Well I would preFER if the public discussion could run in another DIRECTION

> more constructively I don't think it is constructive (-) the way they do it (Researchers: mm) because they enter the discussion with a FIXED opinion which impossible to CHANGE (-) then they do these ACTIONS it is it is NOT I do not think it promotes so well the climate of the DISCUSSION (Researcher: no) (Researcher: mm) but this must DEFINITELY be discUSSED more it is good that there will be more attention given to the topic but not in that WAY

It is obvious that the administrator at the SBA has difficulties with the way Greenpeace takes part in the debate. The adjective "constructive" is a key notion which the SBA representative does not define. A probable assumption is that he prefers statements within the referral procedure (see more in 5.5 on Greenpeace acting outside this procedure). The question is: Are utterances considered constructive only when they are within the referral procedure? Also, are utterances with a general discontentment with GMO crops not constructive?

There is also a hedging in the evaluation of Greenpeace when the administrator, without further explanation, uses the phrase "these actions".

3. *Referrals judging the application*

As mentioned above, the referrals' judgment of the application should give clear approval or disapproval. If there is any doubt, the SBA contacts the referral in question and asks for clarification in order to come to a clear "yes" or "no". The referral may write discursive texts, but the SBA is only interested in approving/disapproving the application. The texts are generally formal; however some contain more polemic statements, for example, this sentence written by a professor in plant breeding in favour of deliberate releases of GMO: "Plant material with the gene has at this time been cultivated on millions of hectares around the world without any negative effects".

This polemic tone might seem a bit odd within its formal structure. One important explanation is the fact that the very same professor also publishes his view on GMO in media, e.g. in April 2002 in the regional newspaper in southern Sweden, *Sydsvenska Dagbladet* [The Daily of southern Sweden]. The professor is used to debates and does not hesitate to express his view, even when it is a bit provocative, as above. It is possible to interpret the sentence above as an irritated (or even ironic) statement about the referral system around GMO crops. The professor seems to take the opportunity to question the requirement of applications for GMO crops.

The judgments of the referrals are summarised in the SBA's decision with lists of those which approve and those which disapprove. Then the SBA makes a risk assessment and concludes, inter alias with reference to previous field trials carried out by the applicant, that the field trial is acceptable from an environmental point of view and – without any argument – that the trial is ethically justifiable. An important reason for the absence of elaborated texts or ethical justifications is that GMO regulation only states that judgments are to be made- it does not say how.

4. *Referrals judging and trying to reformulate the agenda*

The non-government organisations Ecological Farmers and Swedish Society for Nature Conservation (SSNC) accept the agenda of the application in terms of its treatment of bio-technical issues. At the same time, though, these organisations try to set another agenda from a precautionary standpoint, introducing topics such as future ecological consequences, risk assessment, and questioning the need of GMOs in plant breeding. In another words, Ecological Farmers and SSNC interpret the application matrix differently than the SBA, in emphasising the need for a thorough analysis of the ethical aspects. In an interview in September 2002 with Ecofarmers, the representative comments the application procedure in this way:

> it's not hard in any way to get in touch with with (-) the person in charge and those who (–) handle these decisions right (–) and then (-) on the OTHER hand (–) there's no direct (PAUSE) what should i say (-) act- (-) there are no ACTIVE attempts by the authorities (-) TO involve the local PEOPLE for example (–) instead you get the feeling that they think it's nice enough as long as (-) as it IS like (-) a FEW (-) people in charge in some NATIONwide organisations that look at THIS (-) and that there ISN'T a load of (–) discussion at the local LEVEL (Researcher: m) (–) there there i think (-) THERE i think maybe that that (-) people in the board of agriculture have PRETTY much the same attitude as people at (-) x-company or (–) y-company or any of the COMpanies

Being an environmentalist within the referral procedure thus is a bit frustrating for the representative of Ecological Farmers. It seems as if the interviewed individual thinks that an increased commitment of local persons could lead to a greater diversification of GMO opinions as well as a reformulation of the agenda. This utterance can also be read as a critique on the absence of utterances and opinions of citizens in the application procedure, in other words a deficit in democracy.

It could also fit into a political genre like political speech or statement, since there is an obvious critique on the present conditions. This fits in the role of a representative for an interest organisation (even though not a political party). But there is also an interdiscursal connection to a bureaucratic discourse, e.g. a newspaper interview with a representative of an authority. In such a public genre (if one takes on the role of an official representative for an authority), one may present opinions, but it is important that they are hedged, thus allowing one to rephrase them in the case of a negative public response. In this sequence, the interviewed individual underlines the ease with which one can contact representatives of the authorities (to be read as the SBA). Accordingly, the interviewed is very careful when formulating the critique:

> "(–) there's no direct (PAUSE) what should i say (-) act- (-) there are no ACTIVE attempts by the authorities (-)"

Further on there are hedges like: "you get the feeling" and in regards to the alleged impartiality of the bureaucrats at the SBA:

> there there i think (-) THERE i think maybe that that (-) people in the board of agriculture have PRETTY much the same attitude as people at (-) x-company or (–) y-company or any of the COMpanies

5. *Greenpeace – the activist neglecting the procedure*

The overarching topic for Greenpeace is political action in terms of concrete activities on and around the fields intended for deliberate release of canola in Croptown in southern Sweden in April 2002. It is important to bear in mind that before this action, Greenpeace did not take action in the GMO issue, neither in text contributions (e.g. debate articles or press conferences), nor in the form of direct physical actions.

Greenpeace uses the principle of transparency when asking the SBA for the maps of the field trials on the date of decision for the canola case on April 8, 2002, a request which in itself of course is not an activist action. However, the maps are not requested out of pure curiosity, but for a specific activist purpose, since the Greenpeace activities commenced on the fields outside Croptown on the very same day.

An activist organisation of course makes an extensive use of public action in order to promote important topics and opinions. Public action can take the form of physical activities announced via press releases, leaflets and/or oral information. The goal is to spread the actions of the activists to a wider public via media.

The only guaranteed media resource for Greenpeace is its own web site where different texts can be found, primarily press releases functioning both as press releases to all potential media, as well as combined news texts and debate articles for those reading these texts on the Greenpeace web site. The Swedish newspapers, radio and TV are of course important media resources for Greenpeace. However, they are merely potential resources since media coverage is not guaranteed.

Most central for the communication is the choice of vocabulary. Greenpeace does not accept certain key words, for example, it revises the neutral and most used noun *field trial* with the amendment *so called* and reformulates the interpretation of the acronym GMO from *genetically modified organisms* to *genetically manipulated organisms*.

There seems to be a tacit consensus among the referrals that the communication should only take place within the permitting procedure. (Compare the negative evaluation ("then they do these actions") given by the SBA administrator in 5.2 above.) Greenpeace as an activist organisation opposes the referral procedure as the only relevant debate forum, stating in one of its press releases that there is no point in taking part in *an endless dialogue*.

The problem focus for the activist is to create and obtain maximum effect via strategic actions. The activities are spectacular in order to evoke the interest of mass media, however since they compete with other events for media coverage; this can be a difficult enterprise. Examples of strategic actions in the Greenpeace campaign April-May 2002 are: going door-to-door in Croptown, establishing a mobile office in front of the head office of Crops Ltd, handing over an open letter to the managing director of the company, offering ecological coffee to people passing by Greenpeace stands, activists dressing up as bees on the fields intended for deliberate release, sowing ecological seeds from the applying company on the same fields, chaining themselves onto sowing machines, etc.

Since 2004 Greenpeace has also made the choice to influence GMO applications as a referral.

6. *Crops Ltd – the predicted publicity or minimising information and publicity*

Once the applicant receives permission to grow GMO crops from the SBA, which is connected to two conditions for information dissemination for the general public: advertising in local newspaper(s) and informing the boards of the municipalities where the field trials are to take place. However, there are no further instructions on the modes of communicating the permission.

The genre of public notice (in Swedish *kungörelse*, literally 'to make known') is used for public information in the printed press regarding new directions and instructions from authorities. Local authorities are the primary users of these means (although sometimes using proper advertisements as well) to inform changes in parking regulations, rising fees etc. It is worth noting that national authorities often create campaigns when imposing new regulations of interest for many citizens. These campaigns often use combinations of web texts, newspaper texts and information leaflets sent home to the citizens concerned.

When publishing the information about deliberate release of GMOs in the local newspaper using the genre public notice, Crops Ltd writes about the permit as strictly and formally as authorities do about new directions and new laws when using the same genre. If and how the general public is interested in a certain aspect of the planned deliberate release is thus not considered by the applicant.

Interestingly, the permit only prescribes information to the local public in local newspapers. The information could in other words very well have been designed as an advertisement with a thoroughly thought through information structure and layout. But as long as the SBA does not prescribe another genre for the information (like a professional advertisement or an information leaflet distributed to the households in the municipality) it is most unlikely that the genre usage will change. It would also be possible to demand that the applicant- in connection with handing in the application- should make public the areas considered for deliberate release. That would at the very least provide incentives for committed citizens to take part in the discussions, since they would know about the GMO crops with enough time to react.

The public notice and the informing letter both contain pro forma information, relevant and impartial according to the condition in the permit. However, it should be noted that the informing letter also has a paragraph wherein Crops Ltd takes the opportunity to promote a positive self-image to the board of the municipality in Croptown; in other words, mono-directional information on the planned field trials.

7. *Crops Ltd – reluctantly answering to the Greenpeace action or the unpredicted publicity*

In conjunction with a deliberate release of GMO canola in the vicinity of Croptown, the Greenpeace campaign in April- May 2002 altered communicative structures. Usually the applicant only communicates the permission according to the SBA's conditions of information dissemination (see above in section 5. *Crops Ltd*). But in the case of GMO canola in April-May 2002, Crops Ltd had to respond to the utterances and actions of Greenpeace. The company, accustomed to monodirectional communicative procedure, was forced to meet Greenpeace in the public arena.

Of course, Crops Ltd had no reasons to expect this change from informing to debating and being required to argue for the deliberate release of GMO plants, and was neither used to nor at ease with this new position. Therefore, during debate, Crops Ltd emphasises the legality within the procedure, e.g. mentioning in press releases on the internet that the permit for deliberate canola release goes back to a "rigorous set of rules and regulations" and utterances connecting to this legality: "We will not refrain from possibilities of obtaining more knowledge". Legitimacy is anchored around words such as *future*: "We invest in the future" and *tradition*: "Crops Ltd is the only remaining Swedish crop breeding company". The latter utterance is also an indirect threat; if Crops Ltd can not continue with GMO field trials, it might leave Sweden.

The communication deals with comments and opinions connected to the Greenpeace actions as well as to the written texts produced by Greenpeace (leaflets and texts on the Greenpeace web site). It takes place on the web site of Crops Ltd, including a combination of positive self-representation and arguments for key values of the company (see above). Crops Ltd underlines the importance of "an open dialogue with cultivators, general public, authorities and organisations within all areas surrounding the enterprise operated by the company" and also attempts to create an image of enlightening or educating the man in the street: "We want to take our part in the responsibility to provide the general public the basic data needed to take a stance in this issue." Worth mentioning is that Crops Ltd described an informational meeting for local beekeepers and central authorities like the SBA as "a new start for continued dialogue". The description is a bit ironic: the information manager at Crops Ltd denied the author of this article and other Swedish researchers access to an informational meeting in April 2002 regarding the Greenpeace campaign in Croptown. The motivation behind the denial was that the beekeepers did not want the presence of researchers. However, when the research team contacted the beekeepers after the meeting, they declared that they never opposed the presence of the research team at the actual meeting.

Interesting is the wording in the communication or rather the change of established wording. Instead of using *field trial* or *deliberate release,* Crops Ltd constructs a new phrase, *refinement area* (cf. the changes of wording by Greenpeace).

F. Conclusions on citizenship in Swedish GMO discourse

In this section, conclusions regarding types of citizenship will be drawn. It is possible to discern different types of citizenship. The citizenship constructed within the referral procedure I have described represented citizenship as an attempt to formulate the pre-constructed citizenship in section D on the discursive practice. Citizenship in this case is constructed around the application and the utterances from authorities, applying company, and referrals contrary to the public citizenship.

We know that Greenpeace generally is an activist actor, also in this analysed case of GMO canola. Contrary to the procedural structure, this activist structure is not grounded in law but in politics. The main difference is that activist structure is public. An investigation of the mass media coverage of GMOs in Sweden (Möllerström 2004) clearly demonstrated that the GMO topic hardly received any attention at all (with exception of the Greenpeace activities in April-May 2002). GMO is in other words a non-topic. The citizenship emerging from the Greenpeace campaign can be labeled public citizenship. It is created outside the procedure also encompassing genres as letters to the editor from single citizens as well as debate articles.

We should bear in mind that the public citizenship formed by Greenpeace also is a form of represented citizenship, since Greenpeace takes action in its own interest. Greenpeace does not take the role of a democratic initiator trying to help Swedes take sides in the question of genetically modified organisms by providing unbiased information. Instead, Greenpeace acts for its own interests, ideals and ideas, maintaining a form of represented citizenship, even though it is formed publicly. Represented citizenship can also be found at the web site of Crops Ltd: "We want to take our part in the responsibility to provide the general public the basic data needed to take a stance in this issue." And since Greenpeace takes part in the referral procedure since 2004, it seems possible to combine represented citizenship within the system with the outsider position as well as public citizenship.

So – do these different forms of citizenship conflict with each other? And what about the non-existing individual citizenship in this Swedish context? (Of course, this does not preclude the existence of an individual Swedish citizenship in other contexts.) Are there any possibilities for a strong individual Swedish citizenship in the GMO discourse to develop? Being pessimistic (or realistic in the light of what have been described above), the answer would be no. However, in some cases the situation may also be interpreted more optimistically. The opinion of a local citizen living in Croptown has a most specific background. His utterance on GMO crops seems to contradict this optimistic view: "somehow i think that i feel TRUST that it's done in the right WAY you know" However, this exclusion of self-interest and commitment can be explained. The citizen does not want to question GMO crops as he lives in the small municipality of Croptown, dominated by and dependent upon Crops Ltd and its work on plant breeding. But when recording an interview with four persons having lunch in Croptown but not living there, the opinions on GMOs were much more critical. When questioned upon the possibilities of obtaining more information on deliberate releases of GMO, one of the men said:

> [I don't think] that you there's any eh:: then you REALly have to dive DEEP into this if you want to search OUT the ANswers to the questions and I don't think it's so easy for us: to to do I don't know where to TURN even an:: you want to search in THIS then maybe you have to go to the LIBrary if there's anything written at all in SUCH places (-) then THEN it's not so easy at least it's it's not it's not something that you dive into every DAY

My interpretation of this utterance is that the single citizen finds it difficult to know where and how to look for information in order to form an opinion. What is important to bear in mind is that the interviewed was a man in his fifties, probably non- academic. The younger and the more educated (lower age and higher education are often correlated) the citizen is, the likelier they are to know how to obtain information on the topic, and the likelier they are to participate in the public debate.

As mentioned, GMO crops have been a non-topic in Swedish media. And topics not covered by mass media do not easily become the talk of the day among citizens. The reasons for their lack of coverage are hard to pin down. One explanation is that the traditional responsibilities of the SBA are not controversial at all: animal health, welfare, subsidies, economic accounts on agriculture, etc. Hence, the characteristic bureaucracy and dullness attributed to these uncontroversial issues is transposed to GMO crops. In interviews with SBA officials, the impression is that they lack the knowledge and motivation to implement the EU directive on extended involvement of single citizens in GMO issues. In the end, this is a political question. The Swedish parliament and government have the capability to promote the interest and the commitment among citizens by commissioning central authorities in the field (SBA, SEPA, GTAB) to initiate information campaigns. Discussions on the ethical aspects of GMO of course would be a key issue.

The principle of transparency within the Swedish legislative tradition offers great possibilities for committed individuals to perform individual citizenship. However, it will take long time for individual citizenship to develop in Sweden as a norm due to the total dominance of and reliance upon represented citizenship and, as a consequence, the lack of tradition and communicative infrastructure for acting an individual citizenship. Hopefully, it will be possible in the future to combine represented citizenship (based on juridical and administrative thoroughness) with not only public citizenship (based on media debates and activism) but also with an individual citizenship based on the commitment of individuals. It is important to bear in mind that committed single citizens do not gain maximal influence and strength when acting individually. Therefore, the best way to obtain results in societal issues is to unite in an organisation of some kind (e.g. interest group, union, political party). The key issue is not to act individually, but to make use of the opportunities to obtain information provided by the principle of transparency. An authority receiving many requests for texts regarding a certain topic will most likely be influenced by this interest and commitment!

References

Baier, Matthias, Holsánová, Jana, Hydén, Håkan, and Rahm, Henrick (2004): Country report for Sweden: final report of the research project PARADYS to the European' Commission

Fairclough, Norman (1992): Discourse and Social Change Cambridge: Polity Press

Fairclough, Norman (1995): Media Discourse London etc.: Edward Arnold

Fairclough, Norman (2003): Analyzing Discourse London & New York: Routledge

Fairclough, Norman, Pardoe, Simon and Szerszynski, Bronislaw (2006): "Critical Discourse Analysis and Citizenship" In: Hausendorf, Heiko & Alfons Bora (eds.): Analyzing Citizenship Talk: Social positioning in political and legal decision-making processes Amsterdam & Philadelphia: John Benjamins Publishing Company

Möllerström, Veselinka (2004): Swedish media coverage on GMO Unpublished paper Department of Sociology, Lund University

CHAPTER SEVEN

PARTICIPATION IN ITALY: THE PUBLIC AND GENETICALLY MODIFIED CROPS

Elena Collavin

A. Introduction

Distrust of the public, risk, and uncertainty associated with the development and use of technological products elicit calls for the inclusion of lay citizens in the decision-making processes that oversee the adoption of controversial technological products (Irwin 1995). EU policy makers assert the necessity and value of implementing forms of governance that include the broader public in making decisions related to controversial technologies (Abels 2002). Among policy scholars there is a general understanding that increased public participation yields both better and more democratic decisions. However, researchers have only recently begun to scrutinize the effectiveness of actual participatory efforts. In the context of food biotechnologies, a European Union Directive requires all Member States to consult the public before genetically modified crops are cultivated in the open for experimental purposes (EU Directive 2001/18). The various ways in which such consultations with the public have been devised and carried out in different Member States, and the notion of citizenship entailed by those country-specific participative forms, have been the objects of a multinational study (Bora & Hausendorf 2004; Bora & Hausendorf 2006) conducted with both a sociological and socio-linguistic approach. Building on the results of the Bora and Hausendorf study carried out in Italy (Collavin & Pellegrini 2004) the present work proposes data-rooted reflections over the nature of public participation in Italy in the context of food GMOs.

First I will briefly illustrate some of the key features and philosophical assumptions of inclusive forms of assessing new technologies. The Italian case suggests adopting a perspective built on the notion of public participation in conjunction with current processes of representative democracies. In the following I will consider the Italian situation. I will look closely at key texts in the record of public engagement with food biotechnologies in Italy. I will answer the following questions: How has public participation taken form in Italy in the context of food biotechnologies? What has been the impact of public participation in Italy on the current regulation of GM farming? This paper is therefore a contribution from an empirical perspective to the ongoing discussion on participatory science and its current relevance for governance.

B. Participation and power

Biotechnologies have become a key terrain for confronting the challenge that scientific developments pose to democratic forms of government. Worldwide public debate has encouraged theoretical discussions among political theorists (David 2005) and stimulated an array of experimental and empirical attempts to better the decision-making process by admitting – in one form or other – more individuals into the procedure, especially more diverse and dispassionate individuals. The reason for having participation in a democracy is first of all normative. All democratic theories imply some level of participation of the public, at least as citizens with right to elect their representatives. However, for both theorists and policy makers advocating strong democracy, the reasons for greater and more direct participation of the public are primarily functional. Increasing public participation is assumed to democratize decisions, particularly in highly complex domains pertaining to the fields of science and technology (Bechmann 1993). EU policy makers often use "participation" and "democratization" as causally correlated concepts, where the former is assumed to lead to the latter. Participation is given a number of positive normative, epistemological, ethical and societal attributes. A good example of the discursive repertoire (Potter & Wetherell 1987) of this type of participatory stance is offered by the 2001 White Paper on European Governance. The programmatic document begins acknowledging a widening gap between citizens and institutions. With the aim of regaining both the trust and interest of citizens, the White Paper enlists participation as one of the five recommended principles of good governance:

> Participation. The quality, relevance and effectiveness of EU policies depend on ensuring wide participation throughout the policy chain – from conception to implementation. Improved participation is likely to create more confidence in the end result and in the Institutions which deliver policies. Participation crucially depends on central governments

> following an inclusive approach when developing and implementing EU policies. (White paper on European Governance: 10)

Breaking down the implicit assumptions extolled in the above quote, I will list in the form of five propositions the beliefs about participation expressed by EU policy makers: Participation improves the quality of decisions. Participation improves the effectiveness of decisions. Participation improves confidence in the outcome of decisions. Participation increases the level of trust in government. Participation improves the relationship between the citizen and institutions.

Crucially, participation is expected to produce the above mentioned outcomes when applied "from conception to implementation". Good governance then means that citizens should be able to participate at every stage of the political and administrative decision-making pipeline. This philosophy, often referred to as new governance, is inspired by the standpoints of deliberative democracy (Elster 1998), which relies on the model of a citizen who lives up to his or her idealized qualities of being a rational, detached, and morally objective individual concerned with the public good (Price 2000). Citizens characterized as above can represent the public interest in a way that neither appointed politicians nor stakeholders (for example scientific experts, anti-GMO activists and business representatives) can, given their vested interest in the matter. Furthermore, the logic underlying calls for including the public in decisions encompassing highly technical aspects resides precisely in the need to broaden the spectrum of criteria for opting one way or another. Scholars have written about the need to "free the voices" (Irwin 1995) of non-specialists, for such voices provide enriching perspectives to a new paradigm of science which must embrace, rather than erase, the structural uncertainty intrinsic in technological advancement. According to the participatory standpoint, strictly scientific arguments need to be integrated with socially relevant criteria, which are not represented by the expertise of a panel of technocrats. Public participation brings "social intelligence" (Burgess & Chilvers 2006) to the decision, enriching the discussion with considerations that are key to the life of a society but are not given room in technocratic forms of decision-making. The public, as lay citizens with no personal investment (either ideological or financial) in the decision, should play a key role in participative forms of decision-making. However, it is also true that stakeholders, administrators and scientific experts inevitably play an important role in any such effort: to enlarge the pool of decision makers they are the sponsors, the organizers, and the sources of information for the lay citizens participating. Taxonomies of participative modalities (also called "Engagement strategies" and "Participative Technology Assessments") tend to categorize the many forms of public engagement on a continuum that goes from the weakest possible form of participation to the strongest form of engagement. Here I will follow the six steps of classification provided by Burgess & Chilvers (2006). At the weakest end are provisions for informing and educating the public without the public being able to give any feedback. Information can come in the form of TV programs, newspaper articles, leaflets, websites, displays and booklets. Among these forms of public involvement are public meetings (Fiorino 1990) and on line consultations. Forms of consultation, such as questionnaires, surveys, interviews, and focus groups are considered to be one step further. In these cases it is the social researcher who provides the link between the public and the decision-maker, by summing up the results of the consultations in a report for the sponsors. Current forms of public participation are largely limited to these three levels (Burgess & Chilvers 2006). Stronger forms of public involvement are more dialogic, and they aim to create a social space where stakeholders and lay citizens are encouraged to voice their thoughts and experiences "without hindrance" (Burgess & Chilvers 2006: 721). These dialogical forms of engagement strategies are best distinguished looking at who are the key actors involved in the process. Some procedures focus on local stakeholders as representatives of a community, who may engage in the decision-making process for extended periods, developing fruitful relations with the decision-makers. Among these forms are workshops and participatory research (Fischer 2000). In other procedures instead professional stakeholders are involved under the assumption that they have specialist knowledge and can help frame the issue from their own professional perspective. During stakeholder dialogue, through collaborative analysis, or multi-criteria mapping (Stirling & Mayer 2001), decision-makers and expert stakeholders differentiate between the key areas of discussion, and produce documents which offer policy makers a guide to what matters most to those more knowledgeable in the field. Other tools, like consensus conferences (Joss & Durant 1995) and deliberative mapping (Davies & al. 2003; Davies & Burgess 2004) engage not stakeholders but lay citizens to represent the broader public. These forms of participation put the citizens at the center. Citizens are offered first hand information in person by specialists, and have the power to ask for clarification and question the experts interacting with them freely, introducing additional perspectives to the topic. Citizens eventually address the decision-makers with a final document which contains comments and recommendations. Abels (this volume) offers a different typology of a variety of forms of participative technology assessment, categorizing them according to the kind of actors involved in the assessment, and consequentially according to the kind of democratic theory which underlies each different participatory effort. Indeed, while participation and democratization go hand in hand in general terms, participation acquires different meanings depending on how one assumes its requirements are being fulfilled. For instance, any participative effort that puts stakeholders at the center of the process reflects a view of democracy that relies on the competition of different interest groups for its realization. In other words, this practice is inscribed in a view of democracy as pluralism, a condition in which the public good is guaranteed by the competition of citizens united into interest groups who pressure the administration into making the decisions that most suit the groups' best interests. Other participative technology assessments instead stand on a deliberative theory of what democracy should be. Analytic-deliberative processes (Stern & Fineberg 1996) for instance, rely on a structured procedure that allows for evidence to emerge in an unbiased environment. The procedure should foster high quality argumentation free of partisan biases. Ideally, participants should be able to reach consensus on the best possible decision by being rational and open to factual information. These forms of technology assessment rely on the participation of a very small number of lay citizens who are involved in extended dialogical consultations with experts and policy-makers. The validity of the outcome depends chiefly on the quality of the procedure, which is deemed to foster the distillation of worthy arguments and high quality decisional outcomes. Democratization in this case is fulfilled not by admitting more citizens to the decision-making process, but by maintaining a very high-quality level of discussion. As Abels (this volume) remarks, some deliberative forms of decision-making might in fact turn out to be elitist forms of decision-making. Because upholding the high quality of the discussion requires the participation of a handful of articulate, skillful individuals participate, one could question who, among the citizens, might be fit to make a contribution.

The study of concrete episodes of participation highlights some intrinsic problems that are bound to plague any participative effort. Among those, the question of who actually participates in participatory activities is central. Lay people are mostly not eager to put time and effort in demanding deliberative processes in which they feel as they have no immediate stake. This usually leaves the stage to those already committed to a particular course of action. Furthermore, assessments and opinions collected from a representative sample of a population cannot be given too much weight. After all, if those polled know nothing about an issue which requires some thought to be mastered, then how much should their opinion count? (Burgess & Chilvers 2006). These unresolved concerns leave open the issue of how to implement participative efforts to which all parties are willing to subscribe.

Burgess and Chilvers (2006) argue in favor of protracted deliberative processes which can bring a unique epistemological value to the decisions. So far, most current forms of public engagement have been limited to less interactive and dialogical strategies. This fact makes it difficult to empirically assess if strongly deliberative processes do in practice yield better and more widely welcomed decisions. According to Burgess and Chilvers (ibid.), for instance, the unsatisfactory outcome of a broad public consultation such as GM Nation? might be explained by the failure to involve the public in more deliberative activities while relying solely on weaker forms of consultation (i.e. public meetings, press and website information, and online forums). Having followed the debate on food biotechnologies in Italy since 2001, I have concerns with the achievability of effective deliberative forms of decision-making in Italy in the context of GMOs. The first concern regards the expected outcome of the process. Burgess & Chilvers (2006) state that:

> A fundamental purpose of participatory activity from the perspective of the sponsor (and of the participants if they are committed to co-operative social action), is to achieve agreement by consensus, with the end result being commitment both to the agreement and to its purpose.
> (Burgess & Chilvers, 2006: 721)

The expectation of consensus under deliberative models of participative strategies has its roots in a Habermasian notion of cooperative communication (Eriksen 2003). Participants are expected to act as rational beings eager to listen to others and prepared to be convinced by the best argument. In order to achieve such openness and freedom, subjects must relinquish or overcome ideological stances. The debate must be carried out in a condition of serenity and openness. However, in Italy for instance, the discourse around food biotechnologies has taken radically antagonistic modalities which leave little space for an intellectually honest and dispassionate dialogue (Collavin 2007). Cooperation and collaboration presupposed in deliberative forms of decision-making are not easily achievable in a highly controversial and polarized field. Agreement by consensus might not be attainable in the Italian context and perhaps not in other contexts either. For instance there are no indications that prolonged debates in the British context would have produced a further consensus between committed participants [see the discussion of the experiment by Horlick-Jones et al. (2004) and Rowe et al. (2005)]. In the Italian democracy, publicly relevant resolutions (first of all legislation) are still reached by lobbying and bargaining rather than with rational argumentation (Bobbio 1984). Even the outcome of participative processes is the pronouncement of participants but not necessarily the expression of consensus between parties. Furthermore, proponents of participative deliberative processes downplay power inequalities reflected in decision-making procedures, such as the ones involved in allowing the cultivation of GM crops. Sponsored experiments, in which institutions invite citizens and stakeholders to make contributions – without a clear commitment to follow through on decisions made by the public – have little resemblance to real episodes of citizens' struggle to obtain a voice in decisions that are exclusively in the hands of technocrats. The gay community in the U.S. undertook a fierce campaign to influence the decisions to develop, test and distribute new drugs to control H.I.V.. In 1987 in Boston, Aids Treatment Activists welcomed the Food and Drug Administration representatives at a public forum brandishing wristwatches aloft. The message was clear: people affected by the virus did not have time to wait while scientists and the FDA took time to run lengthy testing on new drugs. By 1992 some of the same activists sat as voting members of the committees of the AIDS Clinical Trials Group (Epstein 2000: 15). The inclusion of representatives of the gay pressure groups in the panels of decision-making experts resulted in quicker development and availability of new drugs to those affected by the syndrome (ibid.). This is a case of a community affected by one issue that lobbies to make its voice heard. Public participation in this and many other instances meant forcing the government to take into account measures taken by active minorities, rather than stances voiced during participation in government-organized initiatives. "Participation" should involve having some voice in the outcome. Under the current circumstances, however, participative experiments are oftentimes dissociated from institutional settings and hardly alter the trajectories of institutional decision-makers. Participative forms of appraising new technologies greatly differ in scope and ambition. Abels (this volume) clarifies that thus far, participatory assessments have had an almost exclusive advisory nature, and that participation is still far from integrated into the systematic functioning of representative democracies. To date, participative assessments have not been clearly consequential for the decisions to which they were called to contribute. More should be said about the fact that besides fostering dialogue and broadening views, factual participation should involve handing over some power to subjects that traditionally have been excluded from the decision-making process. Public participation has to do with the inclusion of "hard values" (Funtowicz & Ravetz 1992), and the acquisition of "social intelligence" in the context of otherwise unrepresentative fact-based debates (Burgess & Chilvers 2006). However, broadening the perspective of appointed experts to include a multiplicity of social voices ultimately implies that such voices must be allowed to take an oppositional role within the institutional arena. Participation entails a redistribution of power in society. In the classic formulation offered by Arnstein:

> citizen participation is a categorical term for citizen power. It is the redistribution of power that enables the have-not citizens, presently excluded from the political and economic processes, to be deliberately included in the future. It is the strategy by which the have-nots join in determining how information is shared, goals and policies are set, tax resources are allocated, programs are operated, and benefits like contracts and patronage are parceled out. In short, it is the means by which they can induce significant social reform which enables them to share in the benefits of the affluent society. (Arnstein 1969)

No matter which form it takes, participation not integrated in the institutional deliberation is too weak to bring about the dramatic changes expected in the relationship between the public and their institutions.

C. Public engagement with food biotechnologies in Italy

Having briefly discussed how scholars describe participative forms of decision-making, I will now look at the form that public participation took in Italy over the contested issue of food biotechnologies. Italy is a peculiar case in respect to food biotechnologies regulation. In every other E.U. Member State genetically modified crops are being cultivated for research and in a growing number of cases for commercial purpose as well. In Italy instead both kinds of cultivation are banned[1]. Despite prescriptions in E.U. directives and regulations Italy has managed to de facto outlaw the cultivation of GMOs. Currently, attempting to plant in Italy the same GM corn commonly harvested in Spain is punishable with a hefty fine and possible prison time. Violators also face the prospect of lawsuits for damages brought by local administrations and neighboring farmers. The most recent Eurobarometer on biotechnologies was released in 2006. It reports data collected in 2005. At the time, 34% of Italians who participated in the survey expressed "support for GM foods" (Eurobarometer 64.3: 21). Public support for GMOs is low in Italy, however, other countries expressed even lower support. Nevertheless, lack of support for GMOs as expressed by the results of the Eurobarometer poll on biotechnologies is not associated with their actual cultivation in a country. According to the Eurobarometer, only 20% of the French support GM foods (Eurobarometer 64.3: 21), but in 2007 20, 000 hectares in France were cultivated with GM corn. In Spain, where public support is 34%, just like in Italy (Eurobarometer 64.3: 21), about 75, 000 hectares of corn, corresponding to 25% of all the corn produced were genetically modified. If the Eurobarometer survey provides some evidence of EU citizens' standpoints, then there is a gap between citizens expressed will and their countries policies in respect to GMOs. Democracy is not served by simply following what the majority wants. However, it is remarkable that by far the most ambitious public consultation to date regarding the topic of biotechnologies, "GM nation?", which involved about 36,000 people (Burgess & Chilvers 2006), has left every party involved unsatisfied. After consulting the public, the government decided to go ahead and authorize further experiments and commercial cultivation of GMOs, despite the fact that participating public had clearly indicated its will to halt them. Scholars have remarked that the decisions of the government to allow commercial cultivation of GM crops took little account of the results of the consultation; meanwhile, experts undermined the representative weight of the participants, who they say could not legitimately speak for the British public.

---

[1] Although there are still a few field trials, no new ones could be authorized under the current legislative frame.

D. The public outside the frame: Anti-transgenic declarations

Our study of how decisions were carried out in Italy in respect to authorizing field trials with GM crops showed that despite the requirements of E.U. Directive 2001/18, local citizens were not participating at any level in the decisions made by the designated authority (the Inter Ministerial Commission for Biotechnologies). Citizens were not informed of ongoing experiments – let alone summoned to participate, evaluate or have any influence in the decision (Collavin & Pellegrini 2004). After the late implementation of the 2001/18 directive, Italian institutions provided only pro forma spaces for the expression of public opinions on single experiments with GM plants.[2] Furthermore, contrary to what happened in several Member States, Italian institutions responsible for the authorization of field trials did not organize any form of public discussion, nor did they make any systematic effort to provide the public with information on the subject of food biotechnologies. Institutions did not organize consensus conferences, public meetings, or large scale consultations with the public. Institutions did not ask the general public to express opinions or raise questions. In other words, contrary to the dictate of international agreements and European Directives, Italian institutions did not offer citizens any opportunity to come close to the table of the decision-makers. The main form in which the Italian public participated in the institutional decisions taken on the subject of biotechnologies has been with the issuing of local resolutions against GMOs. These resolutions are not the outcome of referenda held locally, or of organized consultations between citizens, stakeholders, and administrators. Rather, they are declarations issued by mayors and council representatives. The mayor and the council members are elected figures who represent local citizens. As such, they issued resolutions declaring their councils "antitransgenici". The first local administration to issue a formal resolution against GMOs was the council of Bubbio, a small village in the Asti province. The Asti geographic area, in the north-west of Italy, is famous for its food products, in particular for the sparkling wine spumante. Bubbio decided to become a "Council free

[2] On the Italian Biosafety Clearing House website, it is now possible to subscribe to a newsletter. The newsletter would inform all subscribers about new Italian requests for authorizations to carry out open air experiments with GMOs. There is no mention of any commitment or obligation to reply to the comments received on the part of responsible authorities.

from GMOs" on August, 13, 1999. Bubbio's vice mayor at the time, Gianfranco Torelli, is a wine maker, and committed to organic farming and the anti-GMO cause. He promoted the resolution and is an active figure in Italy in opposition to the introduction of genetically modified foods and crops. The official text of the Bubbio resolution contains, in a nutshell, the most widely voiced arguments against GMOs heard in Italy. I thus present it in translation and shall point out its main tenets below. The Bubbio declaration is important for two reasons: The first is that the document exemplifies the main arguments for rejecting food biotechnologies found in Italy. It is a perfect compendium of the main-stream Italian discourse over food biotechnologies. The second reason is that the Bubbio declaration is the first of many resolutions at a local level that currently dictate the destiny of food biotechnology research and farming in Italy. My translation does not correct some linguistic awkwardnesses (i.e. "reproductive chain" for "productive chain" and "irreversible dangers" for, I guss, "irreversible damage".)

Bubbio Council
Asti Province
ANTI-TRANSGENIC COUNCIL

The Council assembly, taking into account the fact that the introduction of the farming of GMOs has raised great doubts and perplexities in public opinion

- for ethical reasons,
- for the consequences on the health of citizens,
- for the irreversible dangers to the ecosystem,
- for the further disparity that it would create between rich countries and developing countries; *Considering* that the new farming model proposed is in clear contradiction with that practiced in our area, which is strongly linked with traditions and with the features of the territory; *Having decided*, in the light of what is mentioned above, by virtue of the scope of its authority, to take a stand against the introduction into agriculture of genetically modified organisms; *Having taken into account* the support of the Council Secretary, in accordance with article 53 of the law 142/90, concerning the administrative regularity of the present document; unanimously and concertedly with votes expressed by raising hands; *decides:*
- to declare the council of Bubbio an "anti-transgenic council"
- to post below the street signs at the entrance of the village the sign "Anti-transgenic council"

- To forbid, in all the territory of the council, experiments, farming, and animal farming of living organisms, both vegetal and animal, obtained using genetic manipulation
- To create an ad hoc council commission initially composed of the vice mayor and two council members, which may be composed in the future of other persons, in order to pursue the following aims:
- To inform, using meetings, postings and letters, the producers in the council territory (winemakers, ham producers, bakers and confectioners) about the risks of the use of genetically modified products in the productive chain (for example eggs from chickens fed with GMO feed, selected yeasts, enzymes, ascorbic acid obtained with methodologies that imply the use of GMOs and so on)
- To inform, using meetings, postings and letters, the resellers in the council territory about the risks of selling foods from producers who have been accused of using genetically modified products in the reproduction chain
- To inform the citizens, using meetings, postings and letters, about the risks linked with the eating of products obtained with GMOs, and to start a serious campaign for alimentary education in the use of traditional quality products
- To see, during events organized by the local association for Bubbio, to an effective promotion of local products promulgating the message against genetically modified products in the most effective manner.

Notably, this is a resolution which provides assessments and details future course of action. This is not an advisory document offered to the Italian government, nor the attempt on the part of a local authority to access the institutional process of decision-making either at national or European level. While I hold this as a key document in the history of participative efforts in Italy in the debate over GMOs, its characteristics do not fit any existing model of participative technology assessment. The text enlists four kinds of reasons for a declaration against GMOs. The first reason is "ethical" which entails that GMOs are unethical. The attribution is not developed any further, as the document focuses elsewhere, but this aspect is mentioned as the first motive for issuing the resolution. In the rest of the document there are mentions of other reasons why GMOs may be considered "unethical." The declaration has polemical features that invoke several argumentative levels in order to attack its target. The first reason why GMOs are unethical most likely has to do with the intrinsic character of genetically modified plants. "Unethical" may refer to the practice of introducing alien genes into an organism, a concern widely voiced. The second reason, "the consequences on the health of citizens", uses an existential presupposition, triggered by the definite article, to attribute with implicit certainty unhealthy properties to GMOs. Noticeably, there is no hedge to the claim. The definite article presupposes the existence of what one must imagine as undesirable consequences for citizens' health. The document's assertiveness characterizes it as not only the definitive resolution of a local authority, but also as uncompromisingly ideological with no concessions to dissonant views. Irreversible dangers to the ecosystem are also pragmatically presupposed. The fourth impetus refers to what can be called the "Social Justice" concern with GMOs. GMOs raise concerns because it is argued that their introduction results in impoverishing already underdeveloped areas of the world, while the western corporations holding the patents for genetically modified plants (Shiva 1999). The Bubbio declaration introduces a fifth argument, although not in the opening list of concerns. This argument is linked to matters of tradition, culture and identity. While these aspects emerge with consistency in the Italian data, they have so far received little attention in the literature on biotechnologies (See for instance Bauer & Gaskell 2002). This concern strongly characterizes the food biotechnology debate in Italy. In the Bubbio declaration GMOs are described as opposed to what farming is in "our" area, where the plural first person possessive indicates a community and an identity which encompasses farming practices. Tradition and territoriality are seen as values "in clear contradiction" with GMOs. Here, GMOs are something bigger and more consequential then pest-resistant crops. GMOs are depicted as the wrong approach to agriculture; they are the product of an entire worldview that is rejected here. The Bubbio resolution represents food biotechnologies as dangerous for health, the environment, and local culture and economy. In particular, GMOs are depicted as a threat to the current way of farming, which is in turn strongly associated with tradition and with the local geography and terrain. On the roads entering each one of the anti-transgenic Italian councils, the one sign announcing the name of the city or of the village is supplemented by another that reads "comune antitransgenico". In the past, many Italian Councils led a campaign against nuclear power using the same strategy. A permanent sign was posted under the city name that read "comune denuclearizzato" a neologism, loosely translatable as "Nuclear free Council". There is no doubt that the anti-nuclear power strategy has inspired the "commune antitransgenico" campaign. According to the official website of the anti transgenic councils, 451 of the over 8,100 Italian councils have declared themselves to be "antitransgenici," (Comune Antitransgenico, n.d.). However, the website of the anti-transgenic councils and regions has not been updated since 2004. Since then more councils have joined the number of the ones who issued similar declarations.

E. Anti-transgenic regions

More remarkably, all Italian regional governments have issued some piece of legislation opposing GMOs. In some regions, GMOs cannot be cultivated and field trials are forbidden (Umbria, Regional Law N.20, 21st August 2001). In others GM foods cannot be served in any publicly owned facility like schools and hospitals (Campania, Law N. 15, 24th November 2001). In the Marche region, producers using food components that are derived from or contain GMOs are excluded from all regional incentives to the food industry. Also, it is forbidden to serve GMOs in any community restaurant depending on or directly owned by the region. (Marche Regional Law N. 5, 3rd March 2004). In other regions still, authorities offer incentives and monetary support to those who commit to GM-free farming practices in order to discourage the cultivation of GMOs and to promote organic and traditional farming (Trento Province, Law N. 4, 28th March 2003). Adhering to the "Italia libera da OGM" campaign, regional and local authorities have also banned GM foods from any publicly run or subsidized canteen. In some regions food caterers who carry GM products cannot participate in public bids. While the legal status of such bans is dubious due to contrary EU regulations, these measures are evidence of a consistent institutional rejection of food biotechnologies. Most importantly, these provisions have come to play a key role in the current legal regulation on GMOs.

F. The Italian law on coexistence

On July 23rd, 2003 the EU Commission issued a Recommendation requiring that each Member State finds ways to guarantee coexistence between genetically modified and non-genetically modified crops. "Coexistence" refers to the need to provide principles for the safe commercial cultivation of both GM and non-GM crops. The Commission issued its recommendation based on the fact that a growing number of GM crops can be legally farmed in all Member States. Given this reality, the Commission asked Member States to put in place measures to prevent non GM and GM plants from cross breeding. The measures include: maintaining distance between GM and non GM crops, devising natural barriers for pollens, and choosing plants that flower in different times of the year. The Italian law N. 5, dated 28 January 2005 turns a previous Government Decree, the so called "Coexistence Decree" (Decreto Legislativo n.279), issued in November 2004, into a permanent law of the Republic.[3] The law regulates the terms under which authorized GMOs may be cultivated in Italy. The parliamentary debate was heated. People both in and outside the Parliament argued that safe coexistence between genetically modified and non-genetically modified crops is impossible in Italy, supported by studies that show how pollen travels long distances. Given the small average size of farms in Italy and other features of the Italian landscape, many argue that it is impossible to guarantee that GM and non-GM crops would not interbreed. The consequences would be contamination of non-GM crops and hence loss and damage for conventional and organic farmers. As a result, the argument goes, the only way to guarantee farmers and consumers GM-free crops is to forbid the cultivation of GMOs in the whole country. The position is incompatible with European legislation, which requires that no barriers be posed by an individual country to products that have been approved for commercial use in the Union (art. 22 of the EU2001/18 Directive). Furthermore, the EU Court has dismissed the arguments when it was put forward by Austria along with a detailed scientific report on the ground that it is not backed up by scientific evidence not Scientifically justified (EU Court overturns Austrian law to ban GM, October 2005). While sharing the same concerns, Italian legislators took a different road than the one taken by the Austrian authorities. The Italian law defines the normative frame for the coexistence between transgenic crops (other than those grown for experimentation) and conventional and organic crops, "with the aim of not compromising biodiversity of the natural environment and to guarantee freedom of economic initiative,

[3] A Government Decree is a temporary law promulgated by the executive branch of the government, which is valid for 60 days. A Decree loses its effect unless it is reissued, if within 60 days the two chambers of the Parliament fail to approve it and convert it into a permanent law.

the right to choose for the consumer, and the quality and typical features of national food production."(Art.1) Art.2 focuses on the "protection of the coexistence principle".[4] The principle states that "different types of crops (transgenic, traditional, organic) must be farmed so that the farming of one type does not compromise the farming of another type of crop". Coexistence must protect "peculiarities and specific producing features" of crops, and must avoid "any form of contact between transgenic and conventional and organic seeds." Article 2-bis specifies that introducing GM crops must not prejudice preexisting farming practices, and that those practices should not need to be changed because of GM crops. Article 3 states that coexistence "must guarantee the right of choice for farmers, other dealers along the food chain, and consumers to choose between conventional, organic and transgenic products, and therefore GMOs must be cultivated in a segregated food chain." The key feature of the law is the following: legislators assign to regions the task of "adopting a plan for coexistence". The plan includes devising the technical provisions for realizing it (Art.4/1). While developing the plan regions must consult with organizations, associations and involved subjects (Art.4/2). Regions can create a monetary fund for the just compensation of possible damages caused by noncompliance with the plan for coexistence (4/3bis). Whoever wants to cultivate GMOs must notify the region, elaborate a coexistence plan, and keep a detailed register of adopted measures (Art.5/3). Regions must collect and retain all the information included in these registers (Art.5/4). Article 6 focuses on sanctions, establishing that those who fail to keep registers are subject to a fine of 5, 000 to 25, 000 Euros. Still, the most important provision of the law deals with transitional norms. Article 8 states that:

> in order to achieve the aims specified in article 1 [that is, safe coexistence], until the adoption of the specific legal provisions of article 4 [that is, regional legislation on coexistence], transgenic cultivation, aside from cultivation for research, is not allowed.

No deadline is specified for the regions to devise coexistence plans. Without fixed dates for the regions to provide legal ways to farm authorized GMOs, their cultivation is effectively banned indeterminately. Cultivating GMOs before the competent region has issued a law

[4] Much like the case of "precaution", "coexistence" has become a "principle" to be safeguarded by legislation. This transformation has played a role in the rhetorical battle against GMOs.

on coexistence is punishable with imprisonment from one to two years and hefty fines up to 50, 000 Euros. The provision has been called "medieval" by a representative of the Italian Association of Biotech Industries (off the record personal communication), and it may well be seen as a Machiavellian way of not complying with the decisions of EU authorities.

G. Field trials: Decree N.72 29/03/2005 for the preservation of biodiversity

As I wrote above, in the last seven years, all Italian regions have issued legislation restricting the cultivation of GMOs in their territory. This sometimes even includes banning farming for research purposes. In Italy, like everywhere in the EU, the authorization for carrying our field experiments is undertaken at national level, not at regional or local level. However, as with farming authorized GMOs on Italian soil, the government referred to the regions the authority to designate appropriate areas for experiments. The chief piece of legislation for the exclusion of field trials stands once again on the process of devolution. 'Devolution' means that national authorities delegate more power to the regions. Rome has the authority to authorizing a trial, but the regions designate suitable areas where a trial can be carried out. In the right circumstances, this might amount to a veto power. As long as no areas have been designated there is no viable place for conducting experiments. The Biodiversity Decree also requires anyone wishing to carry out an open air experiment to provide an additional risk assessment, beyond the requirements of EU legislation, on the basis of criteria specified in the Decree as well as to gauge different potential risks of the trial on a scale from "negligible" to "high". No new trials have been undertaken under these new provisions, most likely because as of this writing, no region has designated appropriate areas for this purpose.

H. National Consultation on GMOs

Between the 15th of August and the 15th of September 2007, the Foundation for Genetic Rights, an Italian anti-GMO think-tank, conducted a "National Consultation on GMOs" (Consultazione Nazionale sugli OGM). The initiative was sponsored by big caliber stakeholders committed to oppose to GMOs. COOP, the largest food chain in the

Country, was among the supporters, joined by 28 other national associations of food producers, farmer unions, consumer associations, and environmental associations. These associations united under the label "Italo-European Coalition Free from GMOs" (Italia-Europa Coalizione Liberi da OGM). The aim of the initiative was to collect three million signed votes against GMOs. The idea driving the initiative was to run an unofficial nation-wide referendum against food biotechnologies, and, with the weight of its results, seal once and for all the fate of GMOs in Italy under an avalanche of citizens' signatures. The foundation sought but did not obtain the direct funding and endorsement of the Italian government (Colombo, personal communication). However, the initiative had the support of several members of the government. The Consultazione Nazionale consisted of hundreds of local initiatives. Anti-GMO public speeches and conversations were held at street fairs and local *fairs* across the country, where organizers distributed material on GMOs and collected signatures. Hundreds of offices of the supporting associations offered their facilities for collecting signatures of citizens who subscribed to the statement:

> Do you want the agro-alimentary sector, food and its genuineness, to be the heart of development made of both people and territories, health and quality, sustainable and innovative, funded on biodiversity, free from GMOs?

In Italian: "Vuoi che l'agroalimentare, il cibo e la sua genuinità, siano il cuore dello sviluppo, fatto di persone e territori, salute e qualità, sostenibile e innovativo, fondato sulla biodiversità, libero da OGM?" The question manages to enumerate in one sentence the key concerns Italians have with food biotechnologies (Collavin 2007). Luca Colombo, the main organizer of the campaign, told me that it is hard to imagine who would not agree with such sentence. Indeed, during the two months of the national consultation the organizers collected more that three million signatures supporting the statement. Although critics in the press trashed the referendum as rhetorical and aimed at indoctrinating (Alpi and Bartolommei 2007), the over three million signatures are very likely to reinforce the inclination of the government to keep defying the prescriptions of EU legislation.

I. Conclusion

In Italy, the synergic union of economic interests, political will, and the inclination of the public is currently banning the cultivation of GM crops. Abiding EU regulations, appropriately labelled GM feed and food authorized by the EU can and are used in Italy. However, in Italy, GMOs are not farmed because open air experiments were effectively halted in 2004. The current arrangement is basically the implementation of a resolution; the country has decided to move in the direction of refusing GMOs. The role of the public in this result is of great significance. Public participation has played a key part in this outcome, but not in any of the manners currently envisioned by political science scholars or policy-makers. In the area of experimentation, legislative provisions and administrative practices have allowed citizens to express themselves on single field trials, yet only recently and in the weakest possible form. In the light of my longitudinal data, it is reasonable to assume that contributions by individual citizens, if there have been any, have hardly influenced the decision-making process. The Italian national government did not sponsor any form of direct involvement of the public in the matter of authorizing commercial growth of GM crops. The contribution of the public has come from outside the relevant legislative frame. In Italy there have been episodes of street protest, and NGOs have lobbied using familiar strategies (e.g. Greenpeace has organized periodic media-savvy stunts at the location of Monsanto in Lodi). However, episodes of people taking to the streets have not been of measurable effect in the legislation. On the contrary, public will, expressed representatively in the form of local and regional deliberations, has been a major factor in the current legal arrangement. The fact that all Italian regions and autonomous provinces have issued legislation against GMOs, and that hundreds of councils have declared themselves "liberi da OGM" and "antitransgenici" has no legal holding. Decisions on field trials are made at the national level, while decisions on allowing the commercial farming of a genetically engineered plant are made at EU level; local Italian authorities have no legal say on either matter. Local resolutions might have been meaningless. However, in this particular case, grassroots bi-partisan resistance to food biotechnologies expressed by local authorities was met halfway by the determination of the national government to resist any cultivation of GMOs. The public through its local and regional representatives had made it possible for several subsequent the Italian Governments to issue laws that currently exclude both commercial and experimental growing of GMOs. The role of local authorities has been more than simply that of support for governmental decisions. The exclusion of GMOs has been achieved through the process of devolution of power to regional authorities which have long declared their opposition to GMOs. While regions have no say over the matter of GM plants, they have been given the power to individuate suitable areas for the cultivation of GMOs. This may equal to a veto power. Given the nature of their territory, the subdivisions of land property, the type of soil, the winds, the water system and the overall necessity to fulfil the precautionary principle, regions may not be able to select any suitable site for coexistence. The same holds true for the commercial growth of GM plants. Regions that have already stated their determination to be GM-free are likely to resist the selection of areas suitable for farming GM crops. Even if the EU authorities were to insist on the individuation of regions of coexistence, the outcome is unlikely to change. Fear of substantial fines, unforeseeable liability in case of transgenic contamination, and above all a general inclination for a non-GM food market in Italy will be enough to discourage any farmer from planting GM crops in the country.

In the light of the Italian case I propose to broaden the notion of public participation as is currently used to include not only sponsored episodes of deliberation, such as consensus conferences or legal hearings, but also instances of participation expressed representatively by local institutions taking up issues outside their domain and jurisdiction. Citizens succeeded in influencing the Italian policy on GMOs via the actions of their appointed representatives at local, provincial, and regional level. Participation so conceived is not only achieved inside the window of opportunity provided to the public by institutions; it is also a form of civil action taken up spontaneously by active minorities and local communities who are outside the decision-making procedures. In Italy local resolutions have had substantial impacts *despite* legal arrangements only because they acted in a synergic manner with the actions of central government. Participation is not necessarily the expression of single individuals who address the relevant institutions, or of citizens organized in interest groups who knock on the door of the decision-makers. In the Italian case, the relevant institutions were left outside the activities of the public who did not even address them. In this case, a "wild" public has not so much taken to the streets or expressed dissent through associations or groups. Rather, it has expressed its mind through countless micro-resolutions of dubious legal standing at the level of local authorities. Furthermore the Italian situation shows that the contribution from the public, offered representatively (not directly) in the form of issuing resolutions at the council and regional level, may produce a force that can effectively resist the dispositions of the European authorities, when it converges with economic interests and political will. Indeed, the way in which decisions on GMOs are made in Italy provides a perfect example of "rubber wall" resistance to the policy adopted at EU level, including its emphasis on public participation. While think-tanks, committees, forums, and policy-makers on the EU level think hard to devise innovative ways of including the public in the decision-making process in order to make more transparent, democratic, and thoughtful decisions, in Italy decisions seem to be made in much more indirect and guileful ways. This produces something of a paradox. While in Italy there has been no platform for the debate over GMOs designed to include the public, it seems that in Italy more then everywhere in the EU, the public's negative response to cultivating GMOs has actually been implemented. In the light of the provisions included in the White Paper of Governance and the Århus Clearinghouse, two exemplary documents of the ideal participatory dynamic at EU level, participation as described in Italy appears turned upside down. At the EU level, participation is conceived of as a top-down process, taking place in a space created and managed *by* institutions for listening to citizens in a regulated setting. Institutions are then called upon to process the input from society, and eventually to issue more inclusive and effective provisions which – it is assumed – will enjoy the support of citizens. In Italy, such spaces have not been created for civil society at any level of the decision-making process. Public participation in Italy has been a force which developed outside the procedures, and rather than being integrated and contributing to the development of more democratic legislation, it is actually adding momentum to the Italian government's resistance to EU policies. Local authorities pursued their own agendas resisting the policies set by the EU.

References

Abels, G. (2002): Experts, Citizens, and Eurocrats: Towards a Policy Shift in the Governance of Biopolitics in the EU, in: European Integration online Papers 6, 19. http://eiop.or.at/eiop/texte/2002-019a.htm

Alpi, A. and Bartolommei, S. (2007): Liberi dagli OGM? Perchè? *Il Sole 24ore*, November 16 2007.

Arnstein, S. (July 1969): *A ladder of Citizen Participation in the USA*. Journal of the American Institute of Planners.

Bauer, M. W. and G. Gaskell (eds.) (2002): *Biotechnology, the making of a global controversy*, Cambridge: Cambridge University Press.

Bechmann, G. (1993): Democratic Function of Technology Assessment in Technology Policy Decision-Making. *Science and Public Policy* 20, 11–16.

Bobbio, N. (1984): *Il futuro della democrazia*. Torino, Einaudi.

Bora A. & H. Hausendorf (eds.) (2004): PARADYS Final Report to the Commission. Unpublished Report.

Bora A. and Hausendorf, H. (eds.) (2006): Analysing Citizenship Talk. Social positioning in political and legal decision-making processes. Amsterdam: John Benjamins.

Bucchi, M., and Neresini, F. (2004): Why are people hostile to biotechnologies? *ScienceSupporting online material*, Doi: 10.1126/science. Retrieved March, 12, 2005 from http://www.sciencemag.org/cgi/data/304/5678/1749/DC1/1

Burgess J. and Chilvers J. (2006): Upping the ante: a conceptual framework for designing and evaluating participatory technology assessments. *Science and Public Policy* 33 713–728.

Collavin E. and Pellegrini, G. (2004): Italy. In Bora, A. & Hausendorf, H., *PARADYS Final Report to the Commission.*

Collavin E. (2007): *Food Biotechnologies in Italy: a Social Psychological Study*. Helsinki University Social Psychology Department.

David, M. (2005): *Science in Society*. Palgrave.

Davies, G and Burgess J. (2004): Challenging the 'view from nowhere': citizen reflections on specialist expertise in a deliberative process. *Health and Place* 10, 349–361.

Davies, G., Burgess, J., Eames, M., Mayer, S., Staley, K., Stirling, A. and Williamson, D. (2003). *Deliberative Mapping: Appraising Options for Closing 'The Kidney Gap'*. Final Report to the Welcome Trust.

Deliberate releases and placing on the EU market of Genetically Modified Organisms (GMOs). Joint Research Centre. Retrieved on March, 3rd, 2007 from: http://gmoinfo.jrc.it/gmp_browse.aspx

Della Vedova, B. (2002, July 30): PAC, una riforma per lasciare tutto come è [CAP, a reform to leave things as they are]. *Il Sole 24 Ore* [Electronic version]. Retrieved October 3, 2003, from: http://coranet.radicalparty.org/pressreview/print_right.php?func=detail&par=27

Elster, J. (1998) (ed.): *Deliberative Democracy*. Cambridge University Press.

Epstein, S. (1996): *Impure Science: AIDS, Activism, and the Politics of Knowledge*. University of California Press.

Epstein, S. (2000): Democracy, Expertise, and the AIDS Treatment Activism. In D. L. Kleinman (ed.): *Science Technology and Democracy*. State University of New York press (15–32).

Eriksen E. O. (2003): *Understanding Habermas: communicative action and deliberative democracy*. Continuum.

EU Court overturns Austrian law to ban GM. (2005, October 5). Retrieved October 6, 2005, from www.europabio.org

Fiorino, D. (1990): Citizen participation and environmental risk: a survey of institutional mechanisms. *Science, Technology and Human Values* 15, 226–243.

Fischer, F. (2000): *Citizens, Experts and the Environment*. Durham NC: Duke University Press.

Fuller, S. (2000): *The Governance of Science: Ideology and the Future of the Open Society*. Buckingham: Open University Press.

Funtowicz, S. O. and Ravetz, J. R. (1992): Three types of risk assessment and the emergence of post-normal science. In *Social Theories of Risk*, eds. S Krimsky and D Golding, pp. 251–273. New York: Greenwood Press.

GM Maize growing in five EU Member States. *GMO Compass*. Last retrieved on October, 3rd, 2007, from: http://www.gmo-compass.org/eng/agri_biotechnology/gmo_planting/191.eu_growing_area.html

Horlick-Jones, T., Walls, J., Rowe, G., Pidgeon, NF, Poortinga, W. and O'Riordan, T. (2004): *A Deliberative Future? An Independent Evaluation of the GM Nation? Public Debate about the Possible Commercialisation of Transgenic Crops in Britain, 2003*. Centre for Environmental Risk, University of East Anglia: Norwich, UK.

Irwin, A. (1995): *Citizen Science*. Routledge.

Joss, S. and Durant J. (eds.) (1995): *Public Participation in Science: The Role of Consensus Conferences in Europe*. London: Science Museum.

Poppe, C., and Kjærnes, U. (2003): Trust in Food in Europe. A Comparative Analysis(National Institute for Consumer Research (SIFO) Professional Report 11(2003). Retrieved May 2, 2005, from: http://www.trustinfood.org/SEARCH/BASIS/tif0/all/publics/DDD/24.pdf

Potter, J. and Wetherell, M. (1987): *Discourse and Social Psychology*. London, Sage.

Price, D (2000): Choices without reasons: citizens' juries and policy evaluation. *Journal of Medical Ethics* 26(4), 272–276.

Regioni Libere da OGM. [website] Retrieved on May, 14, 2003 from: http://www.rfb.it/images/comuni_liberi_da_ogm/italia-ogmfree2.gif

Rowe, G., Horlick-Jones, T., Walls, J. and Pidgeon, N. (2005): Difficulties in evaluating public engagement initiatives: the evaluation of the UK *GM Nation?* public debate about transgenic crops. *Public Understanding of Science*, 14 pp. 331–352.

Shiva, V. (1999): *Stolen Harvest: The Hijacking of the Global Food Supply*. South End Press, Cambridge Massachusetts.

Stern, P. C. and Fineberg, H. V. (eds.) (1996): *Understanding Risk: Informing Decisions in a Democratic Society*. Washington DC: National Research Council.

Stirling, A. and Mayer, S. (2001): A Novel Approach to the Appraisal of Technological Risk. *Environment and Planning C*, 19, 529–555.

Wynne, B. (1995): Public understanding of science, in *Handbook of Science and Technology Studies*, S. Jasanoff et al., eds. (Thousand Oaks, CA: SAGE, 1995), 361.

Yearley, S. (2000): What does science mean in the 'public understanding of science'? In: *Between Understanding and Trust: The Public, Science and Technology*, M. Dierkes and C. von Grote, ed. (Amsterdam: Harwood, 2000): 217–236.

CHAPTER EIGHT

COMMUNICATING QUASI-CITIZENSHIP? PUBLIC PARTICIPATION IN GMO-RELEASE PERMITTING PROCEDURES IN HUNGARY – A CONVERSATION ANALYTIC APPROACH*

Zsuzsanna Iványi, András Kertész and Kornélia Marinecz

A. Introduction

1. . . . *on behalf of the Hungarian citizens* . . .

> [I myself would demand it too, and I think I say all this on behalf of the Hungarian citizens that we indeed would like to know what dangers there are, we like to know what we eat, what we are made to eat. So in any case, I believe that the community has to be involved in these things, and with their consent such laws, such regulations may be brought in, which enjoy the approval of the community] (SS/321–7)

The quotation above comes from an interview conducted with an organic farmer on the topic of biotechnology. The speaker explicitly notes that he is talking not as an individual, but on behalf of a social group he belongs to and is a representative of, namely, the Hungarian citizens. In the following statements this fact is signalled by the use of the first person plural form of the verbs. The general demand for information about the quality of food, and about possible dangers connected to them is presented to be characteristic for the group. The speaker suggests the involvement of the population as a way to satisfy this demand. Moreover, he considers legal regulations concerning the public to be subject of their consent, that is, citizens should be not only informed but also asked for opinion in the matters at issue.

This short sequence raises several questions right at the outset. Nevertheless, within the limited frames of the present study we focus only on some of them, and we do this in line with our linguistic interest,

* András Kertész' contribution to the present paper was supported by the Research Group for Theoretical Linguistics of the Hungarian Academy of Sciences at the Universities of Debrecen, Pécs and Szeged.

at that. What we are primarily interested in is: By what communicative means are the notions and ideas of participation of the public in the process of the legal-administrative procedures constructed in communication?

To answer this question, in the present paper we will apply the technique of conversation analysis. We will show that there is a striking parallel between certain central features of present-day Hungarian society and the results of our conversation analytic investigations. In particular, the communicative means of public participation, which our conversation analytic research revealed and on which we will report, are symptoms of the social setting and, as such, reflect relevant features of the latter. Our main finding will be that communication of public participation between the government and the public as well as between the other involved parties and the public in the decision making procedures we investigated is handicapped in several respects. This exposes the existence of *a very restricted kind of communicative citizenship in Hungary* that we would provisionally call 'quasi-citizenship'.

Before tackling the issues thus indicated, it would be sound to sketch some of the background assumptions that guided our research so as to clarify the key terms we are operating with. This will also allow for the specification of the basic problem of the present study.

2. *Background assumptions*

The central issue of public participation and social positioning in GMO-release permitting procedures in Hungary is the notion of *citizen* in a specific sense. Citizenship is not restricted to nationality or membership in a particular state. Rather, citizenship involves the right to participate in decision making processes, the right to being informed, and the right to act within the given legal framing (Bora and Hausendorf 2006a: 40). Accordingly, citizenship is on the one hand, not independent of the legal system of the country: on the other hand, however, it includes essentially more than the sole following of the laws in that it emerges when people are addressed as citizens by administrative bodies. Such administrative procedures of citizen participation "*provide slots* for people to enter the scene as citizens in the very sense of the word" (Bora and Hausendorf 2006b: 86; emphasis added). These slots can be *filled* by a great variety of different participatory activities during which people act as citizens in the sense mentioned, that is, make particular use of their rights to participate in decision making procedures.

In addition, recent research also assumes a substantial relationship between communication and citizenship. Therefore, we may say that *citizenship is socially realized by being communicated*. That is, citizenship as a *communicative achievement* is constituted during verbal or non-verbal interaction (Bora and Hausendorf 2006b: 86).

Thus, we have sketched the relationship between the legal framing, the notion of citizenship and the specification of the latter as communicated citizenship. Citizenship as a communicative achievement is constructed as a social position in the participatory discourse. (Bora and Hausendorf 2006b: 86). This means the following.

Participants of talk-in-interaction disclose several details regarding their social identity that might be essential for the proper understanding of their contributions (see Sacks 1967, 1972a 1972b, 1992), and also take a stand on the specific communicative situation. In other words, they position themselves and others with regard to the wider social arrangements they are referring to (in our case the GMO-release permitting procedures) and the knowledge participants might have about these.[1] In the process of social positioning they highlight those ones they consider relevant in the specific communicative setting from a variety of characteristics (characteristic features, typical activities, attitudes). Significant aspects of social positioning (see Fig.1.) are the communicated ideas of involvement, and of participation in the given social structure. We will call them *participation concepts* (see Bora and Hausendorf 2006: 26).

Accordingly, the slots left open by the legal framing can be filled by particular participatory activities whose actors realize given *participation concepts* in communication processes.

One of the key features of social positioning is its *dynamics*. This means that the participatory process itself influences the particular social positions constructed communicatively so that they may change continuously. Moreover, the dynamics of social positioning can be grasped as the relation between social positions.

[1] Particular social situation and pre-structured participation concepts in institutional and organizational talk can be considered as prototypes of the situational identities, as for instance teacher-student at school, or judge, solicitor, prosecutor in court. Zimmermann (1998: 90–95) differentiates between three types of identities in social interaction: discourse identities, situational identities, and transportable identities.

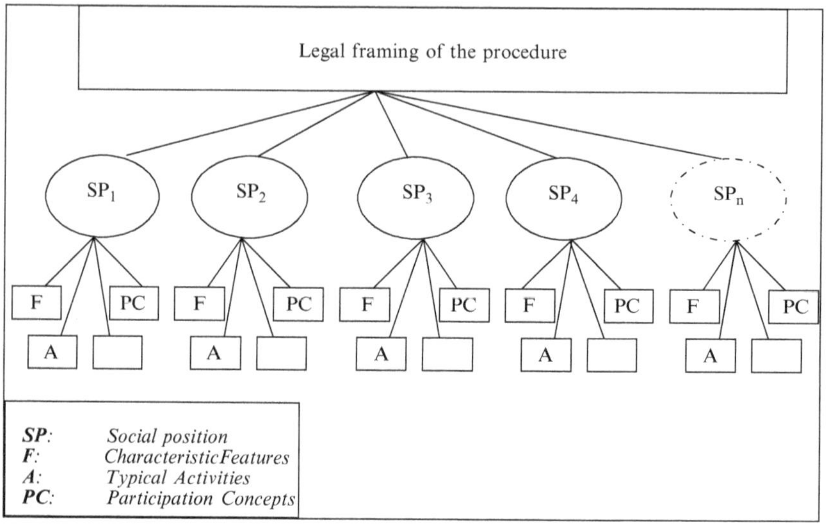

Fig. 1 Significant aspects of social positioning.

Decision making processes are typical cases of the citizens' making use of their rights to act, to negotiate, to declare their interests, to be informed adequately, and, above all, to influence decisions affecting relevant aspects of the society in which they are members. Therefore, the paper centres on the investigation of citizenship as it is communicated in particular decision making procedures.

GMO release permitting procedures were chosen as the subject matter of the investigation as typical instances of decision making processes accompanied by great social, political and economic interest (see Bora 2006).

Therefore, the question arises, in what ways social positioning as the communicative construction of citizenship can be realized in decision-making procedures. The answer is that there is a great variety of ways, which, however, share the fact that they are rooted in communicated *images of self and others*. Social positioning represents a certain kind of conversational work, a kind of "communicative problem" which has to be solved by the participants and the solution of which yields the positions. The techniques of *conversation analysis* appear to be the most appropriate approach for the study of social positioning and participation concepts. The analyst's task is the sequential, process-oriented and thematically ordered reconstruction of the way conversations are organized; of the linguistic means applied by the participants; and of the reality constructed in conversation.

3. *The structure of the paper*

In Section 1. we have already indicated the basic problem which is the focus of the present paper. Now, against the above background, it can be raised more precisely: *by what communicative means and to what extent are the slots left open by the legal framing filled with participation concepts regarding the public during a certain kind of decision-making process with respect to GMO release in Hungary?*

Accordingly, our line of argumentation will be as follows.

Since it might be evident that the ideas and notions of participation we are interested in are rooted in the legal regulation, we start the empirical work in Section 2 with the textual analysis of the relevant law.

Then, in Section 3 we will move on to our recorded data of interviews and conversations so as to find out in what way these ideas and notions are constructed in communication processes. Our method of analysis will be the particular approach to conversation analysis as elaborated in Hausendorf (2000) and summarized in Bora and Hausendorf (2006b)[2]. Our empirical research focuses on communicative processes around biotechnology, specifically in permitting procedures of GMO release in Hungary. We considered two corpora. The first corpus consists of written texts (the relevant legal laws – Act No. XXVII of 1998 on Biotechnology Activities; Act No. LXVII of 2002 on the modification of Hungarian Act No. XXVII of 1998 on Biotechnology Activities – and some newspaper articles). The second corpus involves recorded oral data of altogether 16 hours and 9 minutes.[3]

As a next step, in Section 4 we will compare the findings with respect to the law with those findings obtained by the analysis of the oral data.

From the results of these analyses we will draw conclusions concerning the way in and the extent to which concepts of public participation, as the manifestations of citizenship, are communicatively constructed in the decision making procedure at issue.

---

[2] For further details see the conclusion.

[3] Interviews with persons involved in the procedure as well as with members of the public; lectures on the topic of regulation and permission of genetic engineering (GE) research in Hungary; an informal discussion between a group of students; a moderated TV-talk-show.

B. The written data: social positions provided by the legal framing

With respect to our study, we presume that in the political and social arena of democracy, where public participation is, so to say, a pre-encoded entity, the framework of administrative procedures is given by the relevant legal framing, which outlines the social positions that can be expected to participate in the procedure as well as their relation to each other. Accordingly, we are going to start our examinations with an analysis of the laws on biotechnological activities.

The Hungarian Act No. LXVII of 2002 on the modification of Hungarian Act No. XXVII of 1998 on Biotechnology Activities (set into force in January 2003) clearly refers to those special positions with which the legislation counts during the GMO-release permitting procedure. This is done by naming the concrete positions, those who have these positions and the description of their activities. Our analysis revealed the following positions:

The beginning sentence "The Parliament passes the following law…" secures the *position of the legislator* of the procedure.

The topic of Chapter II is the regulation of the administrative level that deals with GMO-activities. The title (Permission procedure and Administration) indicates the *permissive and administrative position* of the procedure; later on it mentions its name (Biotechnological Authority) and ascribes functions to it: the various genetic engineering (GE) activities have to be reported here, and this authority gives out the required permits.

The Biotechnological Committee (BC) passes judgement on the submitted requests. Its composition (5 delegates of the Hungarian Academy of Sciences, 5 different representatives of ministries and 9 members of 4 different social organizations in different fields, like environmental protection, health care, biotechnology and consumer protection) secures its legislative power on the one hand (as the representatives of the ministries are chosen by the legislators), and on the other hand gets a *scientific position* through its members delegated by the Academy. The membership of the representatives of different civil organisations ensures the participation of the *public*. As in most cases the aim of civil organisations is 'protection' (protection of the environment, of health and of the customer), the composition of the Biotechnological Committee is from the first built upon contradictions:

on the one side stand the potential 'aggressors' and those supporting them, on the other side the 'protectors'. If we project this opposition on the background of GMO-release, the position of the *organised protester* is created as opposed to the researchers and anybody else involved in GE-activities.

From those involved in GMO-activities it is the *utilizer* in the first place who plays a role in the permitting procedure: he/she is going to be the applicant who submits requests and reports for permission to the biotechnological authority and he/she is the one who bears the prescribed duties and rights.

The law regulates the publicity of the procedure, too. Let's have a more thorough look at some crucial points in this respect.

The draft of the permit has to be made public:

> The biotechnology authority shall publish the draft permit in its official journal within forty-five days following receipt of the application (hereunder publishing deadline).

In spite of the apparent supply of information, the location of the announcement (the official journal of the Ministry for Agriculture) clearly shows that only well-informed circles, at best really concerned individuals are addressed, as the official journal is not widely spread, but actually a hardly accessible organ, so it does not reach the public.

Comments on the permit of the application for deliberate release of GMOs can be submitted:

> Comments on the draft permit can be submitted to the Biotechnology Committee and to the biotechnology authority within thirty days following the publication of the draft permit (hereunder commenting deadline)

The general term "comment" suggests that any kind of remarks can be handed in. This subject-less, passive-like construction[4] suggests that the opportunity to submit comments is open to anyone. Though the addressee might thus also include the public, the lack of specification of the addressee connected with the location of the information implies the fact that it could be neglected. The public is suggested to be an irrelevant position in the permitting procedure.

[4] Though there is no Passive Voice in Hungarian, there are several constructions with passive character.

The submitted comments have to be considered:

> The Biotechnology Committee shall examine the comments within ten days following their receipt and forward its opinion to the biotechnology authority (hereunder forwarding deadline). On the basis of the opinion of the Biotechnology committee the biotechnology authority shall finalize or amend the draft permit, or reject the application within five days following receipt of the opinion (hereunder decision-making deadline).

There being no specification about the nature of the comments that would be considered by the Biotechnology Committee suggests that all submitted comments are reasons for reconsideration. Anyway, the lack of specification also excludes any eventual complaints concerning comments not taken into consideration. Furthermore, there is no specification concerning the reaction of the authority or of the BC to these comments – as no duty of reply is mentioned, we may presume that those making the comments never learn about whether their comments were taken into consideration or not, and if not, why not.

The fact that these reconsiderations could lead to the alteration of the permit or even to the rejection of the application (though it is not clear what kind of remarks – professional arguments, or general observations about risks, or whatever – could induce this) signals the right (of the public?) to influence the decisions about deliberate release of GMOs.

An announcement about the permission is issued in the official journal and a summary about the control of GE-activities is published in the Ministry's official journal.

So the public is seemingly not only provided with information, but also has the right to participate. Nevertheless, because of the location of the announcement it is only a very limited circle that becomes aware of the case or has the chance to make use of its right to have a say. Thus the public actually remains uninformed and uninvolved in case of an application procedure. Besides, according to the prescriptions of the law, the *users* and *customers* of the GMOs receive education and information in schools and outside schools about the essence and usage of biotechnology and the effects and risks of the usage of the GMOs:

> In the course of fulfilling state tasks, the Government shall ensure that within the framework of school and not school based education, training and information supply the users and consumers of genetically modified organisms receive information about the essence and applications

> of biotechnology as well as about the environmental, health, economic and social effects and risks of the use of organisms modified in this manner'.

The examination of the way and the extent to which this task is fulfilled in practice goes beyond the scope of the present paper.

As a conclusion it can be said that the law positions the *public* in the permitting procedure in the following way: the public has the right to information, as well as the right to comment on the procedure – and so to influence it. However, its access to information is restricted. Therefore, both an active and a passive part are ascribed to the public with respect to the procedure.

According to what has been said above in Subsections 1.2 and 1.3, the social positions outlined above within the legal framing work as *open slots* which are to be specified, that is filled by more specific content, regarding among others, different concepts of participation in the course of oral interactions. In the next section we will summarize the analysis of the latter.

C. Concepts of participation regarding the public in the oral data

1. *Preliminaries*

It is the orientation to social structures and formations that we are specifically interested in when studying social positioning, thus different participation concepts. While the specific social environment is to be regarded as the framework that opens up certain possibilities of social positions, we assume that this framework is filled with content within social interaction, meaning within communication. Moreover, we are interested in social positioning and concepts of participation regarding the public as the clear-cut manifestation of citizenship only if and in so far as they are constructed within and through communication. Hence, the reconstruction of the significant social positions relies on the fine-grained analysis of the empirical data.

Participants of communication reveal their understanding of the relevant social roles in communicated images of themselves as well as in their images of the other participants. Thus social positions understood as sets of expected typical attitudes, activities, and participation concepts, i.e. sets of expectations, are communicatively constructed (see Bora and Hausendorf 2006a, 2006b).

Since we regard social positions as communicative achievements, we are justified in presuming that there are *communicative means,* by the use of which participants in an interaction construct different positions, and, accordingly, the participation concepts connected to them. So the researcher's analytical job is to *reconstruct the social positions from the structures of communication.* He/she has to show how, by the use of which communicative means, social positions have been communicated by the participants of talk-in-interaction.

In this section we will present the social positions reconstructed in our analyses (3.2.), then we will summarize three basic aspects of the dynamism of social positioning with special respect to the role the public plays, that is, to the concepts of participation regarding the public in our data (3.3.).

2. *The reconstruction of the social positions in the oral data*

In accordance with the basic background assumptions of conversation analysis (for a concise summary cf. e.g. Deppermann 2001), the analyst's task is the sequential, process-oriented and thematically ordered reconstruction of the communicative means, by the use of which participants construct social positions in the course of interaction. As for the reconstruction of how participants solve the problem of social positioning with respect to a specific corpus, i.e. how they construct the relevant social positions in a given communicative setting, in our analyses we applied *the three-level model* put forward in Hausendorf (2000: 106–151) and Hausendorf and Bora (2006).

According to this model, on the highest level there are *communicative tasks*, which are to be solved during the interaction. The middle level includes the *semantic-pragmatic means* by which the solution of the tasks is achieved. The lowest level consists of the *lexical and grammatical forms,* which serve the linguistic representation of the means. These three levels constitute a coherent whole: there are no tasks without means and forms, there are no means without tasks and forms, and there are no forms without tasks and means.

With respect to social positioning there are three communicative tasks, namely, assigning ('*Zuordnen*'), ascribing ('*Zuschreiben*'), and evaluating ('*Bewerten*'). Each of the communicative tasks is to be solved by a limited number of semantic-pragmatic means (e.g. emphasizing, explicit naming, generalizing, suggesting, illustrating by example etc.), whereas the grammatical and lexical forms are, in theory, infinite.

The starting point of the analytical reconstruction is the empirical data, i.e. the observable (audible and visible) forms. Hence the analytical direction is so-called bottom-up: it leads from the forms through the means to the tasks.

We will extend the application of this model in two respects. First, the method of conversation analysis may also be applied to written texts that are in one way or another part of the social setting in which the interaction takes place. Second, different pieces of written and/or oral texts may be related to each other through the particular social setting at issue, although there is a temporal and local distance between them. For example, it is clear that the law regulating GMO-release procedures as a written text is part of the decision making procedure, although it may be the case that in particular communicative situations, it is not even implicitly referred to. Also, different conversations and interviews we analyzed are separate interactions while they are closely connected to each other by being involved in the whole of the decision making procedure at issue. This approach legitimizes the coherent analysis of such different, locally and temporally distant, yet simultaneously interrelated data.

For lack of space we cannot exemplify the analyses themselves; therefore we restrict the discussion to enumerating some of the substantial results we obtained.[5]

In particular, the generalization of our results over the whole oral corpus can be summarized as follows (see also Fig. 2.).

The *legislator* plays an important role in the preparation and the formulation of the law as well as in its passing and amendment. The law on biotechnological activities (disregarding some deficiencies) gets a positive evaluation in the contributions of all the interviewees who handle the topic (persons enacting the positions of *the administrator, the organized protester, the scientific expert and the applicant*). This also suggests a positive evaluation of the position of *the legislator* itself. The text of the law describes the position: it settles the frame and the script of the permitting procedure and the function of its participants (for details see Section 2 above), thus it indicates explicitly or implicitly the *legislator's* expectations and attitude towards relevant actors and roles.

[5] For the details of the analyses see Iványi et al. (2006) and Iványi et al. (2004).

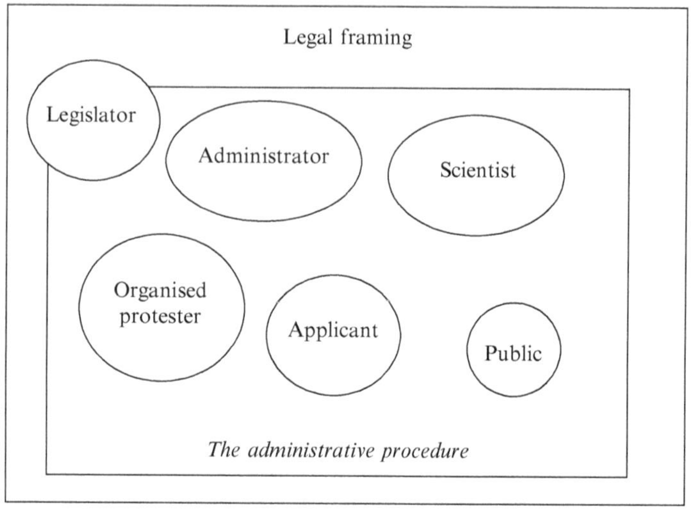

Fig. 2 The social positions.

The *administrator* is responsible for the implementation of the legal regulation; he/she deals with preparing, permitting, evaluating and controlling the applications and the deliberate release of GMOs. In the Hungarian permitting procedure the authority has a leading role. It grants permission of the releases after getting the evaluation connected to the requested application from the Committee for Evaluating and Controlling Biotechnology Procedures, in short the Biotechnology Committee, i.e., BC. Our data shed light on the operation of the *BC*, its composition and the relation of its members to each other: 'greens' vs. non-environmentalists represent the anti- and pro-GMO groups, respectively. Sociological and emotional views vs. expertise are typical attitudes towards GE. These attitudes are meanwhile the reflection of their belonging to other diverse positions (see later).

The position of the *scientific expert* is rather complex. Not only the scientific researchers, but the research-teams carrying out GE experiments are also communicated in the images of self and others as experts, but to a certain extent also all those who are skilled in GE or in the domains of biochemistry, biology or other scientific research.

The position of the organized protesters is represented without exception by environmentalists. Those who let their voices be heard in the context of GE are to different degrees well informed in this domain, whereas some environmentalists are also positioned as scientific experts. The environmentalists assume responsibility for informing the public but they seem to have little success in this task, as they themselves assume the public to be uninformed and ignorant about GE. Though they perceive that the public is only interested in matters with direct consequences, they do little or nothing to reach the locals/farmers, in other words exactly those who would be easy(er) to be mobilized precisely because of the direct impact with the presumed effects of free GMO release in field trials.

The *applicant (company)* – being representative of profit-oriented companies – deals with questions of market and profit and is interested in production as user and distributor as well. The specific economic interest of the company makes the applicant take sides for the production of GMO-s, and (s)he affects (or can affect) the permitting procedure accordingly.

The *public* is represented in several reconstructed categories, such as *the public, the Hungarian people, farmers, locals, the simple people, the cleverer, consumers*. The most frequent assignments in our data are 'public', 'public opinion', 'the population', 'the Hungarian', 'the people', 'the community', and 'the inhabitants'. As more focused specifications of what is generally called 'the public' we differentiate *the locals* and *the concerned/critical individual*. The contribution of the *concerned/critical individual* helps reinforce the picture about the low level of public awareness in Hungary concerning GMOs. There are small farmers among them who are interested in GMO-free bio-production, in the protection of the environment and in health. The 'local experts' are well read in scientific research, they do not dispute the raison-d'être of scientific development, and above all they are all 'concerned', critical personalities, who expect information about GE research in Hungary, want to give their views, and wish to participate in the permitting procedure.

The *locals* stand for a social position whose representatives (primarily farmers) on the one hand deal with local problems: e.g. the production to cover own needs; the protection of their families; avoidance/ replacement of dangerous substances. On the other hand, since they have not learned about the experiments being carried out in their neighbourhood, their 'locality' with regard to GE is only expressed in their shock to hear about the experiments for the first time from the interviewers, their shock at not being informed and so being excluded from the decision making that affects their direct surroundings; their own lives.

3. *The dynamics of social positioning*

The main focus of our analysis was the outlining of the social positions that appear in our data and this has been done relying primarily on the communicated images of self and others of the participants of talk-in-interaction. Their examination in the various pieces of discourse of the analyzed corpus revealed that on the one hand the varying typical features of a certain position – just like the different participation concepts connected to them – emerge not in one, but in many different interactions, and these complete each other. On the other hand, it became obvious that sometimes the images of self in a certain position and the way others see and picture that position overlap, whereas sometimes these contradict each other.

The thorough comparison of the positions reflected in the communicated images of self and others enables the examination of the *dynamics of social positions understood as the relation between social positions.* In Subsection 3.3.1. we will compare the social positions that emerge from different conversations. Subsection 3.3.2. will be devoted to the comparison of the attitudes of the participants reflected in the elaboration of certain relevant topics. Finally, in Subsection 3.3.3. we will exemplify how the sequential and process-oriented nature of the conversations influences the construction of social positions.

3.1. *Overlapping and contradictory features and attitudes – a comparison of the oral data*

This comparison shows how a certain social position is constructed and completed in the contributions of various speakers as representatives of different positions. Certain overlaps come into sight, for instance:

- The public (locals just as the concerned individuals) assume to be uninformed and ignorant about GE, and this feature is highlighted to be characteristic of them from the point of view of the other positions as well.[6]

[6] The overlaps as well as the contradictions with regard to the public are elaborated in greater detail in Section 4.

- The organized protester appears in images of self as having fears and anxieties with regard to GE. These fears and anxieties are also typical of the position in the administrator's view, and they are evaluated as even being exaggerated in the presentations of the scientific expert and of the applicant.
- The scientific expert presents him/herself as being competent in GE and having thorough qualifications, this is confirmed by the attribute "well-informed", which is ascribed to the position both by the organized protester and the public.
- The organized protester attributes to the scientific expert the feature of being "sensitive to real arguments", this corresponds to the scientific experts' self-presentation, according to which "they accept (only) professional argumentation".
- "Follows the EU" is ascribed as a typical approach of the legislator by the scientific expert and the applicant as well as by the organized protester.
- The applicant is presented by the organized protester as being motivated by interests (sometimes even dishonest ones) and this chimes in with the self-presentation of the position, where the applicant admits that he/she is aiming at market and putting his/her own interests, i.e. profit, forward.

But contradictions are also striking, such as:

- The public appears in their self-image as expecting and needing information, however, from the point of view of the organized protester they are only interested in matters with direct consequences and not interested in GE at all. The scientific expert shares this opinion and even emphasizes that because of their lack of interest they do not need (more) information.
- While the organized protester claims that GE does not serve the interests of the locals, the scientific expert and the applicant stress that locals can only profit from biotechnology since dusting becomes unnecessary.
- The organized protester admits to having stiff standpoints, however, the scientific expert and the applicant indicate as a typical feature of the position, the fact that they can be influenced and manipulated.
- The scientific expert highlights "competence and thorough qualifications" in his/her self-image, but the public points out "lack of a

serious scientific approach to GE operation" to be characteristic of the position.

- As opposed to the feature of "working cautiously" in the self-image of the scientific expert, the latter is indicated to "play unfair" in the presentation of the public and is ascribed the typical feature of an "irresponsible way of thinking" by the organized protester.
- The administrator is regarded by all the other positions as being an expert (even the applicant indicates that the representatives of this position understand and support biotechnology). In contradiction with this the administrator emphasizes non-expertise in self-images of the position.

The survey of the whole comparison also reveals certain common features, attitudes or expectations that turn out to be characteristic of several social positions, for example:

- "Lack of knowledge about the consequences of GE" is characteristic of the public just as of the "well-informed" positions of the organized protester, the scientific expert and the applicant.
- Not only the applicant, but also the scientific expert appear to be "motivated by personal interests", i.e. profit.
- The legislator is indicated to be just as "ignorant concerning GE" as the public is (*concerned individuals* and *locals* included). This feature is also, at least to a certain extent, characteristic of the organized protester and the administrator.

3.2. *Similarities and contradictions along relevant topics*

Another aspect of the comparability of the analyzed interviews and discussions in our data (aiming at elaborating on possible linkages between them) is the examination of the participants' attitudes towards genetic engineering and the application procedure along some topics relevant to the research. These topics include interest in GE, information, risks and worries associated with GE, the legal sphere (e.g. regulation, permitting procedure, feedback), the public sphere (e.g. involvement, participation) and expertise. These topic-oriented comparisons also reveal overlaps and contradictions between certain social positions and their typical attitudes. Let us have a look for instance at the problem of the public, focusing on the questions of the lack of information, interest in GE, and participation.

In regard to *lack of information:*

"Ignorance about GE" turns up as a characteristic feature of the public across the different social positions. For example, the organized protester ascribes the public the feature of being ignorant; it is remarkable that in his/her opinion this feature is common to different social positions (the legislator and partly the administrator, but the organized protester, too). Nevertheless, she/he even assumes responsibility for the lack of information, i.e. the ignorance of the public. In the administrators opinion the public is simply ignorant. From the point of view of the scientific expert, the public is ignorant, and it does not demand more information, either. A passive, deprived status without any choice and information is attributed to the public by the applicant.

All the same, locals as well as concerned individuals acknowledge to ignorance, but add that they expect information (see below) and that they would be able to understand comprehensible information.

The question of *interest in GE* is also elaborated upon in a contradictory manner:

"Lack of interest in GE" is presented to be characteristic of the public in the others' descriptions. For example, the organized protester refers to the lack of interest of the public in GE first by emphasizing its sole interest in direct consequences (while with respect to GE these are unknown for the time being), then by stressing its susceptibility to manipulation as regards economic growth, wealth and welfare. The applicant underlines the accessibility of opportunities to make objections to GE: accordingly, the fact that the public never makes use of these opportunities indicates lack of interest. The scientific expert also underscores the lack of interest of the public. Furthermore, the scientific expert expresses his/her belief according to which this situation is going to change in future (suggesting the public being not yet mature enough).

Meanwhile the representatives of the public presented themselves and the position they belong to as being interested in the issue of biotechnology. For example, they expect information or they want to give their views and to be listened to.

What we can observe in this regard is more than a mere contradiction between the image of self and the way others present the position at issue: while – based primarily on the lack of interest – the public appears in others' accounts as consisting of unconcerned individuals, the representatives of public present themselves as being concerned individuals. This conflict of positioning is the consequence of a vicious circle: the lack of information results in an apparent lack of interest as regards the public, and this induces further lack of information. In spite of this cycle, there seems to be some agreement with respect to the topic of *participation*:

The chances for public participation and public voice are deemed slight both by the applicant and partly by the concerned individual. Both of them attribute a passive role to the public.

In the organized protesters' view, the public, lacking the necessary information and therefore ignorant, is unsuited to participate in the process of decision-making. However, he/she does not attach much expectation to the informing of the public: on the one hand there is nobody to give it information; on the other, the really concerned ones are isolated or barely accessible.

3.3. *Sequentiality and interactivity*

Although the method of conversation analysis was extended to the comparison of different oral data in our previous research, we focussed primarily on the intra-textual analyses of our data. The detailed sequential analyses highlight the sequentiality and the interactivity of the construction of social positions in face-to-face communication. All participants have an active part in positioning, since they suggest certain categorisation and establish sequential implications in their contributions, while the other participants either respond (i.e. accept or reject) or neglect them. To exemplify the dynamism of social positioning with respect to the role that the public plays in the decision-making procedure at issue, in the following passages we present excerpts from our sequential analyses. This example shows how the social position of the *concerned individual as the representative of the public* is constructed interactively, turn by turn.

The analysed sequence is part of a moderated TV-talk-show on the topic of genetic engineering. In the preceding parts of the conversation some of the invited speakers have been introduced and have delivered their views regarding GE as well as their fears. In addition, members of the audience have made comments on the subject. Participants of the following extract are the moderator of talk (M), a telephone caller (T1), and two invited speakers: one of them has previously been positioned as a scientist and an organized protester (MV), while the other one is a scientific expert, a biotechnologist (DE).

1. M még annyi türelmét kérhetem hogy egy néző vonalban
2. van aki (.) lehet hogy éppen (.) fontos kérdést tesz
3. fel; halló?
4. T1 jó napot kívánok
5. M csókolom a kezét; [hallgatjuk]

M so much patience may I ask you a viewer is online who just may be asking an important question. hello?
T1 good afternoon.
M kiss your hands; we're listening to you

The moderator (M) interrupts the flow of the discussion and announces a telephone caller to be the next speaker. The categorization *viewer* suggests the position of 'public', while the mere fact of the phone call itself suggests more specifically the positioning of the next speaker as 'concerned individual'. M explicitly expects a question to come (2); this indicates that he presumes the caller to be in need of information.

After a sequence of formal greetings in the opening of the talk on phone, M signals the caller that she gets the floor; he invites her to take the turn.

6. T1 [teri vagyok] gyuláról termeléssel
7. foglalkozunk, bulgár kertészek vagyunk és hiába
8. szeretnénk visszaállni a a a normális rÉgi
9. hagyományos magot nem lehet ám kapni, (.) sehol az
10. üzletekbe; csak ezeket a
11. [génmanipuláltakat (-)

I'm teri from gyula we deal with gardening we're bulgarian gardeners and we'd like in vain to get back to the normal old traditional seeds you can't get them anyhere in the shops; only these genetically manipulated ones

Overlapping, the caller (T1) sets up by introducing herself by her first name and she also gives information regarding her geographical location (6), thus confirming her position of 'public'. She goes on to provide some information regarding her occupation, first by indicating a typical activity – production – and then by denominating the category of the *gardeners*[7] (6–7). The first person plural form of the verbs indicates

[7] "Bulgarian gardeners" is the denomination for gardeners with specific traditions, who typically grow vegetables.

assignment to the category and signals that the speaker is going to talk in the name of the mentioned social group. The categorization first suggests competence and establishes this feature to be the ground of the following contribution; it also gives the reason for the actual issue T1 is going to present: the problem of the seeds. The wish to "get back" to the traditional seeds presupposes that they have at some point given those up (7–8) and alludes to dissatisfaction regarding the change. The listed attributes she uses suggest that the available seeds are not normal (8–9), and then she specifies that the available seeds are genetically manipulated (10–11). All in all T1 presents herself and her position as (even if not necessarily against) at least not enthusiastic about GE.

14. T1 menjek arr[ébb(.) igen (-) ez ez]
15. M [bocs (-) igen igen (.) köszönöm]
16. MV [ez (.) én] [hogyha]
17. T1 [csak ezeket]
18. elnézést kérek nem olyan régen a tEszkóban vásároltunk
19. [paradicsomot] gyönyörű volt tényleg (.) nagyon szép,(.)
20. DE [hehe]
21. T1 hát felvágtuk idehaza (.) és a magok kihajtottak
22. benne; én nem hiszem hogy ez normális; természetesen
23. nem (.)nem ettük meg; nem tudjuk hogy mi ez benne de
24. nem ettük meg; tehát nem (.) valóban úgy van hogy nem
25. értünk hozzá mint amit a közönség soraiból is
26. mondott, mert nagyon kevés a tájékoztató, de én
27. gyere' pici gyerek korom (.) óta (.) ezzel
28. foglalkoznak a szüleim és öh: (-) ilyennel nem
29. találkoztunk [még]

T1: *I should go [farther yes this this*
M: *[I'm sorry yes yes thank you*
MV: *[this I] [if]*
T1: *[only these]- I'm sorry not so long ago we bought at tesco's tomatoes they were beautiful indeed very nice*
DE: hehe
T1: *well we cut them at home and the seeds had sprouted in them. I don't think this is normal. of course we didn't eat them, we don't know what was in them but we didn't eat them. so no it's really so that we are not* well up *on it as someone from the audience has also said, because the information is very sparse but I since my very early childhood my parents have dealt with this and such a thing we hadn't yet met*

After having clarified a problem of some technical disturbance (11–13), T1 would go on (14), when MV overlaps and tries to take the turn (16). Nevertheless T1 reiterates some of her words before the interruption (17, see also 10), this way showing that she will continue the interrupted train of thought. In any case she has noticed MV's intention and excuses herself for not leaving the floor (18). Then she sets about elaborating on the topic of the tomatoes bought at a huge supermarket (18–19). DE's laughter signals that he might know the problem. The strange occurrence of the seeds sprouting inside the beautiful tomato (19–21) recalls the abnormality suggested earlier; moreover, T1 then formulates her doubts explicitly (22). In the following utterances she reveals reluctance to unnatural things (22–24), the adverbial phrase "of course" (22) indicates this attitude to be typical and expectable. T1 agrees with an earlier opinion from the audience regarding ignorance and lack of sufficient information as the reason for the ignorance (23–26); however, the adversative conjunction "but" (26) signals that the consent is only a partial one. In the following adversative clause she then refers to the long tradition of gardening in her family (26–28), suggesting that experience and the acquired competence could compensate for the lack of information, thus also attenuating the previous assumption of ignorance being the cause of the fears and of the standpoint towards GE. In this respect, the fact that they have never come upon such strange behaviour of the tomato seeds (28–29) only stresses the peculiarity of the presented phenomenon.

30. MV [.hh]
31. M most nagyon elhalkult de ez a- engem a a
vet' a mag
32. vásárlásnál nyilván azt [(.)]
33. T1 [igen?]
34. M arra gondolt hogy vetőmagot [ugye?]
35. T1 [vető]magot, igen; nem is
36. kapni[csak]
37. M [milyen] vetőmag amiről ön beszél [ezt nem fejtette]
38. T1 [ezek hOlland]
39. vetőmagok;(.)És génmanipulált ez:(-)mondják a magboltba is]

M: *now you've grown fainter but this I'm the sow' by buying seeds you obviously*
T1: yes?
M: meant seeds for sowing, [didn't you?]
T1: [seeds] for sowing, yes. You can't get [only]
M: [what] kind of seeds you didn't state [that]
T1: [these are Dutch]
seeds; and they are genetically manipulated they say so in the seed shop, [too

MV's breathing in (30) signals her intention to take the turn, which again is unsuccessful. After some comment regarding the quality of the tone M sets on about clearing some details concerning the previously mentioned seeds (31–37), thus getting back to the first topic of the conversation. T1 gives the required information; she then specifies that the seeds she has talked about come from the Netherlands (38). She repeats her earlier assumption, according to which they are genetically manipulated and as a reinforcement of her statement she refers to the seed shop as an additional source of information (39). It is obvious that she regards the seed shop as representing expert, reliable opinion, so this could confirm and strengthen her information.

39. T1 vetőmagok; (.)És génmanipulált ez: (-) mondják a magboltba [is]
40. MV [én]
41. hagy [(.)] nyugtassam meg a hölgyet [(.)] hogy magyarország
42. M [igen,]
43. T1 [igen,]
43. MV egyrészt (.) zöldségek gyümölcsök genetikailag módosított
44. zöldségek gyümölcsök sehol a világon nincsenek még forgalomban;
45. .hh alapvetően szántóföldi növények elérhetők genetikailag
46. módosított változatban, úgy mint kukorica, szója, gyapot,
47. repce, (-) cukorrépa [és hasonlók]

T1: seeds; and they say genetically manipulated in the seed shop,[too
MV: [I] let me reassure the lady that in Hungary
M: [yes]
T1: [yes]
MV: for one vegetables, fruit, genetically modified vegetables and fruit are not in trade anywhere in the world basically plough-land plants are attainable in genetically modified versions, such as maize, soy, cotton rapeseed, sugar-beet [and similar]

At this point, MV interferes and in an overlap (40) she takes the floor. The turn-taking is certified by M (42). MV discloses the purpose of her contribution (41), which is consented to by T1, the addressee of the coming statement (43). Thus MV positions herself as a well-informed expert on the topic, who thus has the competence to reassure, to calm down. Meanwhile, she suggests T1 is uninformed or at least misinformed and this way the public is ascribed the feature of having unjustified worries. By stating that genetically modified variants of vegetables and fruit are not available not only in Hungary, but anywhere in the world (41–44) she actually reveals the information delivered so far by T1, as well as the worries connected to it, to be groundless, in this way shattering the idea of the competence of the 'public' established earlier by the caller. She then goes on to give right information regarding the sorts of organisms touched by genetic engineering

(45–47). The instructing tone confirms the expertise in her self-image and the lack of competence and information in her own image of the public.

47. MV repce, (-) cukorrépa [és hasonlók]
48. T1 [de mondom]azt mondták [a] a magboltban,
49. hogy (.) a magboltban azt mondták itt gyulán hogy ezek a magok
50. is mInd (.) mInd hibrid és genetikailag mani[pulált]
51. MV [a hibrid] és a
52. genetikailag manipulált [az két különböző dolog]
53. T1 [tUdom azt mondtam hogy És] (.) És

MV:rape, sugar-beet [and similar]
T1: [but I tell you]they said in the seed shop that in the seed shop here in Gyula they said that all of these seeds are hybrids and genetically mani[pulated
MV:[the hybrid] and the genetically manipulated [that's two different things]
T1: [I knOw I said And And

Overlapping, T1 takes the turn. She does not give in; she sticks to her earlier information and to its source, the seed shop in Gyula, the competence of which she seems to consider firm and unquestionable (48–50). Moreover, she extends the range of the information, the stress of the determiner "all" as well as its repetition (50) show that not only the earlier mentioned Dutch seeds, but the entire available stock is concerned – this statement is quite the opposite of MV's "not anywhere in the world" (44), so it clearly signals T1's doubt towards the expert's opinion. MV reacts promptly; she immediately interferes and brings in a correction (51–52). The instruction should strengthen her expertise and meanwhile demonstrate the ignorance of the other party, so it should restore the positioning she had previously proposed and built up. Nevertheless, T1 stands up for her image. The overlap following right after MV has repeated the nouns denominating the controversial features of the seeds (52–53) shows that she is fully aware of the argument to come. The emphasis of the verb and of the conjunction "and," as well as the repetition of the latter reveals strong objection to the implied ignorance, namely the mixing up of the notions.

54. M tehát akkor lehet hogy itt annyira keverednek a fog' fogalmak
55. [hogy indokolatlan a gyanakvás]
56. T1 [az elképzelhető, (.) az elképzelhető;]

M: so then maybe here the notions are so confused
[that there is no cause for suspicion
T1: [that's possible, that's possible]

M picks out the idea of the mixed-up notions, which could bring the involved parties to a common point and would unveil the suspicion as well as the worries connected to GE as unjustified (54–55). The passive-like construction does not specify whom it might refer to. Thus he hints again at the lack of information of the "public" touched upon at earlier stages of the discussion, and suggests that it is the cause of the conflict of the different viewpoints. T1 accepts the possibility, though it is clear that her agreement also has a generalized character: it does not explicitly refer to herself.

59. MV hogy (.) ha a vetőmag
60. boltban valóban genetikailag manipulált vagy módosított
61. vetőmagot [áru]sítanak,(.) akkor ezt a vonatkozó hazai
62. T1 [igen]
63. MV törvénnyel Ellentétesen teszik; tehát egész egyszerűen
64. illegális dolgot művelnek, [ami]
65. T1 [hát] már elnézést kérek de sOk
66. mindent illegálisan művelnek ebben az [országban ( )]
67. DE [ez biztos]
68. MV [ez]
69. M [jó
70. bocsánat csak a színfalak mögött én látom hogy
71. ((taps))

MV: *... if in the seed shop it's really genetically manipulated or modified seeds that they sell then this they*
T1: [yes]
MV: do oppose the relevant home rule; so they quite simply do illegal things, [that's]
T1: [well] I beg your pardon but there are many things they do illegally in this [country
DE: [that's sure]
MV: [this]
M: [all right
sorry but behind the scenes I can see that
((applause))

In the conditional clause (59–61) MV seemingly admits to the reliability of the controversial information about the genetically modified seeds on the market in Hungary, thus acknowledging T1's accurate information and competence. However in the following main clause, she then shatters the image of the public when disclosing that this fact implies illegality (61–64). The reference to the relevant legal regulation should again undermine the trustworthiness of the information. T1 immediately interferes (65) and by pointing to the fact that violations of the law occur rather frequently in Hungary (65–66) she actually rejects MV's argument as ineffective. The displayed distrust towards the power of laws finds wide acceptance: DE, the invited scientist verbalizes his agreement (67) and the applause of the audience (71) indicates agreement, too.

The results of these analyses boil down to the following (see also Fig. 3).

First, the 'competence' of the *public*, a feature that is certainly a determinant for the concepts of public participation, was constructed during several turns with the active contribution of the participants. Its dynamism involved the following stages: it was first established as a typical feature of the position; then it was shattered, then doubted or even denied, and then finally strengthened and consented to.

Second, in certain respects some of the social positions (their features and attitudes, their participation concepts) appear to be convergent or even compatible with each other. Yet in other respects social positions are in conflict with each other, their features and/or attitudes are opposite. A significant type of relation is that a certain position (the public) is simply ignored; its legitimacy and its importance within the procedure concerned are played down.

D. Conclusions

The analyses we exemplified in the preceding sections yield our solution to the central problem of the present paper as raised in Section 1.3 along the following considerations.

We presented a twofold analysis of the communicative means by the use of which social positions with special respect to the participation concepts associated with them have been constructed. Extending the methodology of conversation analysis as elaborated e.g. in Bora and Hausendorf (2006b) and Hausendorf (2000), we both analyzed the written text of the law representing the legal framing, and completed detailed sequential analyses of oral discussions on the topic of biotechnological activities and permission procedures. After having carried out the analyses, we must now clarify as to *how the slots* outlined by the law were filled with particular social positions via participation concepts during the oral interactions in the decision-making process we examined. Our answer is: in a contradictory manner, because *three kinds of contradictions* emerge.

The *first kind of contradiction* is inherent in *the text of the law*, because it positions the public in two incompatible ways. Let us see

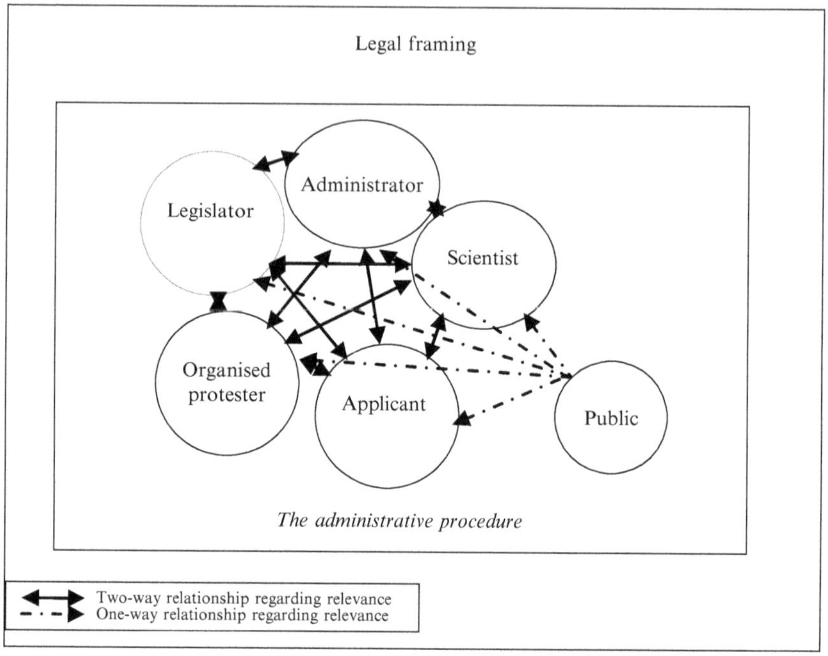

Fig. 3 The social positions and their relations.

a few examples of this contradiction. The first example is that the social position of the public is present in the legal framing. The public has the legally codified right to participate in the permitting procedure through the initiation of the civil companies into the BC, and through the potential submission of comments. Incongruently, from the text of the law it can be concluded that the public bears an insignificant social position and *need not* be properly informed.

As another example we may mention the fact that, although the draft of the permit must be published, by the location of the announcement (the official journal of the Ministry for Agriculture) the text of the law places the information into a context in which it can be interpreted differently. It suggests that it is not the public that is addressed, but rather, circles which are in a special position and which have already been well-informed at the outset.

Third, the law says that the reconsideration of public comments could lead to the alteration of the permit or even to the rejection of the application. This signals the possibility of the public to influence the decisions about deliberate release of GMOs. However, there is no specification concerning the reaction of the authority or of the BC to these comments. Moreover, there is no regulation concerning the publicity of the possible comments or of the reactions induced by them either, although this could theoretically make the whole procedure more transparent.

As our analyses reported on in Section 3 elucidate, the *second kind of contradiction* arises within the *oral data* between certain images of self and those of others. In particular, the *public* is declared to be relevant from the point of view of all positions. Nevertheless, in images of others the *public* (locals and concerned individuals) appears primarily in negative terms: it is presented to be uninterested and uninformed, ignorant, short-sighted, and unable and unwilling to participate in the permitting procedure. Contrarily, although locals and concerned individuals do admittedly appear ignorant in their self-images, they would also like to be adequately informed, to make use of their right to participate, and they demand to be taken seriously by the authorities.

The *third kind of contradiction* emerges between the text of the law and the position of the public witnessed by the oral data. In the oral data locals and concerned individuals dynamically construct social positions, which make them appear in quite a different way than the law suggests.

The fact that these contradictions could be revealed by applying the method of conversation analysis is of central importance for the solution of our basic problem. Namely, it boils down to the assumption that the contradictions are manifestations of *a more basic social conflict* inherent in decision-making procedures in Hungary: while the public positions itself as 'concerned', needing information and wanting to have a say, it is regarded by the law as well as by the other involved positions as 'unconcerned' and thus neglectable. Therefore, *the decisions are not made amid wide publicity*. It is this basic conflict that represents one of the most serious obstacles to practicing citizenship as a communicative achievement in Hungary.

In this respect, the relevance of our conversation-analytic findings is that they have revealed a series of communicative means, which are *indicators* of this deep social conflict. The communicative means of social positioning in the GMO release procedures we focused on reflect substantial peculiarities in the underlying social setting.

As Berényi and Murányi (2004) explain in detail, present-day Hungarian society is, among other things, characterized by the coexistence of certain features of pre-1989 social structure and political culture with those of post-1989 developments. It goes without saying that in the pre-1989 period, not even traces of communicative citizenship existed. After 1989, however, as we have seen, the attempt to lay down the formal foundations of constitutional democracy may have in principle encouraged its development. Nevertheless, due to the complex interrelatedness of pre- and post-1989 characteristics of Hungarian society, the realization of such an attempt at more democratic citizenship proves contradictory, as witnessed by the example of public participation in GMO release procedures. In particular, the inherent incongruities within the text of the law are typical manifestations of this double-facedness of the overall social setting.

Now, we have emphasized that the public is regarded by the law as well as by the other involved positions as 'unconcerned'. Against the social background sketched above, this evidently reflects remnants of pre-1989 social and political culture within the frames of present-day democracy. One might conclude from this observation that communicative citizenship regarding the deliberate release of GMO plants does not exist, and Hungarian people are *not* citizens in the sense introduced in Section 1.2. In fact, it is this conclusion that Berényi and Murányi (2004) draw.

However, our linguistic analyses have yielded findings, which go *far beyond* the above. In particular, we have shown that the public positions *itself* as 'concerned' claiming its right to be well-informed and to be involved in the decisions. This observation is of high relevance, because it exposes the need to move away from the Kádárian attitude. The communist era in Hungary from the sixties on was among other things characterized by authoritarianism, elitism, and exclusionism. This supported the willingness to accept authoritarian methods of decision-making and the preference of informal channels of interest realization. Now, Berényi and Murányi are certainly right in claiming that this attitude still prevails in many facets of society. Nevertheless, our linguistic data have illustrated that the communicative behavior of the public was *different* in the procedures we examined. Instead of passively accepting the decisions made by the authorities, which was the typical attitude before the nineties, the people expressed their need to participate by using a clearly identifiable inventory of communicative means. In short: *people* have *begun* to become communicating *citizens*. Consequently, it is definitely not the case that there is no communicative citizenship in Hungary – communicative citizenship *does* exist, albeit in a specific sense. Let us call it provisionally, until we find a better label, *quasi-citizenship*: a communicative achievement.

References

Berényi, Z. and Murányi, I. (2004): Relationship between legal, political, cultural environment and the dynamics of social positions with respect to citizenship in Hungary. Communicated (and contested? concepts of citizenship. In: Bora, A./Hausendorf, H.: *PARADYS: Participation and the Dynamics of Social Positioning. Final Report to the European Commission*. Bielefeld and Bayreuth, 289–301. (http://www.uni-bielefeld.de/iwt/paradys/English_start.html)

Bora A. and Hausendorf, H. (eds.) (2006): *Analysing Citizenship Talk*. Social Positioning in Political and Legal Decision-Making Process Amsterdam/Philadelphia: Benjamins.

Bora A. and Hausendorf, H. (2006a): Communicating citizenship and social positioning: theoretical concepts. In: Bora A./Hausendorf, H. (eds.) 2006, 23–49.

Bora A. and Hausendorf, H. (2006b): Reconstructing social positioning in discourse: Methodological basics and their implementation from a conversation analysis perspective. In: Bora A./Hausendorf, H. (eds.) (2006), 85–97.

Deppermann, A. (2001): *Gespräche analysieren*. Opladen: Leske + Budrich.

Hausendorf, H. (2000): *Zugehörigkeit durch Sprache. Eine linguistische Studie am Beispiel der deutschen Wiedervereinigung*. Tübingen: Niemeyer.

Iványi, Zs., Kertész, A., Marinecz, K. and Máté, N. (2004): Main Findings of Data Analysis. In: Bora, A., Hausendorf, H.: *PARADYS: Participation and the Dynamics of Social Positioning. Final Report to the European Commission*. Bielefeld and Bayreuth, 257–265. (http://www.uni-bielefeld.de/iwt/paradys/English_start.html)

Iványi, Zs., Kertész, A., Marinecz, K. and Máté, N. (2006): Social Categorization and the Grammar-Pragmatics Relation. An Analysis of Hungarian Data. Sprachtheorie und germanistische Linguistik 16, 111–157.

Zimmermann, D.H. (1998): *Identity, Context and Interaction*. In: Antaki, Ch. / Widdicombe, S. (eds): *Identities in Talk*. London: Sage, 87–106.

PART III

REFLECTIONS ON THE FUTURE OF PARTICIPATORY GOVERNANCE

CHAPTER NINE

PARTICIPATORY TECHNOLOGY ASSESSMENT AND THE "INSTITUTIONAL VOID": INVESTIGATING DEMOCRATIC THEORY AND REPRESENTATIVE POLITICS

Gabriele Abels

A. Introduction

Democracy is a powerful normative concept inherently linked to citizens' participation. A polity with no meaningful citizens' participation we cannot call a democracy. Given the reality of today's mass democracies, government *of* the people is, however, a requirement never met in a direct sense. In mass democracies legitimacy via delegation of power to elected and accountable representatives is *the* key mechanism to accomplish the goal of government *by* the people.

Representative democracy, however, has been harshly criticized for a number of shortcomings, such as political apathy, low participation rates, predominance of party politics, elitist tendencies, lack of responsiveness, under-representation of minorities, etc. Criticisms are raised by diverse schools of thought such as participatory, radical, and also liberal democratic theory. Dahl (1994), for instance, emphasizes the need to balance citizens' participation and system effectiveness. Theorists of radical or participatory democracy emphasize the role of active citizenship whereas theorists of deliberative democracy focus on the quality of public deliberation. According to them, more inclusive politics can lead to better results, because more voices and arguments can be heard and addressed.

Ever since the 1960s, this critique is accompanied by a good deal of 'democratic experimentalism' (Dorf and Sabel, quoted in Papadopoulos & Warin 2007: 445) in order to improve citizens' participation: sit-ins, public inquiries, citizen juries, negotiated rulemaking, collaborative planning, mediations, right-to-know legislation, deliberative opinion polls, focus groups, consensus conferences, and the like. Governance, a concept that has come to the fore both in modern social science and in modern politics, responds to the issue of citizens' participation in a specific way. Instead of focussing solely on institutional politics, it emphasizes the formal and informal aspects of co-operation and co-ordination between a diversity of social actors. Governance involves new modes of policy-making by linking the input (participation) and output (effectiveness) dimensions of democratic legitimacy.

What does this imply for citizens' participation in science and technology policy-making? The development of technology assessment (TA), an instrument to scientifically evaluate the impacts of (new) technologies and to normatively assess these impacts on society, is a key outcome of the intense debate on socio-technological change. While the TA movement started in the United States, it has quickly spread to Western Europe (and beyond). Ever since then, numerous agencies and institutes for TA have been established, many of them by parliaments (cf. Vig/Paschen 2000). However, TA was dominated by scientific experts and the idea of "sound science". Interestingly, participatory claims were extended to the field of science and technology policy from the very beginning (cf. Nelkin 1984). The potential negative impacts of science and technology on society and the environment soon provoked demands for better citizen participation, which until then had been dominated by scientific experts.

While public participation was a vital part of the TA programme from the very beginning, the actual involvement of citizens was marginal. It is only since the 1990s that we can observe programmatic and empirical "democratic experimentalism" in TA leading to the development of so called "participatory" or "democratic TA" (Abels/Bora 2004). The debate and development of participatory technology assessment (henceforth: pTA) builds on three strands: deliberative democracy, "post-normal" science, and risk communication (Burgess & Chilvers 2006: 714). But why is citizens' participation important? First of all, there is the *normative* claim for a democratic function of TA (see, for example, Bechmann 1993; Durant 1999; recently, Hendriks et al. 2007). Active public participation in the assessment and evaluation of (new) technologies is a key mechanism in pTA. From this perspective pTA is "governance by deliberation". Secondly, the participatory claim is defended on *epistemological* grounds. 'The case has been made strongly for widening participation in pursuit of better decisions on the basis of the need to capture knowledge and values that lie behind the professional scientific and technological peer community usually enrolled in assessment processes.' (Burgess & Chilvers 2006: 717) According to such reasoning, different forms of knowledge and values contribute to more rational and effective policies and should therefore be included in the policy-process. This argument still upholds a seemingly clear-cut distinction between experts, who provide 'hard facts', and members of the public, who contribute 'soft values'. Yet this is a problematic polarization. Burgess and Chilvers (2006: 718) emphasize that the complexity of technology development requires the recognition of the 'drive towards harder values and softer facts'. Thirdly, advocates refer to *empirical* evidence illustrating the problem-solving and legitimizing capacity of pTA. However, given the lack of comparative empirical research, this argument requires verification. These three arguments are scrutinized in recent debates on pTA. There is a trend towards developing theoretically sounder arguments in order to justify public participation by linking it more systematically to social and democratic theory – and towards more methodologically sound empirical research. While a great deal of the debate is still normative, a more empirically substantive and functionalist approach to pTA emerges (cf. Abels & Bora 2004; Hansen 2006; Bora & Hausendorf 2006).[1]

The objective of this contribution is, firstly, to shed some light on this programmatic debate on pTA and its link to practical pTA. Secondly, I want to discuss the implications for a more comprehensive institutional design that strengthens the linkage of pTA to representative politics. I reason that most of the pTA literature limits itself to a particular strand in democratic theory only, i.e. participatory and deliberative democracy. They 'serve as self-descriptions of the procedures' (Hansen 2006, 582). I argue that this shortcoming affects the adequate conceptualisation of the empirical plethora of pTA instruments and procedures. Any theoretical conceptualisation of pTA has repercussions on the future institutional design of pTA instruments. The 'institutional void' (Hajer, quoted in Görsdorf 2006) in which most pTA takes place today certainly puts severe constraints on its potential impacts. And this is certainly true not specifically for pTA, but also for innovative participatory procedures in other fields of public policy-making. My key argument is that pTA can and should develop institutionalized links to representative politics, i.e. fill the void.

[1] In the political debate, the well established democratic and empowerment argument is today accompanied by the neoliberal claim which conceptualizes politics as a market of different opinions. PTA is then perceived as an instrument for improving governance practices (cf. Klüver 2006).

B. Participation is not participation is not participation …

The starting point for any such debate is to consider the empirical variety of participatory instruments and their practically (non-) existing links to representative politics. Most research concentrates on single pTA procedures.[2] There is urgent need for more comparative research. Overall, we find a diversity of instruments aiming at the integration of different social actors, especially of the general public, in participatory TA. This diversity can be 'condensed' to a smaller number of specific types. Recently, several typologies have been suggested, for example by Joss (2003), Braun et al. (2002), Martinsen (2006), Burgess and Chilvers (2006), Hendriks et al. (2007), or Hansen (2006).

Abels and Bora (2004) proposed the most differentiated typology (cf. table 1) based on the form dimension of procedures, i.e. the

Table 1: Participatory TA, its participants and models of democracy

Model	Participants (*key actors*)	Underlying model of democracy
Dialogue	*stakeholders*	pluralism + deliberative elements
Narrow pTA	*Scientific experts* and stakeholders	more or less deliberative
Legal public hearing	Lay people and scientific experts (*administrator*)	participatory, in fact: deliberative
Consensus conference	*Lay people* and scientific experts	deliberative
Extended consensus conference	*Lay people*, scientific experts, and stakeholders	deliberative + pluralist elements
Voting conference	Lay people, scientific experts, policy-makers (stakeholders)	deliberative + pluralist elements
Scenario workshop	Lay people, scientific experts, policy-makers, stakeholders	participatory-deliberative + pluralist elements

[2] Nevertheless: there is a surprising lack of knowledge about what actually happens *inside* the pTA. The process is a black box that urgently needs to be opened. Exceptions are Bora & Hausendorf 2006, Görsdorf 2006.

heterogeneity of social actors participating in pTA (stakeholders, the general public/lay people, scientific experts and policy-makers). The seven types also differ with regard to the procedural rules, i.e. the question which of these social groups is in a key position and what the basic procedural rules are. What's more, the typology is based on the assumption of a strong relationship between the form dimension and the functional dimension. This means that depending on who is in a key position and what the procedural rules are, specific types of pTA are more or less equipped to fulfil a number of possible objectives. The *dialogue procedure*, for example, is a partisan procedure since it involves stakeholders only. It may allow for the identification of areas of consensus and lack of agreement between stakeholders; this could be useful for policy-makers especially if it is supported by corporatist traditions of interest intermediation. The expert-stakeholder-procedure (or *narrow pTA*) is fact-finding oriented and aims at identifying consent and dissent on scientific knowledge. This can be helpful for clarifying political options. The *legal public hearing* is a legally framed procedure in which the administrator holds the key position; while affected citizens can bring forward their concerns, only legally relevant arguments can influence the final administrative decision and hence legitimize it. The following two models, the *consensus conference* and the *extended consensus conference*, are 'non-partisan forums' (Hendriks et al. 2007) because lay people act as citizens without a fixed agenda; they question experts and assess the technology under debate. These models allow the fostering and enlightening of public debate by the elicitation of the typical and lay perspective. *Voting conferences* and *scenario workshops* engage a variety of social groups and enable them to look at the issue from different group perspectives. They are hybrid forms because they combine citizen with expert and stakeholder participation (and also direct participation of policy-makers). The crucial function shared by *all* models is democratisation of public policy-making; it is "governance by deliberation".

However, the actual meaning of democratisation and how participation is linked to democratisation and deliberation should not be taken for granted. It raises questions about the model of democracy underlying the various types of pTA. According to the Abels/Bora typology, all models are first and foremost deliberative, i.e. discursive arguing is the basic procedural rule. In so doing, they all rest – at least implicitly – on theories of deliberative democracy. However, the theoretical framework has been extended beyond deliberative democracy since several models incorporate elements of pluralism and/or participatory democracy in

their design. Depending on the underlying model and the way different elements are combined, the role of public participation differs.
I argue that these different forms of participation in science/technology governance, which relate to different functions, have different effects on the institutional void, i.e. for a linkage between pTA and representative politics.

C. Participation revisited or: Which democratic theory for pTA?

Citizens' participation is *the* key feature of pTA; it is equated with the quality of democracy. According to this argument, the quality of democracy improves with the degree or participation achieved. This reasoning goes back to the liberal tradition of democracy as self-determination in which citizens are the best representatives of their own interests. When looking at the literature on democratic theory this equation is all but clear and obvious. Different strands in democratic theory conceptualize the role of participation in different ways.

In principal, the claim for more, better or enhanced public participation can be based on either purely normative or functional reasons. Whereas normative arguments consider participation as a value in itself, functional arguments regard participation as a means to an end, for example, to secure social acceptance of a new technology, to adapt it to consumer needs, or to improve the quality of policy-decisions. The deliberative tradition in pTA clearly concentrates on normative grounds, but combines these with the "quality argument", i.e. the inclusion of all relevant positions (represented by participants) shall allow for finding the best solution. We find this reasoning in recent theoretical publications that assess in particular the deliberative potential of what we have called the consensus conference model (cf. Einsiedel & Eastlick 2000; Smith & Wales 2000). Most advocates of pTA combine normative and functional justifications (cf., for example, Bechmann 1993).

As our typology illustrates, pTA models differ with regard to their empirical features and theoretical background. Scholars of democracy agree that *some* participation is a vital condition for democracy; there is, however, vast disagreement over the ways of participation and over the extent to which public participation is absolutely necessary. At one end of the spectrum we find Schumpeter's concept of elite democracy, at the other end we find Barber's concepts of 'strong democracy'. In what follows I briefly sketch out the main strands in democratic theory with regard to the meaning of participation for democracy as well as with regard to the idea of pTA (for a more detailed discussion see Abels & Bora 2004).

A principal distinction in democratic theory is drawn between empirical and normative theories; *pluralism* is the most prominent theory of what is believed to be the empirical strand. The major advantage of this liberal approach is that it is highly compatible with mass democracy and functional differentiation. Pluralism assumes that citizens actively organize themselves in social groups and act collectively in order to promote their groups' interests. Participation is realized via collective interest group politics; the public good is achieved through the process of interest mediation, but not given a priori. Accountable representatives and a pluralist society guarantee and stabilize democracy, whereas more direct forms of political participation are considered unnecessary or even harmful. For neopluralists the state has to guarantee the free competition among interest groups. Laird has realized the potential of pluralism for pTA. According to him, the asset of pluralism is the specific inclusion of the cognitive dimension. He argues that interest groups have exclusive knowledge in the field to be regulated and also the willingness to learn from others. Therefore, pluralist mechanisms 'make the most rapid progress on substantive mastering of an issue' (Laird 1993: 357). This is an optimistic interpretation. Others argue that 'partisans make poor deliberators because they have committed agenda' (Hendriks et al. 2007: 362). Partisans, or stakeholders, may not have the autonomy to shift their preferences because they may act as delegates with a restricted mandate. This is certainly not a favourable condition for deliberations since it rests on the assumption that deliberators can be persuaded by arguments, and can change their preferences.

The pluralist approach is embodied in the *dialogue model*. In this model, stakeholders, i.e. actors who have a vested interest in the issue at hand and a committed agenda, talk to each other. This dialogue is not purely deliberative; empirical cases illustrate that it often includes elements of bargaining. In this sense, deliberation becomes part of the strategic game played by interest groups – irrespective of whether they come from the private or voluntary sector – and thus involves the question of which resources stakeholders have at hand. A weakness of the pluralist strand is to assume that all relevant interests can be organized and represented; in addition, there is the notion that interest groups are equal. Empirical research illustrates differences with regard to the ability to organize collective interests and with regard to a power imbalance between collective actors. In general, economic interests have an organizational advantage and more access to resources as compared to public interests (e.g. environmental or consumer groups). Yet, to some extent policy-makers can adopt measures to balance out these power differences.

The *participatory* strand in democratic theory has recently been revitalised. In contrast to previous more radical approaches, present participatory theories assume that participatory procedures are complementary to, but never a substitute for, representative democracy. These theories share the argument that the limitations imposed on participation by representative politics lead to a de-politicised public. Instruments for enhanced participation are perceived as a way out and allow citizens to represent their interests. In addition, they assume that interests are not exogenous to the democratic process, but constructed and changed by the democratic process itself. Again, public interests and public virtues are considered to be a result of citizen involvement. A number of objections have been raised against such concepts, for example the idealist concept of humans, the lack of interest of citizens, the disregard of institutions as well as of the complexity of policy problems and a narrow focus on the input dimension of politics.

Participatory theories take a prominent place in the conceptual debate on pTA. Foltz (1999), for example, bases his participatory call on the ideas of Benjamin Barber and Carole Pateman. According to him, an enhanced participation of marginalized groups such as women and people of colour is one of the great assets of participatory procedures. This is certainly the case, at least in those procedures where lay people are recruited by a combination of random and intentional criteria (e.g. sex, age, ethnicity, geographic background) in order to ensure that a diversity of voices be represented in the lay panel. Those procedures based completely on a system of self-selection of participants (e.g. the legal public hearing where those who feel affected can participate) cannot apply such selection criteria and probably also suffer from the general bias identified in the standard model of political participation.[3]

Fiorino (1990) mentions four criteria to measure the democratic character of a participatory process: the direct participation of citizens;

[3] Social stratification criteria such as sex, professional background, level of education, age, and ethnicity influence people's political participation. This pattern is also found in direct democracy. Voting – still the most ubiquitous form of political participations – levels this out to some extent.

the participation of citizens in collective decision-making; opportunities for a face-to-face communication; and citizens should enjoy equal rights with representatives of public administration and technical experts. Fiorino's criteria go beyond the consultative role of participation. Yet, most pTA is advisory. There is only one model, i.e. the legal public hearing, which is firmly connected to a bureaucratic decision-making procedure.[4] While this strong link between the participatory and the decision-making arena may seem positive at first glance, it is exactly this connection which leads to a clear functional deficit. The reason is that administrative decision-making is intrinsically linked to the legal system and its orientation toward the state of the art in science and technology. This allows the administrator to take into account only scientific arguments while other concerns raised by citizens are actually marginalized. They are legally irrelevant, because they are not based on scientific reasoning which is the form of knowledge privileged by the legal procedure (cf. in detail Bora 1999; Bora & Hausendorf 2006). Especially demands for ethical justifications which are so common in participatory arenas – and which are essential elements of citizenship – are not compatible with legal norms and principles; they cannot be turned into valid legal claims (cf. the contribution by Baier in this volume).

Deliberative theory of democracy is a recent development (cf. Warren 2002) and it has become *the* major concept for advocating pTA. Therefore, I will discuss this concept in more detail. First of all, it is important to acknowledge major differences between participatory and deliberative approaches (cf. Papadopoulos & Warin 2007: 450 f). They share the belief that representative politics should be improved by supplementing it with either more direct democratic instruments (the "participationist" argument) or by communication-centred public space instruments (the "deliberationist" argument). In contrast to "participationists", "deliberationists" concentrate on the quality of the discussion. It is important to recognize that citizen participation does not conclusively follow from this throughput-orientation. One could even argue – and this is the standard argument – that the best argumentative quality can only be achieved by expert communication. However, experts always have to address the inherent problem of scientific uncertainty to which pTA claims to be a solution by social inclusion of those affected.

[4] For practical experiences with such procedures in different national and legal contexts cf. to the papers by Baier, Iványi et al., Rahm and Collavin in this volume.

We can distinguish between a weaker or more realistic variation of such procedural theories. The stronger variation rests its deliberative claim on Habermas' discourse theory. Such approaches clearly favour deliberative arguing over all kinds of strategic bargaining. The ideal is that only the best arguments shall prevail in public policy-making. These deliberative approaches are also called procedural democracy, because the main source of legitimacy is the procedures; it shall foster a process of collective reasoning on public affairs leading to the most reasonable arguments. Whereas participatory democratic theory considers participation an end in itself, in deliberative thinking it can be a means to an end: reasonable arguments for better will-formation and policy-making. In some sense, deliberative democracy is a pedagogical concept in its 'transformation of the polity into a school' (Tucker 2008, 129). Proponents of deliberative models acknowledge the complexity of policy issues as well as the prominent role of scientific knowledge granting a vital function to experts in policy-making. However, advocates of pTA call attention to different forms of knowledge, including every-day knowledge, as well as the normative component. Accordingly, deliberative approaches can be combined with participatory elements. The inclusion of those affected and their discursive arguments (or at least the presence of all relevant arguments in the procedure) results in reasonable outcomes. According to the deliberative model, individual preferences undergo a transformative 'purgatory process' in the agora resulting in a common will. According to Abromeit (2002: 103 ff.), democracy is no longer perceived as an instrument of liberal self-determination, but as a means of 'epistemic proceduralism' to achieve sensible politics.

The main argument against deliberative approaches – particularly against the strong variation – is that they build on the idea of ideal discourse freed from social power structures in which participants face each other as equals. In addition, its great strength, deliberation, is also a key problem. From a "participationist" perspective, the communicative and rationalist bias of deliberative procedures may lead to the exclusion of social groups since it places demanding requirements on the participants (such as articulateness, linguistic and cognitive competences). The so-called standard model of political participation also affects deliberative – as well as participatory – procedures. Whenever there is a "natural" self-selection of participants, i.e. when those who feel affected and/or are interested can (and do) participate in pTA, this standard model comes into play and we see a higher degree of participation of those usually privileged (in short: white, middle-aged, middle-class men). Participatory procedures relying on such self-selection modes are sometimes charged to be biased toward the educated middle class (cf. Görsdorf 2006: 179), and, thus, fail to properly represent the public. An example is the UK-based 'GM nation?' debate. It was organized by the government: 675 open public meetings took place across the country with an estimated 20,000 (Hansen 2006: 578) to 36.000 participants (Burgess & Chilvers 2006: 719). Despite the large number of participants, critics spoke of a self-selection and flawed representation, because people who had an interest in the topic where more likely to come to the public meetings. In response, the organizers set up closed focus group meetings with a selected group of citizens supposed to be non-interested and representative of the public. This is not only an example of political and organizational tampering with public procedures but also an interesting example of the confusion of who actually represents "the public".

Nevertheless, in most pTA procedures there is no self-selection by participants: organizers of pTA select members of the public – as citizens – in order to "represent" and speak on behalf of public concerns. This selection process is partly informed in its idea of representation insofar as a random selection of citizens is often combined with social criteria such as sex, age, professional background, ethnicity, and geographical origin. Given that the number of participants in pTA is usually very small (10 to 30 people), numerical representativeness is impossible (cf. Brown 2006). What can be achieved, however, is the representation of a broad spectrum of arguments which then inform and contribute to the deliberation; in a strict sense, deliberation does not even require the presence of the social actors themselves, but the presence of (at the very least) a suitable spectrum of arguments and values in order to come to a rational conclusion.

Recently, Tucker (2008) brought forward some strong arguments, claiming the theory entails oligarchic tendencies. Based on an analysis of the theoretical foundations and of the practice of deliberative democracy in consensus conferences, he argues that deliberative processes are manipulated so that in the end, the deliberating mini-public adjust their preferences to those of the minority of organizers and facilitators of the consensus conferences. While I do not find the empirical cases completely convincing, Tucker has a point. He comes up with some procedural suggestions for diminishing or reducing such tendencies and increasing the autonomy of deliberators.

What is clear from this brief overview is that there is no such thing as *a single* democratic theory. Different forms of pTA can go hand in hand with different strands. All theoretical approaches entail conceptual advantages and problems. Normative selection criteria limit the pTA options available and deny the plurality of pTA procedures. I argue that such normative preferences limit our ability to think about meaningful linkages between pTA and representative politics.

D. Reconciling participatory TA and representative politics – some modest proposals

With the following proposals I intend to make pTA more meaningful, i.e. to improve the resonance of pTA in the social and political sphere. Before I outline my proposals, I have to introduce some underlying key assumptions and problems of pTA.

1. *Assumptions*

The centre of my argument is that pTA can – and should – be linked to representative democracy. Linking pTA to research on direct democracy can be instructive for developing such linkages between different mechanisms of democratic rule. There are, however, substantial differences between decision-oriented instruments of direct democracy and deliberation-oriented instruments of pTA. Plebiscitary decisions, for example, may be subject of judicial review or have clear legal limitations. This is certainly different for the purely advisory pTA outcomes; they have to be linked only to the addressees of pTA advice. While direct democracy is strong with regard to the decisional dimension, it may nevertheless fail on the deliberative dimension of policy-making. This is exactly why we find pTA experiments even in Switzerland (cf. Bütschi et al. 2002).

Direct democracy increases the legitimacy and efficiency of decisions. According to advocates of pTA, this also applies to pTA. Under which conditions can they fulfil such criteria? It is insufficient to evaluate pTA merely by input and process-based input criteria (e.g. representativeness of participants, independence and transparency of the process) or by output-based criteria (e.g. resources, structured decision-making); outcome-based criteria such as the effects of pTA on its social and political environment have to be considered (cf. Rowe & Frewer 2000). This level of evaluation is most challenging. The fact that outcomes are methodologically hard to evaluate (due to long-term impacts and empirical complexity) implies neither that we can nor that we should avoid them. Other evaluation criteria are also important, but they are only part of a broader picture. I do not intend to develop a list of outcome-based evaluation criteria, but to focus on principal-driven and theory-based options for increasing the impact of pTA. I am well aware that so far the elucidation 'of crucial links between participatory processes and participatory outcomes will remain speculative' (Burgess & Chilvers 2006: 724).

Given the reality of pluralist mass democracies there is no alternative to representative politics. Even advocates of a strong participatory model do attest to the need for representative institutions and majoritarian politics. This, however, does not imply that it cannot be improved by changing procedures or by combining it with participatory and deliberative elements. Deliberative elements, for example, are often informal parts of majoritarian politics. The key question is how to combine different modes of governance in such a way that they still adhere to democratic criteria.

Procedures have to be designed to allow the pursuit of the crux of pTA, i.e. *advising policy-makers*. Participatory TA 'aims to provide advice to policy-makers that reflects a wider range of framings, knowledge and values' (Burgess & Chilvers 2006: 713). The encouragement of public debate is a secondary goal.[5] These goals are important irrespective of who actually organises a pTA procedure. Even if some pTA organizers are closer to the public sphere, policy advice – in order to inform and influence policy-making – is still the *key* reason for involving the public (cf. Hansen 2006: 575).

Although impact assessment is a great conceptual and methodological challenge (cf. also Joss & Bellucci 2002), empirical research illustrates

[5] In response to the deficits and failure of most pTA in the political sphere, some advocates have turned to the public sphere (e.g. Joss 2002). If pTA by and large fails in the political arena, it shall nevertheless achieve some kind of resonance in the social environment. For such a function, pTA requires better media publicity. In mass democracies the public sphere is mediated via mass media. Empirical research illustrates that most pTA is hardly covered by the media at all. Often pTA procedures are only reported on in local media, even if the issue under debate is of national concern. There are, however, exceptions such as the 'GM nation?' which was a highly contested procedure taking place in a polarized public sphere, and, therefore, created 'a significant level of communicative resonance' (Hansen 2006: 579).

that pTA so far usually falls short of this advisory function. The policy effects of those pTA models that integrate policy- and decision-makers may be more considerable.[6] Unlike elections or referenda – and also unlike other forms of participatory experiments in other policy fields such as mediation, right-to-know legislation or regulatory negotiations – pTA is *not* typically institutionally integrated into decision- and policy-making processes. In order to make pTA more meaningful and create resonance in the political and social environment, such procedures should not take place in an 'institutional void' (Hajer, quoted in Görsdorf 2006); they require structural linkages to their political and social environment. Yet, drawing these connections is easier for pTA models built (to some extent) on interest group politics (such as the dialogue model), since they are more compatible with "normal" politics. While trying to avoid the pitfalls of technocratic participatory engineering, the crucial question is *how* pTA can be linked to its social and political environment. Such links are always complex and case-sensitive (cf. Bütschi & Nentwich 2002; Hennen 2002). Nevertheless, a consideration of links between procedures and their outcomes cannot be left to individual cases of pTA; neither can they be designed on an ad hoc basis. The objective here is to think about linkages that allow for an integration of pTA into the institutional architecture of polyarchies (Robert Dahl).

That said the rest of the paper addresses this issue while taking the diversity of pTA models into account. I concentrate on the question of the level of pTA, the participants and the addressees. My focus here is on what the design could be rather than on strategic questions of how to achieve such linkages.

2. *What is the appropriate level?*

A key aspect of pTA is the question of social and political regulation of new technologies. Thus, it is important to take into account the authoritative political level of regulation and the corresponding level at which pTA takes place. A local issue such as the decision concerning a waste management site, for example, is best dealt with at the local level, whereas a national issue such as a policy on genetic testing in the

[6] Usually at the final day of a consensus conference the citizens' report is handed over to politicians and the public; in the scenario workshop and the voting conference model, however, policy-makers are active participants in the pTA process.

workplace requires attention at the national level. This is easy. It is usually not so easy to distinguish at which level people are or feel affected, and at which level regulation is adopted. It requires thinking about the connection between pTA and authoritative political institutions at each respective level from the local all the way up to the global level.

Today, technological development is often a highly internationalized endeavour. The human genome project, for example, was an international scientific undertaking involving numerous research teams from many countries. It is an outstanding, yet not unique example of the internationalization of science. Nevertheless, the nation state may still be the authority on the regulatory level. Even if genetic knowledge on the human genome is produced by international research teams, regulation on the use of genetic knowledge, e.g. in pre-natal screening, is still a national issue. Even research is subject to national codes and laws. These examples also illustrate the limits of a state-centric perspective because people can travel to a different country for pre-natal treatment not allowed in their home country. So what is the appropriate level of regulation then? Genetic testing can be framed as medical services and goods. In the European Union products developed in one country can be distributed everywhere in the common market. Yet there are exceptions; medical services are still dominated by national rules whereas the EU has become an authoritative regulator in many fields of technology such as agricultural biotechnology. The latter is certainly a prominent case of transnational political conflicts where corresponding pTA procedures have been conducted at the national level, such as the British 'GM nation' debate, the UK consensus conference on food biotechnology, public debates in the Netherlands, the German procedure 'Diskurs Grüne Gentechnik' or numerous legal public hearings on the experimental release of GMO plants. The GMO debate in the EU (along with the food safety crisis in the 1990s) led to a rhetorical shift in the governance mode towards better public participation along with impressive legal change (a much stricter legal framework for GMOs) and some institutional change, i.e. the rise of a EU food safety regime (cf. Abels 2002). Recently, the first ever pan-European pTA took place, supported, among others, by the European Commission: the Meeting of Minds – European Citizen's Deliberation on Brain Science (www.meetingmindseurope.org). This procedure combines elements of the consensus conference model with the US-American town hall meeting method. It was burdened with several structural flaws common to the consensus conference model (Abels & Mölders 2007). The event was very well-organised, complex and highly structured, as well as co-financed by the European Commission; nevertheless, its impact on EU policy-making is all but clear. That said, it is still an outstanding example of developing pTA beyond the national level.

The EU is certainly a prominent example. It is equipped with a high legal authority that is built on the supremacy of European law over national law, and with dense institutional architecture. It is not the only case of transnational or even global regulation of science and technology (cf. Abels 2007). The Council of Europe, for example, has adopted the 'Convention for the protection of human rights and dignity of the human being with regard to the application of biology and medicine' in 1997, as well as several recommendations on prenatal and genetic testing. According to data from the 'Eurobarometer', all these issues are highly contested in European publics, yet formalized public involvement was left in wanting. The OECD is another prominent example of international regulation among industrialized nations. At the global level the United Nations engaged in the regulation of new technologies. The 1997 'Declaration on the Human Genome and Human Rights' is a good example; furthermore, a declaration on human cloning was finally adopted in 2005. An auxiliary UN regulation is the Cartagena Biosafety Protocol on the trans-boundary movement of GMOs as part of the Convention on Biological Diversity. Again, these are all crucial issues on which no formalized public participation and certainly no pTA, ever took place at the global level. A third example is the WTO and its SPS and TBT agreements, which have repercussions on the global commercialisation and diffusion of GMOs. Due to the wide-ranging effects of WTO regulations as well as its neoliberal orientation and the exclusive character of WTO politics, critics often question its legitimacy.

The cases of the Council of Europe, OECD, UN and WTO substantially differ from the EU case concerning the status of legal regulations. International law is addressed to and places legal obligations on individual states; however, the UN and Council of Europe member states decide when and how to implement international law.[7] This opens up the arena for national politics, and, thereby, options for national pTA. EU law, on the contrary, supersedes national law and is binding, often

[7] The WTO is a partial exception because of its legally binding dispute settlement mechanism which was, in fact, enforced against the EU with regard to strict EU laws on GMOs.

even (in case of regulations as a specific form of EU law) directly in effect without transposition into national law. Its implementation is enforced by the European Commission and, moreover, by the European Court of Justice.

In sum, the globalization of technological development and diffusion challenges the concept of pTA, which has been strongly linked to nation-states. Given that the EU is a peculiar non-state polity, this is an easier – but certainly not easy – task. Pan-European pTA always poses massive constraints on procedures and raises many problems to be solved in order to conduct a pTA. Any participatory procedure beyond the national level is certainly more difficult to conduct, yet there are pressing issues for cross-national deliberation (cf. Levine et al. 2005, 285). Procedures dominated by citizens/lay people (e.g. the consensus conference model, scenario workshop, or voting conference model) have even more issues since they pose, above all, questions of representativeness and size (besides the obvious language problems). Accordingly, procedures based on the dialogue model or on a deliberation between experts and stakeholders are easier to conduct at a transnational level, because scientific communication is always deliberative, and the scientific community is by itself international. Therefore, for scientific experts, a deliberative, trans-national, expert-stakeholder procedure is nothing novel. Secondly, in the EU we do find well organized and professional interest groups. The transfer of competences from the EU to the national level has led to the co-evolution of European federations and associations in many fields of society. The European Commission has actively promoted the establishment of transnational stakeholder organizations. There is, however, an imbalance at the EU level. So far business interests are better organized than public interest groups, a fact which poses some difficulty for transnational deliberation. Nevertheless, such structural imbalances are also found at the national level and are addressed in national pTA involving stakeholders, by different means of selecting stakeholders based on representativeness and how strongly they are affected. The problem of imbalance is certainly more severe at the European level, but it can be dealt with. The major problem is that such stakeholder and expert-based pTA may still receive criticism for not being participatory, for being merely *expertocratic,* or just a refined form of pressure-group politics. This takes us to the crucial issue of who the appropriate participants are in pTA.

3. *Who are the appropriate participants?*

Table 1 illustrates that there are four principal groups of participants in pTA: citizens, stakeholders, experts, and policy-makers. All four groups require in-depth discussion. For example, *citizens* can mean different things. According to pluralist thinking, stakeholders are also citizens. They are people organizing because of a particular shared interest on which they act collectively in order to promote an interest. The will of all is in that case the outcome of many particularistic interests. Against this background, the distinction between citizens and stakeholders is a social construct. Usually the emphasis in pTA is on '*idiots*' – in the original Greek meaning of 'private individuals who are exclusively dedicated to the privacy of one's own' (Lezaun & Soneryd 2006: 3). Lezaun and Soneryd (2006) indicate that it is exactly these 'idiots', i.e. people with *lay knowledge* and *no vested interests*, which are of interest in public participation. Participatory TA, as a form of 'mini-public', shall help to bring about lay perspectives and knowledge. This approach certainly concentrates on the normative rather than cognitive aspects of pTA – although this distinction is problematic insofar as it separates two interrelated concerns. Sometimes citizens may be well-informed and educated in some field related to the topic of the pTA procedure; sometimes they may have a specific personal interest. It is indeed unlikely to consider citizens completely 'disinterested' in the issue under debate since pTA is usually a highly demanding and time-consuming procedure; pTA is also a voluntary procedure so participants need to be 'interested' in one way or another. Especially at the local level, normal citizens may also be stakeholders if the pTA is an issue of local planning, for example. Yet, unlike organized interest groups, such interested citizens will not be committed to any particular agenda.

I have already mentioned that *stakeholders* are, of course, also citizens, but a particular group of citizens. Stakeholders are often defined as organized interest groups such as business associations, companies, environmental or consumer groups, but may also include groups of loosely organized citizens (or even individual citizens) with a vested interest in the particular issue at hand. In pluralist theory, stakeholders – called interest groups, pressure groups or organized interests – are key actors in politics. They engage in politics and seek to influence policy-makers on behalf of their own special interests and simultaneously contribute some form of expert knowledge important for efficient policy-making and implementation. Yet their expertise is always "tainted" by their interests and special agenda. As a result, deliberative pTA aims at separating "tainted" interests (and expertise) from "pure" knowledge by trying to engage interest groups into a *deliberative* mode of communication concerning the best arguments (rather than a mode of bargaining over interests). The discussed pTA models do so in different ways: some models rely on deliberation among stakeholders (dialogue model); some subject stakeholder statements to a deliberative assessment by different social actors such as citizens; some use experts or policy-makers (extended consensus conference model, voting conference model). The deliberative prerogative is always a serious challenge for stakeholders since it changes the rule of pluralist bargaining politics, even more so in corporatist systems for those interest groups who enjoy privileged access. Defending interests always requires some arguing. For stakeholders, engaging in pTA only makes sense if they think it might foster their specific interests, and/or if they are not satisfied with the status quo and hope to change it. When the quality of arguments – not the availability of material resources – is the decisive factor in a deliberative event, there is no guarantee for success. Accordingly, empirical research illustrates that it is difficult to motivate stakeholders, above all well organised interest groups, to participate in pTA at all. They need a strong incentive – such as high costs for non-participation – and they must be dedicated to the deliberative process, since they have alternative options; they may simply choose the exit option if the procedure does not seem favourable to them anymore, and if their options in deliberation are restricted by the mandate (cf. Hendriks 2002; Hendriks et al. 2007). Yet there may be a distinction between varying kinds of interest groups: it is certainly more difficult to argue that profit-oriented private interest groups work in favour of the "common good" than for so-called public interests, whose starting point is their particular interpretation of the common good.

Experts are a key component. They adapt easily to the model of deliberative democracy since argumentative reasoning lies at the very heart of expertise as a form of specialized knowledge. Argumentation corresponds above all with the logic of doing science; hence, we find scientific experts in almost all models of pTA.[8] This is, furthermore, based on the assumption that scientific knowledge is superior to other

[8] The dialogue model is an exception to this rule. Nevertheless, communication among stakeholders in pTA is based on argumentative reasoning and not (at least not primarily) on strategic bargaining.

forms of knowledge. Expertise is, however, not restricted to scientific knowledge. Stakeholders, for instance, can also be experts who provide valuable specialized knowledge. However, this scientific approach certainly privileges some kinds of knowledge. For proponents of pTA, the implicit hierarchy working in favour of scientific knowledge is problematic; they promote the need to "democratise science". This "democratised" approach builds on a difference model of the expert/'idiots' relation, according to which different social actors provide different forms of knowledge. There is no *a priori* hierarchy between these forms of knowledge, but they complement each other and emphasize diverse aspects of social life. The communicative process is then perceived as an opportunity for mutual learning among social actors.[9] The consensus conference model is a good example for such an approach, wherein lay people question expert knowledge and assess it according to the background of their everyday experience.

To involve *policy-makers* in a pTA event (scenario-workshop and voting conference model) is a more recent development. It can be interpreted as a reaction to the so far limited impact of most pTA. Given that policy-advice is a key function of pTA (for a critical debate cf. Saretzki 2007), most pTA has focussed on policy-makers as sheer addressees (or as the organizers, clients or financier of "up-stream" pTA) of pTA outcomes, not as participants in the participatory procedure itself. For a long time, involving policy-makers as participants was regarded as the interference of elite politics; a tainting the "pure" participatory process. Policy-makers are suspected to use pTA as a business-as-usual public relations exercise (especially when they are the clients). Participatory TA then becomes a mere legitimizing and conflict-management device, rather than a means for democratisation of technology governance and empowerment of the technological citizen. Following Tucker (2008), including policy-makers in the procedure itself would probably increase oligarchic tendencies. Yet, the scenario workshop and voting conference model demonstrate that the role of policy-makers in pTA depends upon its procedural framing.[10] Policy-making is always as much a process of arguing as of bargaining among partisan and hence strategic actors. Nevertheless, including

[9] There is no sufficient evidence in the literature if learning actually takes place. Also, the definitions of what constitutes social learning differ.

[10] In these two models, policy-makers enjoy equal rights with other social groups; they engage in a deliberative communication with experts and "normal" citizens.

them in pTA can help to strengthen the accountability relation between partisan actors and their constituency.

It is at least reasonable to assume, the involvement of policy-makers concerned with the debated issue in the representative arena increases the possibility for pTA to impact the policy, in the sense that the policy (-maker) is more likely to take into account the pTA results. This hypothesis certainly requires empirical verification. Policy-maker's participation may be a favourable condition, but is certainly no guarantee for greater impact. This is because policy-maker's decisions are influenced by a number of factors, and even if s/he directly participated in it, a pTA event can only be one of them. Direct policy influence is certainly the strongest form of possible impact; policy-learning, though hard to prove, is another socially desirable form of pTA impact. The case of the German parliamentary inquiry commission (Enquete-Kommission) is an instructive example.

Inquiry commissions are inspired by a more "pragmatistic" model – in the Habermasian sense – of policy advice and public deliberation. Such commissions are a special kind of temporary committee set up by the German Bundestag usually on wide-ranging issues that require long-term attention and a more transparent process of knowledge and preference generation (e.g. life science, civil society, and globalisation). So far, a number of topics relate to socio-technological change, for example, the inquiry commission on 'Law and Ethics of Biomedicine' which was organised for two consecutive legislative terms. Usually, half of the committee members are MPs, half are scientific experts. Each party is allowed to nominate a certain number of delegates proportional to their numerical strength in parliament. Empirical research reveals that the partisan nomination process often results in partisan-aligned scientific experts. Furthermore, they show that extensive exchange and deliberation between the two groups of participants, politicians and experts, can be very intense. In addition, such commissions often have a positive role on general public debate in that they attract some attention to the scrutinized issue.

Yet, the experience with inquiry commissions also tells a story about the limits of deliberation, since MPs are not individuals, but "party animals". Therefore, any outcome of the inquiry process is "filtered" through the party agenda. If there is already a more or less fixed party agenda on the issue under debate, social learning is limited by partisan politics and parliamentary party rules (Fraktionsdisziplin). Individual MPs then perceive the inquiry commission as an arena for partisan politics and their personal career. The structural similarities between the inquiry commission model and those pTA models involving policy-makers are the principal deliberative character of the procedure and the close exchange with other social groups. If social learning and policy impact is unlikely in the inquiry commission under condition of a fixed party agenda, it will be just as unlikely in the pTA process. In both cases timing is a crucial issue, because inquiry commissions can have a policy impact if there is no such pre-fixed party agenda. A decisive difference between these two kinds of procedures is, while most of the inquiry commission deliberation takes place behind closed doors (apart from public hearings and the minutes of meetings), the pTA deliberation is less secretive insofar as policy-makers are urged to deliberate in public and to defend policy positions against arguments by other social groups, such as experts and citizens. This may be helpful in illuminating the political room for manoeuvre, in contrast to expert and lay perspectives. This distinction could be a major advantage of the pTA models. Citizens' reports often conclude with policy proposals to policy-makers that are too general. It seems that citizens often *over*estimate the steering capacity of politics and *under*estimate the problems of decision-making and effective implementation. Again, this is a hypothesis requiring empirical verification.

4. *What are appropriate addressees?*

The "institutional void" in which most pTA takes place gives rise as much to normative questions as to questions of institutional design. According to Hajer (quoted in Görsdorf 2006), the institutional void is an undifferentiated space in a differentiated environment. While my focus has to this point been on the 'undifferentiated space' of different pTA models, in what follows I want to turn my attention to a segment of the differentiated pTA environment, i.e. its political environment. I will not go as far as Leib (2004), who suggests the constitutionalization of deliberative forums, especially the citizen panel, as a fourth, 'popular branch of government'. The key function of the traditional three branches of government is to allow checks and balances. Yet, pTA cannot develop in this direction. Neither do I suggest 'deliberative elections' characterized by a close link of such new deliberative forums to the electoral process, as Gastil (2000) does; this would certainly link deliberative forums strongly to representative politics, despite the fact that we do find examples in the general literature on public deliberation (cf. Levine et al. 2005: 276f.) In comparison to the ambitious proposals above, my suggestions are modest and concentrate on the core function of pTA, i.e. to provide policy-advice.[11] The most prominent means of integrating various expertise and advice in the policy process is to conduct *hearings*. This also means that pTA as policy-advice competes with many other forms of policy input.

First of all, the basis for my suggestions is the question of the addressee of the policy advice at hand. There are good reasons to assume that technological developments are mainly influenced by social systems other than politics, i.e. the economy, and society as a whole. This implies that pTA calls for a different addressee than policy-makers. It undoubtedly highlights the possibility that economic actors such as companies could be important addressees – at least in citizen-dominated models. In models that involve organized interests groups, they serve as "stakeholder-participants". In the programmatic debate, however, there is certainly some shift from advising politicians' (Politikberatung) to 'advising society' (Gesellschaftsberatung) (cf. Saretzki 2007; Joss 2002). The political system is hitherto important for the regulation of technologies and their potential impacts on society. Consequently, the political system is and will remain at least *one* important addressee of pTA. But "the political and administrative system" or "the political environment" requires differentiation between different institutions and actors. So what are the key institutions in polyarchy?

Politics is always partisan and *political parties* occupy a central position in politics. Parties function as intermediates between societal interests and political institutions. Those pTA models that do not directly involve policy-makers – i.e. the majority (e.g. consensus conferences, dialogue model) – often present the results (e.g. a citizen report) to politicians, usually representatives from the ministerial department in charge and selected members of parliament. In so doing they treat these politicians as representatives of the particular organization they come from and not as party representatives. Firstly, pTA – and especially citizen-dominated procedures – could help political parties – if early enough, and that is certainly a problem – to fulfil the

[11] Even if one does not consider advising policy-makers, but advising society as a whole as the major objective of pTA, it still requires thinking about mechanisms and institutions in the differentiated social environment.

interest articulation function of political parties. PTA then becomes a means for securing responsiveness by observing social debates about contested issues before aggregating partisan interests and political programmes. It is much more informative than surveys to monitor the *vox populi* "inspired" by expertise and argumentation. Secondly, pTA facilitators could actively approach party politics in their dissemination strategies and acknowledge that the political sphere is highly partisan. Stakeholder-oriented pTA, in contrast, is less innovative for political parties since there are often previously established links between parties and organized interest groups who seek and sometimes have exclusive access to political parties and state institutions especially in more corporatist systems. Nevertheless, different forms of pTA can be considered part of the intermediation function of political parties.

In democracies, *parliaments* are the key political institution since they embody the idea of the sovereignty of the people. This makes parliaments "natural" addressees of pTA as the "people's voice". Yet, parliaments have to be disaggregated along partisan and functional lines. Many parliaments have established special units for TA (cf. Vig & Paschen 2000). They could be facilitators as well as addressees of pTA. Some of these parliamentary TA units who are chief pTA facilitators have adopted a highly participatory style, for example, the Danish Board of Technology or the Dutch Rathenau Institute, while most units still operate on a more expertocratic TA model. Empirical research on pTA seems to indicate that the policy impacts of pTA conducted by parliamentary TA units are more effective, yet hard data are missing so far. Yet for most parliamentary units such participatory turn seems unlikely. Furthermore, much pTA is, in fact, conducted by other organizations interested in the field, such as foundations, science museums, or professional communication companies, and are often commissioned or financed by private companies, public administrations and ministries or community groups. The point is that such extra-parliamentary pTA can and should be more closely linked to parliamentary policy-making. Parliamentary TA units, in this sense, could be valuable addressees of pTA.

In addition, parliamentary hearings of experts and stakeholders are a regular instrument used by parliaments and parliamentary committees in the discussion of policy proposals. If pTA is available for the policy under debate, one option is to invite representatives of the pTA procedure to hearings and give them a voice. Authors arguing in favour of a reform of parliamentary systems have also made proposals linking parliamentary procedures to those of a participatory nature: The number of interest representatives in public hearings should be reduced while more independent experts and representatives of citizen groups should be invited. Participatory TA dominated by citizens is in line with such general proposals. The outcomes of the pTA could either be presented by a representative of the citizen panel or alternatively by the facilitator. The latter is a second-best solution if there are no representatives of the citizen panel available (e.g. because the pTA took place some time ago). In case of an inquiry commission or a sub-committee working in the field, a pTA representative could have an observer status.

Hearings are not solely a privilege of parliaments: *ministries* and public administrations conduct hearings as well. Given their informational and knowledge-based advantage, policy proposals are actually typically prepared by ministries (they hardly originate in parliament). In Germany, for example, all federal ministries have to consult "groups with a vested interest" as well as experts when preparing legislative bills and orders. This open door policy is outlined in the common rules of procedures for all federal ministries. Again, representatives of especially citizen-dominated pTA could be consulted as well.

Public administrations, including national or even supranational bodies, are often concerned with contested technologies or issues related to the governance of science e.g. food, technical standards. One the one hand, public administrations are involved in case-by-case legal-administrative decision. One the other hand, regulatory bodies may also have a mandate for rule-making. With regard to rule-application and decision-making, we find one pTA model directly related to this: the legal public hearing (cf. in detail Bora & Hausendorf 2006; cf. also Münte and Baier in this volume). In contrast to the different forms of hearings discussed above, these hearings take place at a local level as part of an administrative authorisation process; everybody who feels affected can have access and voice in these public hearings. In this sense, it is the most participatory procedure. Such public hearings are indeed wide-spread in planning and not specific to governance of science. However, empirical research illustrates some structural problems in this procedure as a result of strict legal framing in contrast to citizens' political concerns. The legal framing allows taking only science-based concerns into account in the final decision. All other kinds of objections (e.g. ethical objections) are procedurally excluded. This procedural limitation turns out to be the fundamental problem for the throughput-legitimacy of this pTA type. This implies that public participation interferes much too late in the legal public hearing. A different approach is to introduce public participation in negotiated rule-negotiation. This is common for independent regulatory agencies in the United States and is also preferred by some authors as a model for Europe (Majone 2005). However, the American experience illustrates that rule-making entails arguing as well as bargaining. Usually, public interest groups play a marginal role in negotiated rule-making whereas business interests prevail. Even if results of pTA could be taken into account in rule-making, this kind of deliberation places higher demands on representatives of pTA than actual hearings since rule-making involves bargaining. This bargaining necessitates the legitimization of resources. Yet such resources are too weak in pTA since the participants, especially in lay-people dominated procedures, do not actually represent anybody: there is no principal-agent-relationship required for bargaining mandates. Furthermore, there is certainly no accountability relationship between citizen-participants in pTA and the general public. Therefore, the role could be at best advisory, but not a seat right at the negotiating table.[12]

Participatory TA can also be extended to the social field. For example, due to social conflicts surrounding new technologies in the life sciences and biomedicine, many countries have set up *special committees*, such as national ethics councils and the like. While representatives of the public as well as organized interests are sometimes – or often – included in the committee, experts in the sense of scientific experts are at the heart of such committees. These committees have a purely advisory function. Also, many committees try to include the public via public meetings. One means to fill up the institutional void could be to link pTA, if thematically appropriate, to such committees. Again, hearings are an easy way. The advantage of such a linkage is that these committees explicitly offer space for the utterance of ethical and social reasoning that is often underlying citizens' concerns, but which is excluded in the science-based legal-administrative context. Furthermore, the results of pTA procedures could have an agenda-setting function for national ethics committees. They could draw attention to

[12] A further option for creating relationships with policy-makers is the introduction of the notice-and-comment provision in rule-making. They allow citizens to respond as individuals, and require the administration to respond to them (cf. Levine et al. 2005: 277).

public concerns raised in citizen-dominated pTA and, in this sense, serve again as a means for the observation of society.

Finally, *economic actors* could be addressees of pTA. Some pTA has been commissioned by companies (e.g. the Dutch Unilever dialogue among stakeholders). This is a difficult situation since economic actors have an economic interest in pTA and will strategically make use of it for their own purposes. Nevertheless, if pTA can be a means of 'observing society' for policy-makers, it could have a similar function for economic actors. Citizen-dominated models are especially of interest here, since citizens are also consumers. PTA then fits into a more customer-oriented policy.

Securing democratic legitimacy has also become a most important issue at the supranational EU level (cf. Dahl 1994). Some of my suggestions can be transformed to the supranational level of the EU given its institutional density. With the European Parliament, the Commission and regulatory agencies we find more or less functional equivalents to national parliaments and public administrations. The European Food Safety Authority (EFSA) is a good example. Its role in the management of food-related health risks is solely advisory (regulatory decisions are taken by EU policy-makers), yet in some fields EFSA introduced public consultations before giving advice. In this sense, results like reports from national pTA events, if there is not transnational pTA available, can be a second-best solution and can be taken into account by supranational institutions again, preferably via hearings. The institutional prerequisites are certainly very different in other international environments.

E. Conclusions

Today, there are a number of very different participatory arrangements. While lay-people or citizens are often in a key position, that is not always the case. In some models stakeholders, i.e. organised interests, are key actors or at least important participants. They share the assumption that policy-making can be improved and can be made more efficient by integrating a deliberative element. Hence, they take a strong connection between the input- and output-side of democratic legitimacy for granted. Actually, not all pTA is purely deliberative; some models include elements of bargaining, while others have a stronger participatory approach. The formal aspect of different pTA models affects how procedures relate to institutionalized elite politics.

Participatory TA certainly is a striking example of political experimentation in the field surrounding the governance of science. It can be a testing ground for combining deliberation with the reality of representative politics in mass democracies. Yet, so far there is an apparent lack of such combination and structural linkages: usually pTA takes place apart from, and furthermore hardly noticed by, elite politics. One can blame the elite side for not being responsive enough. But one can also look at the pTA side to find structural barriers. A closer look at the variety of models illustrates that some of them are easier to link to the institutional environment of representative politics. A key objective of this paper was to outline some modest proposals for structural linkages between deliberative and representative modes of the governance of science.

Looking at the underlying democratic philosophy, it is clear that different pTA models are inspired by different strands in democratic theory. The deliberative approach is certainly the strongest and the most demanding one for representative elite politics. Then again, the complexity of pTA cannot simply be reduced to just one democratic approach. Some hybrid models demonstrate creative linkages between pluralist and deliberative approaches. There are, however, different options for linking even deliberative approaches to institutions of representative democracy. Participatory TA then becomes an important means for the observation of society and its dynamics against the background of uncertainty and complexity. The key advantage, particularly of citizen-dominated models, is to provide for well-informed mini-publics.[13] There is no single best way to encounter the institutional void of pTA. Yet: the reality of representative politics is a starting-point for thinking about socially and politically meaningful pTA.

References

Abels, Gabriele (2002): Experts, Citizens, and Eurocrats: Towards a Policy Shift in the Governance of Biopolitics in the EU. *European Integration online Papers* 6, 19. Internet: http://eiop.or.at/eiop/texte/2002-019a.htm

[13] However, this does not mean that the products of deliberation in pTA are of good quality. Information and quality of deliberation are interconnected but still different aspects of the deliberative process. The quality of products is certainly not a guarantee for policy-impact, yet the quality of advice is important for efficient problem-solving. This is so far an under-researched topic. For future pTA research, this requires a more systematic study of what happens inside the participatory process and, simultaneously, what happens in its political environment.

Abels, Gabriele (2007): Trade and Human Rights: Inter- and Supranational Regulation of ART and GM Food. In: Montpetit, Eric, Rothmayr, Christine, and Varone, Frédéric (eds.), *The Politics of Biotechnology in North America and Europe: Policy Networks, Institutions and Internationalization*. Lanham, MD, 35–59.

Abels, Gabriele and Bora, Alfons (2004): *Demokratische Technikbewertung*. Bielefeld.

Abels, Gabriele and Mölders, Marc (2007): Meeting of Minds – kritische Beobachtungen zu Form und Funktion der ersten europäischen Bürgerkonferenz. In: Decker, Michael (eds.), *TA in einer globalisierten Welt*. Berlin, 381–390.

Abromeit, Heidrun (2002): *Wozu braucht man Demokratie? Die postnationale Herausforderung der Demokratietheorie*. Opladen.

Bechmann, Gotthard (1993): Democratic Function of Technology Assessment in Technology Policy Decision-Making. *Science and Public Policy* 20, 11–16.

Bora, Alfons (1999): *Differenzierung und Inklusion. Partizipative Öffentlichkeit im Rechtssystem moderner Gesellschaften*. Baden-Baden.

Bora, Alfons and Hausendorf, Heiko (2006): Participatory Science Governance Revisited: Normative expectations versus Empirical Evidence. *Science and Public Policy* 33, 478–488.

Braun, Kathrin; Herrmann, Svea Luise; and Könninger, Sabine (2002): *Deliberative Modelle als Mittel der Demokratisierung von Bioethik- und Biomedizinpolitik*. Internet: http://www.sciencepolicystudies.de/Expertise%20Braun.pdf

Brown, Mark B. (2006): Citizen Panel and the Concept of Representation. *Journal of Political Philosophy* 14, 203–225.

Burgess, Jacquelin and Chilvers, Jason (2006): Upping the ante: a conceptual framework for designing and evaluating participatory technology assessments, *Science and Public Policy* 33, 713–728.

Bütschi, Danielle, Joss, Simon, and Baeriswyl, Michel (2002): Switzerland: New paths for public participation in direct democracy. In: Joss, Simon and Bellucci, Sergio (eds.), *Participatory technology assessment – European perspectives*. London, 126–139.

Bütschi, Danielle and Nentwich, Michael (2002): The role of participatory technology assessment in the policy-making process. In: Joss, Simon and Bellucci, Sergio (eds.), *Participatory technology assessment – European perspectives*. London, 235–256.

Dahl, Robert A. (1994): A democratic dilemma: system effectiveness versus citizen participation. *Political Science Quarterly* 109, 23–34.

Dahl, Robert A. (1998): On Democracy. New Haven, London.

Decker, Michael and Ladikas, Miltos (2004): EU-Projekt: Technology Assessment in Europe; Between Method and Impact. In: *Technikfolgenabschätzung – Theorie und Praxis* 13, 71–80.

Durant, John (1999): Participatory technology assessment and the democratic model of the public understanding of science. *Science and Public Policy* 26, 313–319.

Einsiedel, Edna F. and Eastlick, Deborah L. (2000): Consensus Conferences as Deliberative Democracy: A Communications Perspective. *Science Communication* 21, 323–343.

Fiorino, Daniel J. (1990): Citizen participation and environmental risk: a survey of institutional mechanisms, *Science, Technology, & Human Values* 15, 226–243.

Foltz, Franz (1999): Five arguments for increasing public participation in making science policy. *Bulletin of Science, Technology & Society* 19, 117–127.

Gastil, John (2000): *By Popular Demand: Revitalizing Representative Democracy through Deliberative Elections*. Berkeley, CA.

Görsdorf, Alexander (2006): Inside Deliberative Experiments: Dynamics of Subjectivity in Science Policy. *Policy and Society* 25, 177–206.

Hansen, Janus (2006): Operationalising the Public in Participatory Technology Assessment: a Framework for Comparison Applied to Three Cases. *Science and Pubic Policy* 33, 571–584.

Hendriks, Carolyn (2002): Institutions of Deliberative Democratic Processes and Interest Groups: Roles, Tensions and Incentives, *Australian Journal of Public Administration* 61, 64–75.

Hendriks, Carolyn M., Dryzek, John S. and Hunold, Christian (2007): Turning Up the Heat: Partisanship in Deliberative Innovation. *Political Studies* 55, 362–383.

Hennen, Leonard (2002): Impacts of Participatory Technology Assessment on its Societal Environment. In: Joss, Simon and Bellucci, Sergio (eds.), *Participatory Technology Assessment. European Perspectives*. London, 257–275.

Joss, Simon (2002): Toward the Public Sphere – Reflections on the Development of Participatory Technology Assessment. *Bulletin of Science, Technology & Society* 22, 220–231.

Joss, Simon (2003): Zwischen Politikberatung und Öffentlichkeitsdiskurs – Erfahrungen mit Bürgerkonferenzen in Europa. In: Schicktanz, Silke and Naumann, Jörg (eds.), *Bürgerkonferenz: Streitfall Gendiagnostik. Ein Modellprojekt der Bürgerbeteiligung am bioethischen Diskurs*. Opladen, 15–35.

Joss, Simon and Bellucci, Sergio (2002): *Participatory Technology Assessment - European Perspectives*. London.

Klüver, Lars (2006): *New trends in public participation*. PATH conference, http://www.macaulay.ac.uk/pathconference.

Laird, Frank N. (1993): Participatory Analysis, Democracy, and Technological Decision Making, *Science, Technology & Human Values* 18, 341–361.

Leib, Ethan J. (2004): Deliberative Democracy in America: A Proposal for a Popular Branch of Government. University Park, IL.

Levine, Peter; Fung, Archon and Gastil, John (2005): Future Directions for Public Deliberation. In: Gastil, John and Levine, Peter (eds.): *The Deliberative Democracy Handbook*, San Francisco, 271–288.

Lezaun, Javier and Soneryd, Linda (2006): Government by Elicitation: Engaging Stakeholders of Listening to the Idiots? CARR Discussion Paper No. 34. London.

Majone, Giandomenico (2005): *Dilemmas of European Integration. The Ambiguities & Pitfalls of Integration by Stealth*. Oxford, New York.

Martinsen, Renate (2006): Demokratie und Diskurs: Organisierte Kommunikationsprozesse in der Wissensgesellschaft. Baden-Baden.

Nelkin, Dorothy (1984): Science and Technology Policy and the Democratic Process. In: Peterson, James C. (eds.), Citizen Participation in Science Policy. Amherst, 18–39.

Papadopoulos, Yannis and Warin, Philippe (2007): Are innovative, participatory and deliberative procedures in policy making democratic and effective? *European Journal of Political Research* 46, 445–472.

Rowe, Gene and Frewer, Lynn J. (2000): Public Participation Methods: A Framework for Evaluation. *Science, Technology, & Human Values* 25, 3–29.

Saretzki, Thomas (2007): … address unknown? Was heißt "Gesellschaftsberatung" und was folgt daraus für Wissenschaft und Demokratie? In: Leggewie, Claus (eds.), *Von der Politik- zur Gesellschaftsberatung: Neue Wege öffentlicher Konsultation*. Frankfurt/M., New York, 95–116.

Smith, Graham and Wales, Corinne (2000): Citizens' Juries and Deliberative Democracy. *Political Studies* 48, 51–65.

Tucker, Aviezer (2008): Pre-emptive Democracy: Oligarchic Tendencies in Deliberative Democracy. *Political Studies* 56, 127–147.

Warren, Mark (2002): Deliberative democracy. In: Carter, April and Stokes, Geoffrey (eds.), *Democratic theory today. Challenges for the 21st Century*. Cambridge, 173–202.

Vig, Norman and Paschen, Herbert (2000): *Parliaments and Technology. The Development of Technology Assessment in Europe*. Albany NY.

CHAPTER TEN

PARTICIPATION AND BEYOND: DYNAMICS OF SOCIAL POSITIONS IN PARTICIPATORY DISCOURSE

Alfons Bora and Heiko Hausendorf

The title of this chapter, "Participation and beyond", is meant in a two-fold sense. Firstly, social positions in participatory discourse *go beyond participation* in the literal sense; actually, dynamics of social positioning processes emerge when "participation" is put on the agenda. As a communicative achievement, participation appears in an amazing variety of concrete discourse events that result from institutional arrangements, administrative procedures, national and political cultures and the concrete communicative forms of face-to-face interaction, written, printed or electronically realized discourse. "Participation", therefore, calls for closer inspection, theoretically as well as empirically and this is what we propose to examine by means of our understanding of participatory discourse.

Moreover, there is, secondly, a normative sense of "Participation and beyond" that we would like to emphasise also. "Participation" is one of the dazzling key words used to emphasize new forms of governance practice, which are said to allow participants to engage in and to be treated by others in terms of practices of citizenship. From this point of view, "participation" appears to be one of the prominent solutions when a lack of democracy has been a subject of complaint in the last decades. However, given the programmatic experience of participation and participatory discourse, especially in the field of new technologies, one might conclude that "participation" hasn't kept all the promises connected with this political idea. Inspecting participatory discourse theoretically and empirically might, therefore, as well give us the idea of going *beyond participation* in terms of normative reasoning about participatory governance. That is what our title also indicates as a concern of this chapter.

Our argument in this chapter will, first of all, be a theoretical one. We will introduce participation as communication. Guided by this starting point, we will then focus on the communicative structures of participatory discourse. It is argued that social structures in participatory discourse can be considered as social positions. Social positions are, as will be elaborated, distinct sets of communicated social expectations. As such, they bear on a social positioning dynamics that can be assumed theoretically in pursuing the idea that participation is communication. The theoretical assumption of dynamic process of social positioning, in turn, calls for empirical analyses of participatory discourse. This is the reason why some findings of the PARADYS project – a project that other chapters in this volume refer to as well – will be brought in.[1] The introduction of case materials of this kind is a necessary step to understand participatory discourse both theoretically *and* empirically. The substantial empirical research in participatory discourse appearances across different European countries conducted within the PARADYS framework provided evidence of interesting difference in the dynamics of social positioning processes: There are exclusive as well as inclusive dynamics in participatory discourse with respect to the repertoire of typical social positions. We will illustrate this finding in some detail because it is of special interest when the intention is really to go *beyond participation*.

A. From Participatory Governance to Participatory Discourse

In what follows, we propose to consider participation as communication. Participatory Governance then becomes tangible as a certain type of discourse: defined by administrative efforts/procedures to allow the public take part in political decision-making-processes. Participatory discourse, therefore, can be seen as the communicative side of participatory governance. A broad variety of forms of participatory discourses have emerged – as distinct forms of communication they constitute a starting point and subject of research. Let us start by briefly discussing the concept of governance and the necessity to study the micro-structures of governance. From this point of view it will then become

[1] Paradys (Participation and the Dynamics of Social Positioning) was funded by the European Commission (contract No. HPSE-CT-2001-00050) in the years 2001–2004. The project consortium – being co-ordinated by the authors of this chapter – comprehended research teams from Hungary, Ireland, Italy, The Netherlands, Sweden, the UK and Germany. Readers interested in these results may find the final report of the project http://www.uni-bielefeld.de/iwt/personen/bora/Projekte/PARADYS/final-report-update.pdf

clear why it is necessary to turn our attention to the aspect of communication.

The concept of *governance*, originally deriving from economic analysis, namely the control over corporations, but in the meantime re-defined through a longer debate in political science, is frequently associated with questions of different international regimes and of global order (cf. for example Held 1995, Kohler-Koch & Eising 1998, Zürn 1998, Kooiman 2002; Rosenau 1995). It is usually understood as a means of political, legal, and social regulation beyond markets and hierarchies (Amin 1997). Since the late 1990's, the World Bank has made use of the concept, commonly describing governance as the exercise of political power to manage a nation's affairs. For our purpose, it is mainly the dimension of public governance that is relevant. It signifies the coordination of new forms of social cooperation, i.e. more horizontal activities between state institutions, non-governmental organisations, private enterprises, and civil society actors. In this perspective, public governance covers aspects of the state, the market, *and* civil society. In contrast to previous lines of regulatory theory, the use of the term 'governance' indicates that new forms of – non-hierarchical, de-centralized, co-operative, enabling – regulation replace older models of central regulation. The governance concept, as Christian Joerges wrote with respect to the EU white paper on governance,

> refers to both activities *and* actor configurations. 'Governance' is to be equated neither with the actions of governments and administrations, nor with law-making activities, nor the law implementing activities of authorities and courts. It is all this, 'too'. But it is a specific feature of modern regulatory policy that it builds, to a large degree, on knowledge available not within the administrative machinery but in society, which it is likewise dependent upon the management capacities of enterprises and non-governmental organisations. Regulatory policy can neither be reduced to the execution of the will of the sovereign by that sovereign's administrative bodies, nor can it be delegated *ab ovo* and *in toto* to non-governmental actors. The complexity of modern governance structures is a response to the problem situations of society and of the political systems. (…) Accordingly, official and technical authorities must engage in new linkages; governance structures in which both private actors and 'civil society' *participate* [our emphasis, AB/HH] in the 'carrying out of public tasks' have to emerge. (Joerges 2001)

Against this background we understand *governance* as a *co-operative social relation between governmental institutions and the actors of 'civil society'*. Dealing with the participatory dimension of governance, we are primarily interested in the role of the citizens and of their participation in governance. We do not want to claim that this relationship is entirely new or that sociological and political theory before the governance debate did not reflect on these issues. Rather we would like to interpret the theoretical interest in governance as an expression of a shifting focus and emphasis in both theoretical and practical respects. Governance in this sense has a dimension that refers directly to questions of civil society and democracy (Hirst 1994, Zürn 1998, Brunkhorst & Kettner 2000, Vandenberg 2000, Edeling et al. 2001, Grote & Gbikpi 2001).

At the end of the last decade, an extended discussion about what has since been called the 'democratic deficit' of the EU has spread through scientific and political debates (Scharpf 1999). In the working document on 'Science, society and the citizen in Europe' (European Commission 2000) the Commission has pointed out the relevance of participatory procedures and the need for new forms of dialogue between science and society. This position corresponds with the one laid down in the white paper on European governance (European Commission 2001), where a close connection between institutional and democratic challenges has been established. One of the most striking features of these umbrella policy papers is their "participatory speech" (Abels 2002: 10) This line in participatory science governance has been followed in all relevant papers since then.

> As a more recent example, the green paper 'Governance of Britain' published by the UK government in 2007 and aiming at major constitutional reforms can be mentioned. It is, among other measures, currently being followed within a consultation process about a 'National framework for greater citizen engagement' (Ministry of Justice 2008)

In its ministerial foreword this document states, that

> Active participation by as many people as possible is essential for a healthy democracy as it encourages a shared understanding, builds cohesion and instils confidence in the institutions and the people who are elected to represent us. (...) the Government recognises that the demands on our democracy are evolving. People are less engaged with the formal democratic process. Some, particularly disadvantaged groups and younger people, are increasingly unlikely to vote at elections. Others are channelling their political activity beyond voting and party politics to protest groups and single issue campaigns. The Government wants to address these challenges by increasing opportunities for people to participate in the decision-making process between elections and in ways that encourage participation by those whose voices are not often heard. (Ministry of Justice 2008: 1).

These examples indicate that in most political contexts and in various social fields, participation is a relevant tool for decision-making (Abels & Bora 2004). This holds true for science and technology policy, in particular. The increasing relevance of participation in this area is conceptually based on a certain critique of expertise and on a discourse about "democratising expertise" (Liberatore & Funtowicz 2003; Nowotny 2003.) Participatory procedures, as a common hypothesis puts it, are more likely to be able to evoke the motivation to engage in decision-making, to broaden the basis of knowledge and of the values involved, to initiate learning processes, to produce new possibilities of conflict solution, to realise common interests, and last but not least to increase acceptance and legitimacy of a decision (Durant 1999; Fischer 1999; Joss & Bellucci 2002). In science and technology policy, such participatory procedures have been developed and implemented in the last few decades. Decision-making processes, such as the licensing of plant GMOs (genetically modified organisms), for example, often carry components of citizen participation. This participatory turn expresses a deep-rooted change in science and technology governance.

However, besides all possible advantages of participation, it is also necessary to see its weaknesses. Participatory procedures–one might argue–will not generate enough commitment amongst all parties, unless they lead to a real win-win-solution. Participants' loyalty to their organisational background will even force them to leave the procedure if serious conflicts arise. The functional differentiation of society may create insurmountable barriers in communication (Bora 1999). Furthermore, these procedures often provoke questions regarding their political representativeness, imbalance of power, a lack of political mandate for those involved etc. One reason for these problems is the lack of embedding of participatory procedures in the institutions of representative democracy (Abels & Bora 2004).

Even more important than the institutional context, however, are perhaps the internal structures of participation, its *micro-structures* as we will call them in what follows. These micro-structures are provide key insights for understanding how participatory governance models function and for clarifying their strengths and their weaknesses. There are a number of reasons for this argument: Firstly the performance of participatory governance models is theoretically grounded in the achievements of interaction and discourse on the micro-level between the actors involved in the procedure. Secondly, the external effects of participatory procedures strongly depend on communications processes between the participants of the procedure and the addressees of the advice produced in these processes of participatory governance. Thirdly, the discursive micro-structures of participatory governance have significant influence on the social positioning of the participants themselves, as we will demonstrate in this chapter. Against this background it seems to be necessary to study discursive processes in participatory and cooperative governance on the level of micro-structures.

Our interest in participatory discourse therefore is a sociological and sociolinguistic one: In sociological terms, we are interested in the intersection between different social systems such as science, politics, economy, law etc. on the macro-level, *and*, at the same time, in an intersection between different communicative manifestations: embracing organization (membership), interaction (co-presence) and society (social belonging). These intersections, however, only become manifest on the level of concrete relations between social actors or addresses, i.e. on the communicative level of what may be called the micro-structures of governance. In sociolinguistic terms, we are interested in the concrete forms by means of which this participatory discourse comes into being: as a communicative process manifested at the surface level of spoken or written discourse. It is at this level where the social reality of social systems (science, politics, economy, law, etc.) and their way of emerging (within organisations, interactions, society) becomes tangible in terms of communicative micro structures: answers and questions, clarifications and requests, reproaches and rejections, statements and responses, i.e. the communicative *Gestalt* of social structures.

What is it that you can learn from social micro-structures of governance? It is not more and not less than the social constitution or construction of "participatory governance". That is it what we are interested in as sociologists and sociolinguists and that is the reason why we start off by looking at participatory communication before coming back to participatory at the end of this chapter. So, our direction is in the first step to move from a focus on participatory governance (a notion and a subject of political theory) to participatory discourse (a notion and a subject of sociology and sociolinguistics).

B. Communicative Structures as Social Positions

Turning to participatory discourse one encounters a broad variety of concrete communicative events, including gatherings, hearings and meetings that serve as oral arenas of debating between experts, politicians and the public and that include written objections and letters from concerned citizens and their responses by administrators, "frequently asked question" pages on governmental websites – to name but a few prominent manifestations of participatory discourse. These examples shed light on the micro structures of participatory discourse partly depending on the participants' co-presence (in the case of face-to-face interaction) and partly depending on communicative 'reachability' in the case of written, printed, broadcasted or electronically published discourse. The social construction of "participatory governance" occurs within this micro cosmos of concrete communicative events. But how can we account for this social construction process? Let us, briefly and in a sketchy way, turn to a concrete field of participatory discourse that we've dealt with empirically at some detail: the field of Genetically Modified Organisms (GMOs) and its administrative regulation through case-specific licensing procedures (cf. Hausendorf & Bora 2006a, 2006b, Bora forthcoming).

There is a striking finding once one starts to look at the micro cosmos of participatory discourse empirically: Across all case-specific differences and details one will find recurrent patterns of questions and answers, reproaches and rejections, arguments and statements in very different empirical materials. Beyond the individuality expressed through each of the participants' physical and cognitive presence, there seem to be social voices that come to be heard; they display arguments, points of view, issues and topics as implications of engagement and involvement already known from and already heard in other discussions and debates. The micro structures of participatory discourse seem to be pervaded by regularities of this kind. They reveal a kind of orderliness beyond the fortuitousness of a single communicative here-we-and-now achievement. It, therefore, appears appropriate to address such regularities in terms of *social positions*. There is, for instance, an "Administrator" position with the communicated self image of a neutral, impartial, unbiased decision-maker who is obeying the law and political will and who is well monitoring the licensing procedure. There is, for instance, a "Concerned Citizen" position with the communicated self image of an active, elite, critical and engaged, sometimes also excluded individual aware of his/her rights and wanting to participate as citizen in important decisions. And there are further social positions recurring in our materials such as a "Local We" position, an "Organized Protestor" position, a "Scientist" position, a "Politician" position and an

"Industrial Actor" position (see below). Whenever social positions of this kind are activated in participatory discourse similar social expectations are communicated concerning legitimate other participants to be included, legitimate issues to be discussed and legitimate ways of proceeding.

Although specified in a "personal" way, the social positions mentioned above do not refer to empirical persons. Social positions are to be rigidly understood as social structures. Therefore, they are not linked to individuals and their personal attitudes and beliefs. Persons may change and often do change between social positions and may even take more than one position during the course of one and the same communicative event. Instead of referring to empirical persons, social positions are meant to describe properties of communicative moves made in participatory discourse no matter by whom. Communicative moves manifest social expectations concerning next moves: What comes next (as a thematic focus, issue or topic)? Who comes next (as speaker)? In which way can speakers' next moves be connected to their current utterances (as legitimate moves)? Sociolinguistic approaches such as conversation analysis have put forward this idea in terms of sequentiality: Social micro-structures are sequentially implicative (cf. Hausendorf & Bora 2006). That means that social expectations become themselves 'expectable'– and a next move can, therefore, display itself as a connecting "next" one. The chronological passing of time is, in this way, transformed into a sequential order of communicated expectations. A social position is a coherent set of communicated expectations of this kind and, in this way, it is a genuine aggregation of social structures as will be pointed out in what follows.

Alongside a wellproven tradition of sociological thinking, we assume that social structures, in general, emerge as communicated expectations. Expectations limit the number of possible linkages. Not everything is communicatively possible when an expectation has been manifested explicitly or implicitly in discourse. Expectations are, therefore, the building blocks of material, social structures. Expectations, generally, within a social theoretical perspective may refer to three possible dimensions; the issue dimension (*Sachdimension*), the social dimension (*Sozialdimension*) and the temporal dimension (*Zeitdimension*) (cf. Luhmann 1995). That means that they may refer to themes, issues and topics; they also may refer to actors and their social roles; and they may refer to the temporal organisation of communicative moves and their linkages. The social world is full of very different combinations of such social expectations, some of which are more closely interlinked than others. There are typical sets of coherent communicated expectations typically emerging within and, at the same time, establishing a certain social structure. In order to describe these sets, we use the term social position.[2] *A social position is, accordingly, a differentiated set of social expectations.* As a set of communicated expectations, it takes a certain and distinguishable form (Gestalt) that applies a typical social semantics (of, for instance, "administration", "justice", "protest", "local concern", "scientific truth" or "political power") and that can be referred to by social categories such as "Administrator" or "Concerned Citizen".

Let us, briefly, illustrate our understanding of social positions as sets of communicated expectations by giving a concrete picture drawn from the materials of participatory discourse we have researched. The following table provides a description of the above mentioned social positions by summarizing the kind of social expectations that were typically communicated when the respective social position is activated. The social positions make the columns of the table. In order to allow for comparisons between the different positions the three structural dimensions (issue, social and temporal dimension) have each been worked out in more detail with regard to the characteristics of participatory discourse. The different structural dimensions make the lines of the table. What has, then, been entered in the boxes are key words that should summarize the associated kinds of communicated social expectation. This table should enable the reader to gain a general sense of our approach to social positions:

Note that this characterisation of social positions is understood as a description by means of which the participants themselves try to make clear and account for their engagement in participatory discourse. It is, therefore, not the analyst from her/his bird's eye perspective who decides that, for instance, the "Concerned Citizen" acts on behalf of a general concern about GMOs, but it is the participants' communication of such an expectation that leads to the reconstruction of some kind of a "Concerned Citizen" position, which is then interlinked with

[2] In earlier texts, also the term "discourse" was used by Bora (1999). – The concept of "frame" does not actually meet our theoretical interest, because a frame suggests, that there is something else that happens "within" the frame–two levels of reality, therefore. Social positions as sets of structures (expectations, as we explained) do not insinuate such a second level of empirical reality.

Table 1: Social Positions as Communicated Social Expectations

Social Positons → Structural Dimensions ↓	The administrator	The local "We"	The concerned Citizen	The organised protestor (Environmentalist)	The scientist	The politician	The industrial actor
Relevant actors	Applicant, experts, politicians, public/ citizens	Applicant; local authority; organised protestors; scientists	Competent authority, citizens	Competent authority, all other actors (if necessary for organised protest)	Scientific commu-nity, public/ citizens,	Public/citizens, science/ experts, industry	Consumers, distributors, authorities, general public
Image of Self	Authority, controlling experiments; guided by law; responding to citizens	Membership in a local community	Generally concerned about GMOs; alert and involved; independent	Advocating interests; proactive minority in service of the common good; representing public concerns	Advice to the decision-makers on scientific and technical aspects; realistic, rational	Leader, decision-maker; responsibly recognising public concerns; emphatic; bound by legal rules	Competent, attentive, trustworthy; open-minded, scientifically expert
Relevant issues	Legal aspects, risk issues	Integrity, autonomy of the local community; information	Risk and need for GMOs in general; scrutiny of authority; safety and health; peoples' rights	GMOs in general; environment; justice, equity	Risk, knowledge and facts;	Risk regulation; protection of (lobby) interests	Safety, health, development/ progress; facts and risk, trust/ legitimacy;

Image of others	Public/ citizens as passive figures; community potentially ignorant or unconcerned or guided/ misled by activists	Applicant as: intruder, expert, and partner; lack of information	Unfair, corrupt, neglect citizens' rights	Competent authority as relevant partner; public and citizens as audience and resource	Public uninformed, manipulated by activists; organised protest exaggerates risks;	Only vague/ ambiguous figures: citizens are non-experts, consumers, as "wise", but lack of information; scientists "divided"	Organised protest has covert, material interest; public lack trust; regulators (administration, politics) are tough but fair, sometimes too reluctant
Valid communication	In principle top-down; hierarchical distribution of legal competences; arguing; open, insofar as arguing	Direct and open dialogue; equity, mutual respect; locals decide about support/ rejection of field trial; negotiation	Challenging powers in charge; make scientists and decision-makers accountable	Strategic interaction; lobbying, campaigning; media activities	Arguing; anchored to facts and expert knowledge	Campaigning and public action; and negotiation with relevant actors, "harmonising", then decision-making	Campaigning; arguing about facts; information; promotion, strategic communication

(Continued)

Table 1: (*Contd.,*)

Social Positons → Structural Dimensions ↓	The administrator	The local "We"	The concerned Citizen	The organised protestor (Environmentalist)	The scientist	The politician	The industrial actor
Problem focus	Compliance with legal require-ments; decision-making according to legal provisions (risk-related)	Community; information and autono-mous decision	Economy threats democracy; public partici-pation needed, therefore also information relevant	Lack of power and influence on regulation and legislation; political support	Getting the truth to the unedu-cated and manipu-lated public (deficit hypoth-esis); risk assessment	Maintaining multilevel democratic discretion while recognising the public concern	Establishing conditions of truth and trust to facilitate economic goals
main system reference	Law	Politics (local)	Politics (participatory)	Politics (strategic)	Science	Politics (strategic)	Economy

further communicated expectations that go together to form a coherent set of expectations.

Social positions as defined and described in table 1 can be seen as a way of summarizing fine-grained and substantial empirical analyses of data from participatory discourse. As such, they have to demonstrate their value both methodologically and empirically. It has to be documented and it has to be accounted for by means of concrete bits of data that how communicative moves can be considered as establishing the schematically anticipated kinds of expectations. We cannot to follow up this matter here.[3] We would rather emphasize the *theoretical* implications of this approach: It is in terms of social positions as communicated social expectations that "participatory governance" is socially constructed. Social positions, therefore, can contribute to understand theoretically how participation is brought into being through discourse: Whatever is to become communicatively relevant within the participation process has to emerge in terms of a social position. This argument can best be proven by looking at the many ways in which the social subsystems that are said to be relevant for participatory discourse (see B above) recur as communicated expectations within the different social positions: Look, for instance, at social positions such as "Administrator", "Scientist", "Politician" or "Industrial Actor" which obviously relate to law, science, politics and economy. But look, for instance, at the line "Main System reference" in table 1 in order to see that "politics" is not restricted to the "Politician" position!

Apart from empirical insights into the forms of participatory discourse we can learn from social positions how social macro-structures in terms of social subsystems (and their organisations) and social micro-structures in terms of concrete communicative events (as face-to-face interactions) become intertwined. Social positions seem to work as intermediate social structures located somewhere between the imponderables and fortuitousness of co-presence and mere communicate reachability on the one hand and the clear-cut definition and fixation of organizational membership on the other hand. It is a certain type of social belonging that is expressed through social positions, and social belonging is neither defined by membership nor by co-presence and/or communicative reachability. Whenever participation is set on

[3] Readers may refer, for instance, to the final report of the PARADYS project, chapter 'Methodology'.

the agenda ("participatory governance") intermediate social structures in terms of social positions can be expected. Participatory discourse, accordingly, appears as a social positioning process. This is inevitable due to the nature of social structures that are involved. It is, to some extent, expectable and predictable at least from a sociological point of view.

As an intermediate social structure (manifested in terms of social positions) participatory discourse has its own dynamics: This dynamics starts when social positions come into being as communicated expectations, including images of self and others. It depends on the micro structures of communicative events. Take, for instance, the many ways, in which the "Administrator" position can be activated with regard to possible slots for participants to engage themselves (s. below D). Led by a social positioning approach, administrative procedures and their regulatory conditions prove to be ways of activating the "Administrator" position. Take, for instance, the many ways in which citizens can try to participate in a political decision making process. Led by a social positioning approach, these different accounts for engaging prove to be ways of activating different social positions in terms of "Local We", "Concerned Citizen" or "Organised Protestor" position. Social positions as intermediate social structures can indeed be anticipated. Even the type of social positions might be predictable (at least with regard to some of our social positions, namely the "Administrator" position or the "Scientist" position). But the dynamics of the social positioning process cannot be anticipated. For social positioning depends on the concrete communicative manifestation of social expectations. This is the point where empirical analysis, at the latest, has to step in. And this is what seems mostly neglected in political sciences when discussing the pro and con of "participatory governance" on a more abstract level.

C. The Dynamics of Social Positioning in Participatory Discourse

A social position is, above all, not linked to any kind of professional occupation, organizational affiliation or to any otherwise ascribed status of a person. There is no theoretical reason whatsoever to suppose, for instance, that a person working as a researcher is always and everywhere taking a "scientist" (or "researcher" or even "expert") position.

We could easily provide empirical evidence for this argument (cf. the "professor" in the data published in Hausendorf & Bora 2006). The question whether or not one of these social positions is being activated can only be answered empirically by looking at concrete forms of communication as the genuine medium where social expectations are manifested in order to become social structures. Accordingly, social positions have to be conceived as communicative constructions in terms of audible and visible manifestations. Social positioning is a process in time, taking place turn-by-turn in a sequential order and, in this way, is by no means predictable. This is what we will turn to as to the *dynamics* of social positioning processes.

Let us start off by emphasizing that social positions and their dynamics, in fact, are the two sides of the same analytic coin. *Dynamics* is another term for the relation between manifestations of social positions in time. This becomes obvious when we notice that each single position in itself emerges within a sequence of foregoing and following moves, which may manifest the same or another social position. Accordingly, manifestations of social positions are sequentially implicative by nature (see above): they take up and reflect implications from previous and foregoing positioning moves and they establish themselves implications for next and subsequent manifestations of social positions. Social positions can only be realised as part of such a dynamics of social positioning. This comes into view when we study the different ways by means of which participants in their own turn react to an already activated position frame, confirming this position or attempting to activate a different position. It is, then, easy to see that the social positions that we have suggested (see above), in principal, represent some kind of stabilization that the dynamic manifestation of positions has reached at a certain state. Social positions such as "Administrator", "Local We", "Concerned Citizen" or "Industrial Actor", therefore, represent communicatively proven prerequisites for strings of participatory discourse. It is, then, due to the dynamics of these social positions that participatory discourse in each and every concrete appearance results in a social positioning process.

When starting to analyze participatory discourse as a social positioning process a variety of different dimensions of dynamics come into sight. For illustrative purposes, we merely want to pick out one dimension of dynamics, namely a dynamics that emerges across different communicative events of participatory discourse, starting with, for instance, the public announcement of a GMO field trial, including written objections and exchanges between the parties involved and maybe ending up with the final decision.

Understanding this dimension of dynamics across different communicative events implies the need to attend to the development of social positions in their sequential order, i.e. on the way in which social positions draw on preceding communicative events and contribute to establishing expectations and sequential implication for next step social positioning. Questions arising here might be: How do "officially", sometimes also "legally" and/or "politically" manifested social positions (maybe in policy accounts, announcements or files) frame the kind of social positioning that are possible for others downstream, who may be expected to continue participatory discourse by writing a letter, posing a question on the web, making an objection in whatever form or organising some kind of public/local meeting? What are the expectations for next turns that have been established in terms of possible and allowable social positions?

Next step moves (manifested by, for instance, a letter, an electronic question or comment, a formal objection) can then be looked at with regard to the manner in which they cope with these expectations: In which way do the next step social positions respond to the foregoing expectations: contesting, neglecting, continuing, suspending or replacing such implications? Note, that these manifestations themselves establish new and further expectations in terms of social positions for next moves to be made – and that and how these expectations were dealt with within the following move, for instance, within the response given to the objections by the "Administrator" position or within the public appearance maybe performed by the "Industrial Actor" position.

Dynamics across communicative events can develop *within* an administrative licensing procedure implying that the different events are part of the procedural framing. They can develop as well in merely *indirect* relation to a concrete licensing procedure implying that social positioning processes take place, for instance, due to framings by the "Organized Protestor" position, i.e. outside the procedural framings established by the "Administrator" position.

In our empirical research, we have followed up both the administratively initiated dynamics and the dynamics outside the pre-structured steps of the official licensing procedure. Without going into details concerning the results of this research, it is of special interest for our argument here that we found evidence for *inclusive* and *exclusive* dynamics of participatory discourse: As far as the outcome or result of participatory discourse is concerned, there is mutual exclusion of social positions as well as mutual inclusion of social positions.[4]

Mutual exclusion means that there is no evidence for resonance between the social positions involved in the dynamics. They prove to be impervious to each other, maybe even in the sense that the continuation of communication is refused. Mutual inclusion means that there is indeed evidence for the demonstration of mutual resonance between the social positions involved. A certain social position finds resonance within another social position in the sense that it is made a relevant contribution worth to be dealt with in further proceedings. This might be the case due to the genuine force of face-to-face interaction within a public arena of debating. This might as well be the case due to a social position's power to force other positions to adopt its own semantics. The continuation of discourse exchange and dialogue typically co-occurs with this type of inclusion of social positions.

In order to illustrate dynamics of mutual inclusion vs. mutual exclusion we will introduce a few findings from our empirical research. We begin with dynamics of mutual exclusion that emerge with the constitution of participatory discourse in terms of the "Administrator's" first framing activities. It is of special interest for our approach to reconstruct how the first opening up of the participation process provided by the "Administrator" position establishes a frame according to which people, the public, citizens or whoever is allowed and expected to be included in whatever way in the procedure. For this frame defines

[4] The terms inclusion and exclusion are in this context used in the same way as above in the theoretical foundations, namely based on systems theoretical ground. These terms describe the fact, whether the communications of a position can be treated as relevant and communicable in the structures of a second position, or not. In contemporary systems theory, the term inclusion refers to the question of how human beings are connected with social (i.e. communication) systems, namely by addressability. "Addressing" in this context means, that the social structures (i.e. the communicated expectations) contain positions and roles for human actors. Inclusion then is a general concept, treating the problem of addressability of persons in a communication system: Who is, when and under which conditions a relevant speaker?

We describe social systems as communication systems, and inclusion as an aspect of communication, namely as taking persons into account as relevant communicative addresses. In so doing, we can analyse citizenship as an empirical "question of voice", a theoretical demand that Hubert Heinelt (2002) has recently formulated.

"Inclusion" and "exclusion" are, accordingly, more abstract notions for what is often referred to as *compatibility, convergence* vs. *conflict, contradiction, neglecting* of/between social positions.

the procedural slot for social positions expected to be relevant to participation.

Whereas the procedural framing in general is facing more and more homogeneity across Europe, the concrete shaping of these slots still differs. Particularly, the German and the Dutch situation allow for insights in this process since we had access in both countries to the sequence of written discourse steps and could study the procedural slot provided by Administrator position, the written objections filling in this slot and the responses by authority or ministry coping with these objections. To a certain extent, the picture in both countries is similar rather than different: It is through the administrator position that the procedure is opened up by providing slots that are significantly broad, vague, and unspecific. Those who can hand in written objections come into view as "third parties", added on to permission-asker as first party, and permission-giver as second party. Except from the indication that it is the public with the reference to "any one" in the text, it is difficult to identity who is expected to fill in this slot. The notion of "objection" (and of "opponent" or "objector") merely indicates that it is some kind of opposition (if not protest) that gives cause for making objections and participating in the procedure. It is, therefore, merely from between the lines that we might conclude that this way of defining the slot can in itself be regarded as a procedural reflection of foregoing experiences with the "Organised protestor" position.

Interestingly enough, the authors of objections obviously do not restrict themselves to the administrator's image of 'objector' but seemingly tend to compensate for the significantly under-specified slot by positioning themselves in an eye-catching way – as local 'we', concerned citizen, and/or organised protestor with associated types of communicated concerns. On the one hand, there are remarkable differences as to the distribution of these second step positionings between the Netherlands (NL) and Germany (D) (D: 'local 'we' among others, NL: no instance of local 'we' but dominant appearance of organised protestor). On the other, there are no differences between both countries as far as the positioning mechanism of the procedure is concerned: In both cases, the administrator's significantly under-determined opening up of the participation process, in fact, seems to invite and to provoke authors to position themselves according to different social positions. So, the eye-catching appearance of manifestation of social positions as such can actually be related to the nature of this sort of procedure. What does then happen to these positions in the next step taken by administrator position?

Although inviting different kinds of social positions, the administrator clearly reduces the scope of possible social positions to a very narrow concept of 'concerned citizen', understood in terms of critical scientific and/or technological competence. Other facets of the concerned citizen position – let alone the other present social positions – do not find any resonance in the "responses" given by the authority. Other positions are deemed unworthy of response in terms of "economical, ethical, and ideological aspects", which have to be left out in favour of "soundly motivated objections" (from the Dutch data). There are formulaic expressions used by administrators which fulfil the specific function of making clear what counts and what obviously does not count: Examples are "It is known that..." as a hint to missing scientific competence on the objector's side and "Strictly speaking, such an objection does not come under the range of Decrees GMO" as a hint that the objection fails to meet the expected requirements.

To sum up: The overall result is that dynamics cannot develop beyond the narrow frame established by the administrator's position. Although systematically invited, other positions than a reduced concerned citizen position are not made available to the relevant parties. Using an emphatic notion of dynamics in the sense of an unpredictable, in a way surprising process, we can also say: that the "administrator" position obviously succeeds in rejecting any kind of dynamics that goes beyond the 'normal' procedural course of events. This is not due to a personal mistake in administrative behaviour. It is, rather, the effect of the legal framework in which the administrative procedure is embedded – the 'iron cage' of the law as it were (cf. Bora, forthcoming). The only social position within this framing that finds resonance is citizenship understood as technological and scientific competence ('technological citizenship' in some of the country reports). We are, therefore, led to assume that this type of dynamics is one of mutual *exclusion* as far as the administrator position proves to be impervious to other positions, in particular to various citizen positions ("Local 'We' ", "Concerned Citizen", "Engaged Citizen".) On the other side, the "Scientist" normally is fully complementary with the "Administrator" position. Both go together well in establishing and maintaining the dynamics of mutual exclusion.

Dynamics of mutual *inclusion* can, in contrast, often be found in the course of participatory discourse events in a merely indirect relation to the concrete licensing procedure. Strictly speaking, this holds true as far as the administrator position, in fact, takes a back seat within these discourse events. When the administrator position is still concerned with these events, there is reason to assume that the type of dynamics is again that of mutual *ex*clusion. Before turning to dynamics of inclusion we will, briefly, illustrate this effect. Take, for instance, the following sequence of written discourse that obviously illustrates this type of exclusive dynamics when the "Administrator" position is involved. It stems from the UK material. The government website invites "local people" to make "representations" via DEFRA (=Department for Environment, Food and Rural Affairs) to those experts within ACRE (=Advisory Committee on Releases to the Environment) who are responsible for informing and implementing government policy decisions. First step: Invited by government as a mixture of administrator and politician position. A citizen then writes a letter, which positions the writer as "concerned citizen". The writer presents his/her concern about GM crops, not as an issue of self-interest, but as an issue for the businesses and livelihoods of those around him, his/her fellow citizens. Second step: Concerned citizen takes up the invitation. In turn, the government response positions the member of the public as requiring or needing further information, and positions the government department as formally and courteously providing that information. Third step: Concerned citizen is re-positioned according to the administrator/politician position. This three-step-sequence nicely documents that and how dynamics of mutual exclusion might work.

According to this observation, evidence could, indeed, be provided for mutual *inclusion* type of dynamics when administrator and/or politicians' position were *not* involved.[5] This evidence can be taken from Italian and Swedish participatory discourse fragments. The Italian data

[5] It is essential to see at this point that we are speaking about positions and *not* about actors. The above mentioned results, therefore, suggest: a more open framing without an administrator *position*, which would define the communication rules, gives greater chances for inclusion. At the same time – and in line with this result – some evidence can be provided (from the German situation, for instance) that such open framing (public debate or similar context) should in every case necessarily include *actors* from the competent authorities. Without their inclusion as actors representing members of authorities such events would rarely be of any relevance for citizen *positions*, as can easily be concluded from their conceptualisation of "relevant actors"!

fragments nicely show that and also show how the "Organised Protestor" position can find resonance with the "scientific expert position", although we know from other dynamics that this is typically a constellation of potential exclusion. This example shows the possibilities of dynamics in the sense of the unpredictable course of events when the narrow frame of the procedure in the "Administrator's" sense did not restrict them. Further evidence for inclusive dynamics can be taken from Swedish data documenting that organised protestor's activities force the industrial actor to adopt semantics from concerned citizen ("debating company") – displaying a dynamics of self-presentation within one and the same social position.

Turning to the Italian example, our data stem from a situation in which people taking the "Organised Protestor" position did not address themselves to the administration but – outside the narrow procedural frame – to those conducting the trial, namely the scientists in charge and the University (Agriculture faculty) hosting the experiments (both taking the position of "scientific expert"). In the course of the communicative exchanges between these parties, written documents were sent to the University by the protestors and were discussed with faculty members. What can be taken from these exchanges is that although the social positions of "organised protestor" and "scientific expert" are to some extent contradictory (see our description of social positions above), there emerges some kind of dialogue between the manifestations of these positions that goes beyond a simple confrontation and that does not end up with some kind of communicative breakdown. On the contrary, organised protestor arguments find resonance on the side of scientific expert and organisational consequences are taken into account at the scientific expert side. This might be a telling case, because it is the contextualization of the debate *outside* the narrow boundaries of the administrative procedure that allows for this kind of dialogue.

Turning to the Swedish example, there was a Greenpeace campaign in indirect relation to a GMO field trial, which found much resonance in the media. And, what is of special interest here, as a direct result of this campaign the applicant company developed a new type of self-presentation with an interesting semantic shift: It presented itself as a "debating company". So, in terms of social positioning, we notice a dynamic change in presentation of "industrial actor" by adopting semantics from "concerned citizen" – triggered and provoked by "organised protestor's" activities. This seems to be a typical example of how mass media oriented "organised protestor" can evoke a dynamics of social positionings that reaches beyond the procedural frame established and controlled by "policy maker" and "administrator". A similar kind of dynamics could be noticed in our Dutch materials when politician positions seem to learn from organised protestor position how to cope with concerned citizen arguments in public debate. And, vice versa, such a change in dynamics appears to occur when organised protestor positions seem to learn from "Administrator" positions in previous licensing procedures how to bring in certain kinds of written objection that have proven to resonate and in this sense have proven to be successful in the formal procedure.

Both the Italian and the Swedish examples clearly illustrate dynamics of mutual *inclusion* between social positions. Summarizing these findings and the ones reported previously, we should keep in mind that participatory discourse, obviously, is an open-ended discourse. Participatory discourse might result in an inclusion of affected social positions, as could be assumed to be intended by the programmatic claim of participation, but it might as well result in an exclusion of social positions. Above all, it is a sort of discourse that bears on its own genuine dynamics. And these dynamics can prove to be inclusive and can prove to be exclusive.

It should be stressed that, from our theoretical point of view, there is no *a priori*-preference for inclusive or exclusive dynamics. The distinction between inclusion and exclusion is per se a neutral one due to the analytic interest in the reconstruction of dynamics of social positioning processes. Participatory discourse is a notion that covers both the case of exclusion as well as the case of inclusion. Whether inclusion is preferred or not depends on a variety of reasons which need not spelled out here. For us as analysts, it makes no difference, for instance, whether an "Industrial actor's" shift towards a "debating company" that reflects and integrates "concerned citizen's" arguments is merely strategic or not. It shows – as a part of inclusive dynamics – an interesting shift in the social semantics of the "Industrial actor" position, and that is what counts analytically. In the same way, a condition of communicative contradiction that is, for instance, implied in the invitation-objection-response sequence between "Administrator" and "Concerned Citizen" position need not be treated as a failure or collapse of participatory discourse. It reveals a prototypical concomitant phenomenon of exclusive dynamics between social positions, and that is what counts analytically.

The entire process looks, of course, very different when you take a governance point of view. The emergence of inclusive and exclusive dynamics might, then, be a crucial factor for the evaluation and the review of participatory discourse. Concerning the demand of "good" governance practices (see above B), the question arises, what kind of procedural and institutional framework will foster what kind of dynamics. This is a challenge, especially for the "Administrator" position and its implementation in participatory discourse. The change of regulatory conditions of licensing procedures in Germany is a markedly telling case in this regard: The public hearings taking place between competent authority and objectors (called "Erörterungstermin") that had been a distinct part of the administrative licensing procedure until 1993 often, ended up with a communicative breakdown going far beyond what could be dealt with by means of face-to-face deliberation and debate (Bora 1999). Having experienced this sort of failure, this kind of public hearing was excluded from the licensing procedure in 1993. In our terms, it can therefore be said that exclusive dynamics have, in fact, made a difference to participatory governance practices! This is the reason why we will now return from the participatory *discourse* perspective to the participatory *governance* perspective in our closing remarks.

D. From participatory discourse to participatory governance

After having described the characteristics of participatory discourse on the level of micro-structures, we will now turn back to participatory governance and its institutional context. We will also speak about the role of citizens and of political discourse in this context. The analysis of micro-structures allows for better understanding the strengths and weaknesses of participatory discourse. In our empirical work we were able to demonstrate that participatory discourse promotes both inclusive and exclusive dynamics in the process of communication. In our empirical approach, we noticed both effects without normative preference for either inclusive or exclusive dynamics. We tried to make clear that both forms are directly linked to the framework of the particular participatory procedure, to its legal and institutional framework and to the expectations that are connected with participation in the respective situation. Participation *per se*, we tried to argue, does not guarantee an advance in democratic culture nor is it *as such* suited to cope with the 'democratic deficit' that we mentioned in the beginning of our article. If our argument proves to be reliable, certain normative consequences might be drawn with respect to further institutional and political-cultural developments *beyond participation*. Such conclusions are, obviously, not more than first suggestions. They are, therefore, open to any kind of critical discussion. They are, nevertheless, based on empirical observations. Against this empirical background they try to explore new ways for democratic engagement, particularly in the governance of science and technology.

We would like to make three points:

1. *Institutional context and legal framework*: Although being a central issue in many policy papers (e.g. the EU White Paper on Governance and the UK Green Paper mentioned in section A, or the Århus convention, for instance) and in a broad scholarly debate, the function of citizen participation in the particular legal provisions for the administrative procedure still is underdetermined. This vagueness has been demonstrated in empirical research. It stems from an unsolved tension between the two declared aims of participation, the first of which is scrutiny of administrative behaviour, and the second is the realisation of civil rights. The first aim is due to the logic of the legal-administrative procedure based on scientific knowledge and expertise, i.e. on the issue dimension. The second relates to aspects as "voice" and "standing", i.e. to the social dimension. As a consequence, the procedure opens slots for a social subject engaging in activities oriented to general welfare, or for his/her own fundamental rights, generally informed about matters of common interest (such as administrative procedures), who, independently of specific interests or preferences, is ready to intensely go into the matter, sufficiently competent to critically assess the project applied for on a scientific level. The legal-procedural frame of the licensing procedure entails all these motifs without clearly focussing on one of them.[6] The main effect of this functional indeterminacy is a more or less unclear impression of some sort of critical control. In the empirical practise, the focus is on scientific expertise. Local issues

[6] In the legal discussion mainly six reasons are usually enumerated for citizen participation: information of the administration, information of the citizens, scrutiny, protection of fundamental rights, representation of interests, legitimation/acceptance. These aims are often being presented as a list, as if there was no internal tension between some of these goals, cf. Bora (1994).

become relevant only insofar, as they can be understood as matters of scientific discourse. One would therefore, argue against the background of these findings that in every case of participatory governance the precise function of participation should be clarified with respect to the particular procedure and with respect to the constitutional and legal framework. Only with such clarification, can the particular form and institutional context be adequately discussed (cf. Abels & Bora 2004).

2. *Informed citizens*: The issue of sufficient information refers to two dimensions, namely to information about the particular procedure on the one hand, and to information about the issue in question on the other (the GMO field trial, for instance). Information about the procedure and transparency about the co-ordinates of the decision-making are the conditions for trust. Understandable information for local laypersons is necessary. Problems resulting from the actual handling of the procedure in the first place concern local people. These persons regard themselves as having the right to communicate to the authority everything they consider as problematic about the field trial. In the administrative decision, this position is usually rejected as irrelevant. This problem results from a general lack of information about the administrative procedure in its particular form. It is combined with a complete lack of information about administrative procedure in general. Therefore, we would recommend that in a particular case of participatory governance the competent authority, instead of communicating formal openness, informs the public about the legal conditions underlying the case, about the government's general attitude towards the subject matter, about the structure of the given procedure, the criteria for decision making, the thematic level relevant in the procedure, and about the potential impact of objections on the procedure. Information should also touch the question of which institutions are involved in decision-making.

With respect to information about GMO field trials the data show that a merely formal public announcement is not an appropriate way of informing the public. Moreover, the information in the official documents is mostly inappropriate. The papers are not understandable for laypersons, and there is no possibility of receiving personal answers to questions about the project. Direct information about the project by the applicant, for example: in the form of parish meetings, could help in informing the local public. Even if these meetings have proven to be not completely successful in some case studies, mainly for reason that relate to the restricted version of "locality" in these meetings, they might nevertheless help in communicating the issue, if only through being presented in a way that supports inclusive dynamics. One could also think about a local information forum organised by relevant actors involved in the case.

3. *Political discourse and responsibility/accountability*: "Alternative" models and fora of participation have been discussed in recent years, as we mentioned in section A. It is obvious that these suggestions implicitly or explicitly formulate the idea of a distinctive form or arena of communication. According to the empirical data, something like public opinion and local voice will not trigger resonance in the administrator or scientist position within the universe of legal-administrative procedures. From our comparative view, moreover, the experience from the Netherlands and Sweden, but to some extent also from the British case shows, that a more "policy-oriented" political institutional context gives the opportunity to establish a different kind of communication (cf. also Bora, forthcoming). Although not being free from problematic dynamics, the "public debates" allow for a greater degree of open communication between different social positions. The danger here is one of tightening the legal-administrative ties around the political discussions. One should, therefore, think about possible forms of participatory procedures, which separate the different functions.

Therefore, in addition to administrative procedures, a separate forum might be established for open dialogue about the matter between citizens and public authorities. Such a forum would have to be detached from the legal-procedural framework of the administrative procedure. It could in the same instance be closely related to the procedure, thereby allowing use to be made of results from the discussions taking place in this decision-making forum. In such an "alternative" arena, the authority can provide information about the issue at stake, about the legal provisions and the structure of the decision-making process. The information can be given in a non-technical and understandable way. Resonance within the structural expectations of citizen positions will therefore be possible. Based on this, the administration can try to correct misunderstanding, to explain its point of view, and to discuss, for instance based on a draft decree or a similar kind of document, the prospective line of decision on the basis of legal requirements and the scientific state of the art. In case of GMO field trials, for instance, even formal or informal negotiations between the applicant and local citizens may be possible with respect to details of the trial (questions of bio-safety, the protection of interests of organic farmers in the neighbourhood or similar issues). In addition, with respect to the legal level of decision-making, the authority would be capable of taking into account arguments and suggesting modifications to the intended project. The administrator would have to deal with the consequences of the decision with respect to the expectations and relevance of citizen positions. Such a forum should, therefore, be established very early in the lifespan of the procedure. It would allow the authority to adequately react to the diffuse communication of the citizen positions without compromising the specificity of the administrative decision–making according to the legal requirements.

In addressing and recommending these "alternative" forms it is, nevertheless, very important to clearly identify a critical point. In spite of the fact that they may have a productive function in improving the opportunities for local and concerned citizen positions, they may also provoke exclusive dynamics, if they are not designed very carefully with respect to their function. In this respect, a warning against any euphoric attitude is necessary. An international overview (Abels & Bora 2004) over a range of "alternative" procedures, such as the consensus-conference, the scenario-workshop, the public dialogue, the voting conference, participatory technology assessment, and others, has shown that there are good reason to be cautious in this respect.[7] It would certainly be misleading merely to install one of these procedures, hoping that it will solve the structural problems on the level of micro-structures. An important result of our research is the necessity of a precise structural analysis of the communicative situation at stake and of a functional analysis of the possible purpose participation is supposed to fulfill in this situation. Any step back behind these requirements will inevitably result in functional problems similar to those we have found in our data.

We would therefore argue that any *raisonnement* about the implementation of "alternative" institutional forms for citizen participation in administrative decision-making be prepared and accompanied by

[7] A number of very valuable studies have been conducted on the issue, some of them in a comparative design, e.g. the EUROpTA study. See, for an overview, the AssesSTGov-Report by Abels and Bora (Abels & Bora 2005) They have brought a tremendous amount of new knowledge about participatory procedures. Our point here is that is inevitable to apply a communication research approach in order to be able to document the empirical function and performance of participation. Any other level of reconstruction will merely reproduce scientific (if not political) prejudices in this respect.

a precise scientific analysis of the function and structure of participation in the particular model. Whether or not the particular solution in a given institutional and political-cultural context with a particular subject matter at stake will be more or less participatory, remains open under these conditions. The question of how much and which form of participation is adequate in a concrete case has to be always dealt with anew. There is no theoretical reason to presume any normative priority for more participation. Insofar, we would like to encourage the scholarly debate to step beyond participation – without giving up the normative intentions connected with participatory governance.

References

Abels, Gabriele (2002): Experts, Citizens and Eurocrats - Towards a Policy Shift in the Governance of Biopoliticis in the EU. Europeans Integration online Papers (EIoP) Vol. 6 No. 19. (http://eiop.or.at/eiop/texte/2002-019a.htm)

Abels, Gabriele and Bora, Alfons (2005): Public participation, stakeholders and expertise: Multi-actor spaces in the governance of biotechnology. State-of-the-art report (PDF). Bielefeld University: Institute for Science and Technology Studies. (http://www.uni-bielefeld.de/iwt/personen/bora/pdf/PublicParticipation.pdf)

Abels, Gabriele and Bora, Alfons (2004): Demokratische Technikbewertung. Bielefeld: Transcript Verlag.

Amin, Ash (ed.) (1997): Beyond Market and Hierarchy: Interactive Governance and Social Complexity. Cheltenham: Elgar.

Bora, Alfons (1994): Grenzen der Partizipation? Risikoentscheidungen und Öffentlichkeitsbeteiligung im Recht. In: ZfRSoz (15), 2, 126–152.

Bora, Alfons (1999): Differenzierung und Inklusion. Partizipative Öffentlichkeit im Rechtssystem moderner Gesellschaften. Baden-Baden: Nomos.

Bora, Alfons (forthcoming): Technoscientific normativity and the 'iron cage' of law. Manuscript. Bielefeld 2007. 24 p. (accepted for publication in Science, Technology & Human Values) (http://www.uni-bielefeld.de/iwt/personen/bora/pdf/Alfons-Bora .technoscientific%20normativities.pdf)

Bora, Alfons and Hausendorf, Heiko (2006): Participatory science governance revisited: normative expectations versus empirical evidence. In: Science and Public Policy 33 (2006), 7, 478–488.

Brunkhorst, Hauke and Kettner, Matthias (eds) (2000): Globalisierung und Demokratie. Wirtschaft, Recht und Medien. Frankfurt/M.: Suhrkamp.

Durant, J. (1999): Participatory technology asssessment and the democratic model of the public understanding of science. In. Science and Public Policy, Vol. 26, No. 5

Edeling, Thomas, Jann, Werner and Wagner, Dieter (eds) (2001): Modern Governance. Koordination und Organisation zwischen Konkurrenz, Hierarchie und Solidarität. Opladen: Leske + Budrich.

European Commission (2000): "Science, Society and the Citizen in Europe". Commission Working Document.

European Commission (2001): "White Paper on Governance COM (2001) 428". Brussels, July 25th 2001.

Fischer, F. (1999): Technological deliberation in a democratic society: the case for participatory inquiry. In: Science and Pubic Policy, Vol. 26, No. 5.

Grote, Jürgen R. and Gbikpi, Bernard (eds) (2001): Participatory Governance. Political and Societal Implications. Opladen: Leske + Budrich.

Hausendorf, Heiko and Bora, Alfons (eds.) (2006a): Analysing Citizenship Talk. Social positioning in political and legal decision-making processes. Amsterdam: John Benjamins.

Hausendorf, Heiko and Bora, Alfons (2006b): Reconstructing social positioning in discourse: Methodological basics and their implementation from a conversation analysis perspective. In: Hausendorf, Heiko; Bora, Alfons (eds.): Analysing Citizenship Talk. Social positioning in political and legal decision-making processes. Amsterdam: John Benjamins, 85–97.

Heinelt, Hubert (2002): "Civic Perspectives on a Democratic Transformation of the EU". In Participatory Governance. Political and Societal Implications, J. Grote and B. Gbikpi (eds), 97–120. Opladen: Leske + Budrich.

Held, David (1995): Democracy and the global order: from the modern state to cosmopolitan governance. Cambridge: Polity Press.

Hirst, Paul (1994): Associative democracy: new forms of economic and social governance. Cambridge: Polity Press.

Joerges, Christian (2001): "Economic Order" - "Technical Realization" – "The Hour of the Executive": Some Legal Historical Observations on the Commission White Paper on European Governance. Contribution to the Jean Monnet Working Paper No.6/01, Symposium: Mountain or Molehill? A Critical Appraisal of the Commission White Paper on Governance. http://www.jeanmonnetprogram.org/papers/01/012201. html

Joss, Simon/Bellucci, Sergio (eds.) (2002): Participatory Technology Assessment. European Perspectives. London (University of Westminster).

Kohler-Koch, Beate and Eising, Rainer (eds) (1999): The Transformation of Governance in the European Union. London: Routledge.

Kooiman, Jan (2002): Governance: A Social-Political Perspective. In Participatory Governance. Political and Societal Implications, J. Grote and B. Gbikpi (eds), 71–96. Opladen: Leske + Budrich.

Liberatore, Angela and Funtowicz, Silvio (2003): 'Democratising expertise', 'expertising' democracy: what does this mean, and why bother? In: Science and Public Policy 1 June 2003, 146–150.

Luhmann, Niklas (1995): Social systems. Translated by John Bednarz, Jr., with Dirk Baecker; foreword by Eva M. Knodt. Stanford, Calif.: Stanford University Press

Ministry of Justice (2008): A national framework for greater citizen engagement. A discussion paper - published July 2008. London

Nowotny, Helga (2003): Democratising expertise and socially robust knowledge. In: Science and Public Policy 1 June 2003, 151–156.

Rosenau, James N. (1995): Governance in the Twenty-First Century. In: Global Governance 1, 13.

Scharpf, Fritz W. (1999): Governing in Europe: Effective and Democratic? Oxford.

Vandenberg, Andrew (ed.) (2000): Citizenship and Democracy in a Global Era. New York: St. Martin's Press.

Zürn, Michael (1998): Regieren jenseits des Nationalstaates: Globalisierung und Denationalisierung als Chance. Frankfurt/M.: Suhrkamp.

ABOUT THE AUTHORS

Gabriele Abels, professor of comparative and European politics at the Institute of Political Science, University of Tübingen. Her research interest are in the field of European integration, technology assessment, participation and democratization, gender studies; recent publications: Demokratische Technikbewertung (Bielefeld: Transcript 2004 together with Alfons Bora); Trade and Human Rights: Inter- and Supranational Regulation of GMOs and ART. In: E. Montpetit, C. Rothmayr, F. (Eds.): The Politics of Biotechnology in North America and Europe: Policy Networks, Institutions and Internationalization (Lanham, MD: Lexington Books 2007); Citizen Involvement in Public Policy-making: Does it Improve Democratic Legitimacy and Accountability? The Case of pTA. Interdisciplinary Information Sciences 13 (1) 2007: 103–116.

Alfons Bora is professor of sociology at Bielefeld University (Germany). Since 1999 he has been holding a chair for technology assessment. He is a member of the German Ethics Council. He studied law and sociology, received his PhD from the University of Freiburg (Germany) and his habilitation from the Free University of Berlin. He worked as a researcher at the Max-Planck-Institute for Foreign and International Penal Law, research unit for criminology, and at the Social Science Research Center Berlin (Wissenschaftszentrum Berlin, WZB). Recent publications include: Technoscientific normativity and the 'iron cage' of law, forthcoming in *Science, Technology & Human Values*, Summer 2009; with Heiko Hausendorf, *Analysing Citizenship Talk. Social Positioning in Political And Legal Decision-Making Processes*, Amsterdam: Benjamins 2006; with Heiko Hausendorf, Participatory science governance revisited: normative expectations versus empirical evidence. In: *Science and Public Policy* 33 (2006), 7, 478–488; with Gabriele Abels, *Demokratische Technikbewertung*, Bielefeld: transcript 2004.

Matthias Baier, LL.D., Uppsala university, PhD in sociology of law, Lund university; Lecturer at the division of sociology of law, Lund university since 2003, tenure. He has been researcher in the PARAYDS program 2001–2004 and in the Baltic Master program 2005–2006. He is currently sociology of law coordinator for the Lund University Centre of Excellence for Integration of Social and Natural Dimensions of Sustainability (Lucid), a ten year grant 2008–2018. His main interests are in socio-legal aspects on participation, environmental problems and in mass media and the law. He is author of *Norm och rättsregel* (Norms and rules), a thesis on environmental problems and norm formation; "A visual self image of the legal authority", *Social and legal studies*. 2002 with Bo Carlsson; the textbook *Om normer* (*On norms*) with Måns Svensson, fortcoming spring 2009 and editor of *Participative aspects on law – a sociolegal perspective*, forthcoming winter 2008.

Elena Collavin is a social psychologist. She lectures at the Communication Department of the University of San Diego, California. She applies discourse analysis and ethnography to the study of social controversies. Her doctoral research focused on the public debate surrounding food biotechnologies in Italy. She is currently researching the practices and discourses of food in Italy and in the United States in a comparative perspective. Her Doctoral thesis "Food biotechnologies in Italy: a social psychological study" was published by the University of Helsinki in 2007. In 2008 she published one article on the rhetoric of food marketing and (with Alessandro Tavano) a book chapter on the pragmatics of the Friulian language.

Heiko Hausendorf received his PhD from the University of Bielefeld (Germany) and holds a chair in German Linguistics at the University of Zurich (Switzerland) since 2007. Till then he was a professor of German Linguistics at the University of Bayreuth (Germany). His research topics are located in the field of sociolinguistics and linguistic pragmatics with a special interest in conversation analysis. Main focuses of research are: methodology of text and discourse analysis; language and social belonging; social categorization and positioning; narrative interaction; talk in institutions; language and discourse acquisition. Selection of recent publications: Zugehörigkeit durch Sprache. Eine linguistische Studie am Beispiel der deutschen Wiedervereinigung. Tübingen: Niemeyer 2000. Analysing Citizenship Talk. Social Positioning in Political and Legal Decision-Making Processes. Amsterdam et al.: John Benjamins 2006 (ed. volume, in co-operation with Alfons Bora). Vor dem Kunstwerk. Interdisziplinäre Aspekte des Sprechens und Schreibens über Kunst (ed. volume). München: Fink 2007.

Textlinguistik fürs Examen. Göttingen: Vandenhoeck & Ruprecht 2008 (in co-operation with Wolfgang Kesselheim).

ZSUZSANA IVÁNYI is an associate professor of German linguistics at the University of Debrecen. Presently (2008) she is the head of the Institute of German Studies and also the director of the Graduate School for German Linguistics of the University of Debrecen. Her research focuses on conversational analysis, on different problems in verbalization and on social positioning as exemplified by following papers: Iványi, Zs. et all.: Social Categorization and the Grammar-Pragmatics Relation. An Analysis of Hungarian Data. Sprachtheorie und germanistische Linguistik 16.2. (2006), S. 111–158. Iványi, Zs. et al.: Bürgerbeteiligung – Traum oder Realität? Soziale Positionierung in Genehmigungsverfahren zur Freisetzung gentechnisch veränderter Organismen in Ungarn – ein konversationsanalystischer Ansatz. In: Sprachtheorie und germanistische Linguistik 17. (2007), pp. 47–62, 101–123.

LES LEVIDOW is a Senior Research Fellow at the Open University, UK, where he has been studying agri-environmental issues since 1989. A long-running case study has been agbiotech – innovation, safety regulation and public controversy. This research has focused on the European Union, USA and their trade conflicts. The controversy provides a case study of concepts such as regulatory science, sustainability, European integration, governance, transnational civil society and organizational learning. Results have been published in special issues of two journals (*Science & Public Policy*, and *Journal of Risk Research*), as well as in numerous articles. He is co-author of *Governing the Transatlantic Conflict over Agricultural Biotechnology: Contending Coalitions, Trade Liberalisation and Standard Setting* (Routledge, 2006). Likewise co-author of *GM Food on Trial: Testing European Democracy* (Routledge, forthcoming, 2009). He is also Editor of the journal *Science as Culture*. See Biotech Policy Group website, http://technology.open.ac.uk/cts/bpg

KORNÉLIA MARINECZ is a high-school teacher for German language and literature, visiting lecturer at the Department of German Linguistics of the University of Debrecen. Fields of research: pragmatics, sociolinguistics, conversation analysis. Recent publications: Iványi, Zs./Kertész, A./Marinecz, K./Máté, N. (2006a): Personal reference, social categorization and the communicative achievement of citizenship: Comments on a local public meeting on GMO field trials. In: Bora, A./Hausendorf, H. (eds.): *Analysing Citizenship Talk*. Amsterdam/Philadelphia: Benjamins. (2006), 223–250. Iványi, Zs./Kertész, A./Marinecz, K./Máté, N. (2006b): Social Categorization and the Grammar-Pragmatics Relation. An Analysis of Hungarian Data. *Sprachtheorie und germanistische Linguistik 16 (2006)*, 111–157. Iványi, Zs. / Marinecz, K. (2007): Bürgerbeteiligung – Traum oder Realität? Soziale Positionierung in Genehmigungsverfahren zur Freisetzung gentechnisch veränderter Organismen in Ungarn – ein konversationsanalytischer Ansatz. *Sprachtheorie und germanistische Linguistik 17.1 (2007)*, 47–62 und *17.2 (2007)*, 101–123.

PETER MÜNTE is assistant professor at the Institute for Science and Technology Studies at the Bielefeld University. His fields of research are governance of science and technology, participative politics, sociology and history of science, methodology of sequential analysis and case reconstruction. Recent publications include: Peter Münte, Andreas Franzmann (2007), "Von der Gelehrtenrepublik zum Dienstleistungsunternehmen' – Ausschnitt aus einer Deutungsmusteranalyse zur Erschließung kollektiver Bewußtseinslagen bei Protagonisten der gegenwärtigen Universitätsreform", in: Andreas Franzmann, Barbara Wolbrink (eds.), Zwischen Idee und Zweckorientierung: Vorbilder und Motive von Hochschulreformen seit 1945, Berlin; Peter Münte (2007), "Strukturelle Motive der Beziehung von Wissenschaft und Herrschaft: Zur wissenschaftssoziologischen Bedeutung der Analyse von Widmungsbriefen am Beispiel der Widmung Christiaan Huygens' an Leopold de' Medici in Systema Saturnium", in: Ulrich Oevermann, Johannes Süßmann, Christine Tauber: (eds.), Die Kunst der Mächtigen und die Macht der Kunst. Neue Studien zur Kulturpatronage, Berlin.

PATRICK O'MAHONY is a Senior Lecturer in Sociology in the School of Sociology and Philosophy at National University of Ireland, Cork. His research interests cover social theory, political sociology, especially the sociology of democracy and the sociology of nationalism, environmental sociology, sociology of science and technology and philosophy of social science. He is currently working on a book on the theory of the public sphere. Recent publications include acting as lead editor of a collection of essays on Irish Environmental Politics after the Communicative Turn to be published by Manchester University Press in 2009, an article on media coverage of the human genome to *Social Studies of*

Science in 2005 (with Mike Schaefer) and co-authoring of a book on the Nationalism and Social Theory with Gerard Delanty for Sage.

GIUSEPPE PELLEGRINI holds a PhD in Sociology and teaches Methodology and Technique of Social Research at the University of Padova. He deals with connections among science, technology and society, with particular attention to dynamics of communication and public participation. He is member of the scientific committee of Observa - Science and Society and Co-founder of the Italian Association for Social Studies of Science and Technology. He published Technoscientific Innovation. Responsibility and new Models of Democracy (ed.), Rubbettino 2008; Biotecnologie e Cittadinanza, Gregoriana Editore, 2005; "Evaluating Public Communication of Science and technology" with F. Neresini in Bucchi M. and Trench B., Handbook of Public Communication of Science and Technology, Routledge 2008; "From Representation to Deliberation - New Perspectives of Communication Among Actors in Science and Technology Innovations" in Cheng D. et al. (eds.) Communicating Science in Social Context, Springer Verlag, 2008.

HENRIK RAHM holds a PhD in Scandinavian Languages. His research interests encompass genre, discourse and intertextuality also in other fields than GMO discourse: student texts, mass media texts, advertisements and texts from health care authorities. Rahm is lecturer in language, communication and media at Malmö University. Since fall 2007 he is on leave for a research position at the Swedish research centre Vårdal Institute in a multi-disciplinary project on municipal palliative care, mapping and analysing modes of communication and genres used between professions and organisations. Among his publications are: Rahm, Henrik (2006a): *Getting attention in the media Interdiscursivity and ideology in advertisements* In: Lassen, Inger, Strunck, Jeanne and Vestergaard, Torben (eds.) *Mediating Ideology in Text and Image* Amsterdam & Philadelphia: John Benjamins. Rahm, Henrik (2006b) (together with Jana Holsánová and Kenneth Holmqvist): "Entry points and reading paths on newspaper spreads: Comparing a semiotic analysis with eye-tracking measurements" In: *Visual Communication,* 5 (1), February 2006, SAGE Publications.

INDEX

INTERNATIONAL STUDIES
IN
SOCIOLOGY AND SOCIAL ANTHROPOLOGY

21. FUSÉ, T. (ed.). *Modernization and Stress in Japan.* 1975. ISBN 90 04 04344 6
22. SMITH, B.L. (ed.). *Religion and Social Conflict in South Asia.* 1976. ISBN 90 04 04510 4
23. MAZRUI, A.A. (ed.). *The Warrior Tradition in Modern Africa.* 1977. ISBN 90 04 05646 7
25. SMITH, B.L. (ed.). *Religion and the Legitimation of Power in South Asia.* 1978. ISBN 90 04 05674 2
31. LELE, J. (ed.). *Tradition and Modernity in* Bhakti *Movements.* 1981. ISBN 90 04 06370 6
32. ARMER, J.M. *Comparative Sociological Research in the 1960s and 1970s.* 1982. ISBN 90 04 06487 7
33. GALATY, J.G. & P.C. SALZMAN (eds.). *Change and Development in Nomadic and Pastor-al Societies.* 1981. ISBN 90 04 06587 3
34. LUPRI, E. (ed.). *The Changing Position of Women in Family and Society. A Cross-National Comparison.* 1983. ISBN 90 04 06845 7
35. IVERSON, N. (ed.). *Urbanism and Urbanization. Views, Aspects and Dimensions.* 1984. ISBN 90 04 06920 8
36. MALIK, Y.K. *Politics, Technology, and Bureaucracy in South Asia.* 1983. ISBN 90 04 07027 3
37. LENSKI, G. (ed.). *Current Issues and Research in Macrosociology.* 1984. ISBN 90 04 07052 4
39. TIRYAKIAN, E.A. (ed.). *The Global Crisis. Sociological Analyses and Responses.* 1984. ISBN 90 04 07284 5
40. LAWRENCE, B. (ed.). *Ibn Khaldun and Islamic Ideology.* 1984. ISBN 90 04 07567 4
41. HAJJAR, S.G. (ed.). *The Middle East: from Transition to Development.* 1985. ISBN 90 04 07694 8
43. CARMAN, J.B. & F.A. MARGLIN (eds.). *Purity and Auspiciousness in Indian Society.* 1985. ISBN 90 04 07789 8
46. SMITH, B.L. & H.B. REYNOLDS (eds.). *The City as a Sacred Center. Essays on Six Asian Contexts.* 1987. ISBN 90 04 08471 1
47. MALIK, Y.K. & D.K. VAJPEYI (eds.). *India. The Years of Indira Ghandi.* 1988. ISBN 90 04 08681 1
48. CLARK, C. & J. LEMCO (eds.). *State and Development.* 1988. ISBN 90 04 08833 4
49. GUTKIND, P.C.W. (ed.). *Third World Workers. Comparative International Labour Studies.* 1988. ISBN 90 04 08788 5
50. SELIGMAN, A.B. *Order and Transcendence. The Role of Utopias and the Dynamics of Civi-lization.* 1989. ISBN 90 04 08975 6
51. JABBRA, J.G. *Bureaucracy and Development in the Arab World.* 1989. ISBN 90 04 09194 7

52. KAUTSKY, J.H. (ed.). *Karl Kautsky and the Social Science of Classical Marxism.* 1989. ISBN 90 04 09193 9
53. KAPUR, A. (ed.). *The Diplomatic Ideas and Practices of Asian States.* 1990. ISBN 90 04 09289 7
54. KIM, Q.-Y. (ed.). *Revolutions in the Third World.* 1991. ISBN 90 04 09355 9
55. KENNEDY, C.H. & D. J. LOUSCHER (eds.). *Civil Military Interaction in Asia and Afri-ca.* 1991. ISBN 90 04 09359 1
56. RAGIN, C.C. (ed.). *Issues and Alternatives in Comparative Social Research.* 1991. ISBN 90 04 09360 5
57. CHOUDHRY, N.K. (ed.). *Canada and South Asian Development. Trade and Aid.* 1991. ISBN 90 04 09416 4
58. RAZIA AKTER BANU, U.A.B. (ed.). *Islam in Bangladesh.* 1992. ISBN 90 04 09497 0
61. AHMAD, A. (ed.). *Science and Technology Policy for Economic Development in Africa.* 1993. ISBN 90 04 09659 0
62. VAJPEYI, D.K. (ed.). *Modernizing China.* 1994. ISBN 90 04 10046 6
63. BRADSHAW, Y.W. (ed.). *Education in Comparative Perspective.* New Lessons from around the World. 1997. ISBN 90 04 10734 7
64. UDOGU, E.I. (ed.). *Democracy and Democratization in Africa.* Toward the 21st Century. 1997. ISBN 90 04 10733 9
65. BEHAR, J.E. & A.G. CUZÁN (eds.). *At the Crossroads of Development.* Transnational Challenges to Developed and Developing Societies. 1997. ISBN 90 04 10732 0
66. LAUDERDALE, P. & R. AMSTER (eds.). *Lives in the Balance.* Perspectives on Global Injustice and Inequality. 1997. ISBN 90 04 10875 0
67. LOVEJOY, P.E. & P.A.T. WILLIAMS (eds.). *Displacement and the Politics of Violence in Nigeria.* 1997. ISBN 90 04 10876 9
68. JABBRA, J.G. & N.W. JABBRA (eds.). *Challenging Environmental Issues.* Middle Eastern Perspectives. 1997. ISBN 90 04 10877 7
69. SASAKI, M. (ed.). *Values and Attitudes Across Nations and Time.* 1998. ISBN 90 04 11219 7
70. SPERLING, J., Y. MALIK & D. LOUSCHER (eds.). *Zones of Amity, Zones of Enmity.* The Prospects for Economic and Military Security in Asia. 1998. ISBN 90 04 11218 9
71. NANDI, P.K. & S.M. SHAHIDULLAH (eds.). *Globalization and the Evolving World Society.* 1998. ISBN 90 04 11247 2
72. ARTS, W. & L. HALMAN (eds.). *New Directions in Quantitative Comparative Sociology.* 1999. ISBN 90 04 11411 4
73. ISHWARAN, K. (ed.). *Ascetic Culture: Renunciation and Worldly Engagement.* 1999. ISBN 90 04 11412 2
74. PATTERSON, R. (ed.). *Science and Technology in Southern Africa and East and South Asia,* 1999. ISBN 90 04 11413 0
75. ARTS, W. (ed.). *Through a Glass, Darkly.* Blurred images of cultural tradition and modernity over distance and time. 2000. ISBN 90 04 11597 8
76. GERRITSEN, J.W. *The Control of Fuddle and Flash,* A Sociological History of the Regulation of Alcohol and Opiates. 2000. ISBN 90 04 11640 0
77. LEE, W.C. (ed.). *Taiwan in Perspective.* 2000. ISBN 90 04 11849 7

78. LUMUMBA-KASONGO, T. (ed.). *Dynamics and Policy Implications of the Global Reforms at the End of the Second Millennium*. 2000. ISBN 90 04 11847 0
79. HARRIS, R. & M. SEID (eds.). *Critical Perspectives on Globalization and Neoliberalism in the Developing Countries*. 2000. ISBN 90 04 11850 0
80. HOWARD, G.J. & G. NEWMAN (eds.), *Varieties of Comparative Criminology*. 2001. ISBN 90 04 12245 1
81. NDEGWA, S.N. (ed.), *A Decade of Democracy in Africa*. 2001. ISBN 90 04 12244 3
82. JREISAT, J.E. (ed.), *Governance and Developing Countries*. 2002. ISBN 90 04 12247 8
83. KEITA, M. (ed.), *Conceptualizing/Re-Conceptualizing Africa*. The construction of African Historical Identity. 2002. ISBN 90 04 12420 9
84. BERG, R. VAN DEN, *Nyoongar People of Australia*. Perspectives on Racism and Multiculturalism. 2002. ISBN 90 04 12478 0
85. DOGAN, M. (ed.), *Elite Configurations at the Apex of Power*. 2003. ISBN 90 04 12808 5
86. SENGERS, G., *Women and Demons*. Cult Healing in Islamic Egypt. 2003. ISBN 90 04 12771 2
87. WILSON, H.T. *The Vocation of Reason*. Studies in Critical Theory and Social Science in the Age of Max Weber. Edited and with a Foreword by T.M. Kemple. 2003. ISBN 90 04 13631 2
88. ZEGEYE, A. and R.L. HARRIS, *Media, Identity and the Public Sphere in Post-Apartheid South Africa*. 2003. ISBN 90 04 12633 3
89. INGLEHART, R. (ed.), *Human Values and Social Change*. Findings from the Values Surveys. 2003. ISBN 90 04 12810 7
90. BEN-RAFAEL, E. (ed.), *Sociology and Ideology*. 2003. ISBN 90 04 13104 3
91. AL-HAJ, M., *Immigration and Ethnic Formation in a Deeply Divided Society*. The Case of the 1990s Immigrants from the Former Soviet Union in Israel. 2004. ISBN 90 04 13625 8
92. AMINEH, M., *Central Eurasia in World Politics*. Conflict, Security, and Development. 2004. ISBN 90 04 12809 3
93. VINKEN, H., J. SOETERS & P. ESTER (eds.), *Comparing Cultures*. Dimensions of Culture in a Comparative Perspective. 2004. ISBN 90 04 13115 9
94. ASSIÉ-LUMUMBA, N.T., *Cyberspace, Distance Learning, and Higher Education in Develo-ping Countries*. Old and Emergent Issues of Access, Pedagogy, and Knowledge Production. 2004. ISBN 90 04 13121 3
95. HARRIS, R.L. and M. Seid, *Globalization and Health*. 2004. ISBN 90 04 14145 6
96. DOGAN, M. (ed.), *Political Mistrust and the Discrediting of Politicians*. 2005. ISBN 90 04 14530 3
97. MÉRIOT, S.-A., *Nostalgic Cooks*. Another French Paradox. 2006. ISBN 90 04 14346 7
99. EISENSTADT, S.N., *The Great Revolutions and the Civilizations of Modernity*. 2006. ISBN 90 04 14812 4
100. NIEUWENHUYS, E. (ed.), *Neo-Liberal Globalism and Social Sustainable Globalisation*. 2006. ISBN 90 04 15159 1
101. SCHRYER, F., *Farming in a Global Economy*. A Case Study of Dutch Immigrant Farmers in Canada. 2006. ISBN 90 04 15170 2

102. SHLAPENTOKH, D. (ed.), *Russia between East and West.* Scholarly Debates on Eurasianism. 2006. ISBN 90 04 15415 9
103. DAY, R.B. & J. MASCIULLI (eds.), *Globalization and Political Ethics.* 2006. ISBN 90 04 15581 3
104. ESMER, Y. & T. PETTERSSON (eds.), *Measuring and Mapping Cultures.* 25 Years of Comparative Value Surveys. 2007. ISBN 978 90 04 15820 7
105. PATTERSON, R. (ed.), *African Brain Circulation.* Beyond the Drain-Gain Debate. 2007. ISBN 978 90 04 15885 6
106. AMINEH, M.P. (ed.), *The Greater Middle East in Global Politics.* Social Science Perspec tives on the Changing Geography of the World Politics. 2007. ISBN-13: 978 90 04 15859 7, ISBN-10: 90 04 15859 6
107. SASAKI, M. (ed.), *Elites: New Comparative Perspectives.* 2007. ISBN 978 90 04 16402 4
108. RIETJENS, S.J.H. *Civil-Military Cooperation in Response to a Complex Emergency.* Just Another Drill? 2008. ISBN 978 90 04 16327 0
109. SASAKI, M. (ed.), *New Frontiers in Comparative Sociology.* 2009. ISBN 978 90 04 17034 6
110. SCIULLI, D., *Professions in Civil Society and the State.* Invariant Foundations and Consequences. 2009. ISBN 978 90 04 17831 1
111. BEST, H. & J. HIGLEY (eds.), *Democratic Elitism.* New Theoretical and Comparative Perspectives. 2010. ISBN 978 90 04 17939 4
112. BORA, A. & H. HAUSENDORF (eds.), *Democratic Transgressions of Law.* Governing Technology through Public Participation. 2010. ISBN 978 90 04 18043 7
113. HUSSAIN, I., *Afghanistan, Iraq and Post-conflict Governance.* Damoclean Democracy? 2010. ISBN 978 90 04 18033 8
114. NIEWÖHNER, J. & T. SCHEFFER (eds.), *Thick Comparison.* Reviving the Ethnographic Aspiration. 2010. ISBN 978 90 04 18113 7